let's talk about FOOD

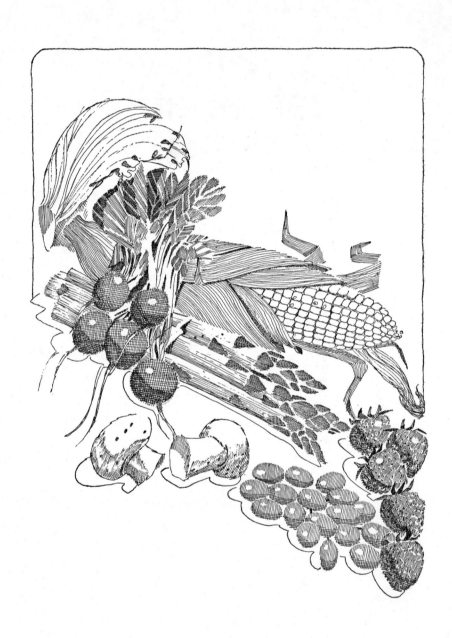

let's talk about FOOD

ANSWERS TO YOUR QUESTIONS
ABOUT FOODS AND NUTRITION

Edited by
Philip L. White, Sc.D.
Secretary, Council on Foods & Nutrition
Director, Department of Foods & Nutrition
AMERICAN MEDICAL ASSOCIATION
and
Nancy Selvey, R.D.
Nutritionist, Department of Foods & Nutrition
AMERICAN MEDICAL ASSOCIATION

PUBLISHING SCIENCES GROUP, INC.
Acton, Massachusetts
a subsidiary of CHC Corporation

Printed in the United States of America.

International Standard Book Number: 0-88416-008-4

Library of Congress Catalog Card Number: 73-85401

contents

1 SOME BASIC CONCEPTS

2 ADEQUATE DIET

3 WEIGHT CONTROL

4 SPECIAL DIETS

10 FOOD SAFETY AND CONSUMER PROTECTION

foreword

Americans enjoy the most diverse food supply in the world. The combinations of foods that can be enjoyed as snacks and meals are virtually unlimited. Seasonal variation in availability of fresh produce is a thing of the past, the change in quality and price in the winter months notwithstanding. Despite the abundance and variety of foods available, too many Americans eat their way into malnutrition and/or obesity, apparently oblivious to the great market of nourishing food available. Poor food choices may stem from inadequate income or lack of knowledge, but often the poor choices result from indifference. One's health is a blessed heritage that ought not be jeopardized by careless food habits.

Personal habits are molded by a variety of events and experiences; once formed, habits are difficult to change. Each of us cherishes individuality and freedom to make choices. So it is with food habits; they are formed very early in life and remain fixed as individual statements until events of great significance change them. The change may be to the willing acceptance of foods that once were shunned or may be to quite innovative patterns of eating.

We have many among us who choose alternate lifestyles that may include rather strange dietary practices. So long as these food patterns cause no physiological harm, we need not concern ourselves. When, on the other hand, harm can be anticipated, the medical profession feels compelled to speak, suggesting modifications that promote adequate nutrient and caloric intake.

There is much that is confusing in the world of foods and the science of nutrition. Difficult words or unfamiliar chemical names, the hard sell of merchandising, the counter current of organic or natural food movements, the ever-present condemnation of one or another food component (sugar, fats, food additives) as a supposed cause of disease. . . How can one cope with it all? Who knows what is right or wrong? Where does one turn? The purpose of this book is to help sort things out—to provide information that will increase understanding and place the issues or concerns into better perspective.

Much of the material for this book was extracted from a column which appears in *Today's Health,* a magazine published by the American Medical Association. Additional topics of current interest have been included to widen the scope of the book.

We acknowledge the editors of *Today's Health* for their splendid cooperation through the many years of serving readers who addressed questions on nutrition to the magazine. The column and the book are compiled from contributions made by nutritionists on the staff of the AMA Department of Foods and Nutrition. We gratefully acknowledge the contributions of Margarita Nagy, Herman Louise Dillon, Diane Robbins, and especially Judy Boeck who helped organize the First Edition of *Let's Talk About Food* in 1967. Therese Mondeika, Assistant Director of the Department, has been a major advisor and contributor to the column since its beginning.

Philip L. White, Sc.D.
Nancy Selvey, R.D.

-1-
some basic concepts

The fundamental concepts in nutrition need not be confusing, but too often we get hopelessly tangled up with complex names and terms and lose interest. One does not need to be a nutritionist to gain an appreciation of basic concepts in order to enjoy the benefits of better understanding.

Commercial interests would have us believe that only calories, proteins, and vitamins are important in health—calories for all of us who count them, vitamins for whatever ails us at the moment, and plenty of protein for us and our dogs. We believe that selling bits and pieces of nutrition only confuses people and makes the process of education that much more difficult.

We would like to improve your appreciation of nutrition concepts. Understanding the answers to the questions of this chapter will prime the reader for the remaining sections. One should remember the following abbreviations:

FDA	Food and Drug Administration
gm	gram
I.U.	International Unit
kg	kilogram
mg	milligram
RDA	Recommended Dietary Allowances
μg	microgram
USDA	U.S. Department of Agriculture

Why are metric units (e.g., gram, milligram) used? The metric system, used throughout the world, is based on the decimal system or multiples of 10. Units can be changed from large to small or vice versa simply by moving decimal points.

Since the FDA has adopted metric units for its nutritional labeling system, and since nutritionists have long used metric units in referring to nutrients, we use them, too, and explain them below.

METRIC WEIGHTS
1 kilogram = 1,000 grams
1 gram   = 1,000 milligrams
1 milligram = 1,000 micrograms

Conversions
1 kilogram   = 2.2 pounds
1 pound   = 454 grams
1 ounce   = 28 grams
3½ ounces   = 100 grams
8 ounces   = 227 grams

METRIC VOLUMES
1 kiloliter = 1,000 liters
1 liter   = 1,000 milliliters

Conversions
1 gallon   = 3.79 liters
1 quart   = .95 liters (950 milliliters)
1 pint   = .48 liters (480 milliliters)
1 cup   = .24 liters (240 milliliters)
1 tablespoon = 15 milliliters
1 teaspoon   = 5 milliliters

RECOMMENDED DIETARY ALLOWANCES (RDA)
The RDA Chart is reproduced inside the front cover of this book

What does "Recommended Dietary Allowances" mean? Is it a good reference for nutrient needs?

The Recommended Dietary Allowances (RDA) were established by the Food and Nutrition Board of the National Research Council. The RDA are a "formulation of nutrient allowances for daily consumption . . . adequate for the maintenance of good nutrition in essentially all the population in the United States." Thus, the RDA are the levels of nutrients recommended as desirable goals in nutrition for almost every healthy person.

In the words of the Food and Nutrition Board, the RDA levels "are meant to afford a margin of sufficiency above minimal requirements and are therefore planned to provide a buffer against the needs of various stresses and to make possible other potential improvements of growth and function." Hence, the RDA were designed to provide for maintenance of good nutrition not only for the average person but for substantially all persons. They also cover persons who may have a greater need for certain nutrients. This explains why it is not reasonable to increase nutrient intake to double or triple the RDA by using multivitamin or mineral supplements.

Judgment must be used in evaluating the adequacy of dietary intake of nutrients against the RDA whether for individuals or populations. Failure to meet RDA levels should not be equated with malnutrition. The RDA are merely points of reference or goals. Knowledge of a person's physical condition as well as laboratory tests are also necessary for proper interpretation of nutritional status. When anyone's nutrient intake falls *well below* the RDA, however, steps should be taken to find out why. Dietary faults should then be corrected.

Most health and agricultural agencies use the RDA as reference standards for adequate nutrient intake. The four-group food plan commonly used in nutrition education was developed from the RDA and enables those who follow it to achieve adequate nutrition. The RDA also provide the basis for national and international planning of food supplies for populations and are used as a guide for the interpretation of food consumption for such groups.

The ultimate evaluation of a person's nutritional status requires more than casual observation. Feeling "below par" is not sufficient evidence to justify a verdict of malnutrition. Inadequate rest or poor exercise habits as well as unapparent illness can rob anyone of vitality, even those persons with the best dietary habits. If one attempts to achieve the goals set by the RDA, however, one is almost assured of being well nourished.

4

U.S. RDA

The U.S. RDA Chart is reproduced inside the back cover of this book

What is the U.S. RDA, used on food "nutrition information" labels?

This abbreviation stands for "United States Recommended Daily Allowances." In general, the U.S. RDA represent an adaptation of the RDA (explained above) for use in labeling nutrition information on food products.

Labeling of nutrition information is a service to consumers which many food processors are now adopting. A processor may voluntarily provide nutrition information. If he does, he must follow a standard label format. He is required to provide the information if a nutritional claim is made in promoting the food. If a nutrient is added to the food to enhance its value, the product must be labeled in the detail required by the appropriate regulation. In order to standardize the method of giving such information on food labels, the FDA devised the U.S. RDA system.

The values chosen are thought by authoritative sources to adequately provide the nutrient needs of our population.

The nutrition information panel of the label must give the caloric, protein, carbohydrate, and fat content of one serving. Protein and seven vitamins and minerals must be listed as percentages of the U.S. RDA. If the U.S. RDA for a nutrient is less than 2 percent, the processor has the option of using zero or stating "contains less than 2 percent of U.S. RDA for . . . ."

In addition to the seven required vitamins and minerals and the other nutrients and calories mentioned above, the processor may mention twelve additional nutrients: vitamins D, E, B_6 and B_{12}, folic acid, phosphorus, iodine, magnesium, zinc, copper, biotin, and pantothenic acid, as well as cholesterol, polyunsaturated and saturated fats, and sodium. It all sounds rather complicated, doesn't it? It needn't be if you keep your wits about you, tear out the back cover, and keep your portable calculator with you at all times.

Oh, yes, one more feature. When a food product is fortified to contain 50 percent or more of a U.S. RDA, it must then comply with yet another regulation. Under these circumstances it must also be identified as a food supplement. You may have seen the dual label on highly fortified breakfast cereals.

To simplify, we offer the following hypothetical example of the nutrition label for Peanut Butter Binky:

Nutrition Information
(Per Serving)
Serving Size = 1 oz
Servings per Container = 13

Calories	136
Protein	8 grams
Carbohydrate	8 grams
Fat	8 grams

Percentage of U.S. Recommended Daily Allowances (U.S. RDA)

Protein	20	Riboflavin	12
Vitamin A	15	Niacin	20
Vitamin C (ascorbic acid)	15	Calcium	2
Thiamin (vitamin B_1)	10	Iron	7

This means that one serving of the food contains 20 percent of the U.S. RDA for protein, 15 percent for vitamin A, and so on.

The U.S. RDA replaces the old Minimum Daily Requirements which were previously used on labels of breakfast cereals and vitamin and mineral supplements.

CALORIE TABLES

How accurate are calorie tables?

The values for food energy (calories) are estimates at best. A great many factors determine the accuracy of the estimates. The two most important determinants are the exactness of the laboratory determinations and the constancy of food composition.

Calories are an expression or measure of the energy which can be derived from food. Fats, carbohydrates, and proteins are the major energy-providing compounds. (The other source of calories is alcohol.) The energy available in a food can be evaluated by combustion of the food in a calorimeter or by assigning caloric equivalents to the fat, carbohydrate, and protein in the food. While these methods correspond rather well, the results obtained on random samples of a given food are still only average values for all other examples of that food. Foods of constant composition, such as oils, could be expected to provide the food energy listed in calorie tables; however, there are not many foods of constant composition. The majority of the foods listed in conventional tables of caloric values can be quite variable in composition. This is especially true in the case of food concoctions, i.e., stews, hash, casseroles, etc.

An additional difficulty is introduced when food energy is given in terms of calories per serving. A "serving" to the untrained individual is little more than a portion of unknown dimensions. Consider also the myriad designations: grams, ounces, pounds, pints, quarts, gallons, cups, serving, glasses, tsp., tbsp., small, medium, large, slice, thin slice, average piece, $3^1/_4$ " × 4" square, fractions of (as $^1/_8$ of 9" pie), stalk, head, pat, bottle, strips, and, finally, a scant $^1/_2$ cup. Whether the values are for the raw or cooked food or for "as purchased" or "edible portion only" is sometimes overlooked in tables. (The dietitian, however, is trained to appreciate standard servings and is skillful in working with weights of food generally expressed in grams or ounces.)

A major difficulty in selecting foods for a weight-reducing diet from tables that list only the energy value of foods is encountered when low-caloric foods are selected without regard to nutrient values. There is a temptation to assume 100 calories as a "cut-off" point. Foods for a calorie-restricted diet should be chosen on the basis of nutrient concentration first and caloric value second. Nutrients assume increased importance when the total food intake is restricted.

Calorie tables can be useful but they must be used intelligently. The USDA's booklet *Nutritive Value of Foods* is a good calorie and nutrient guide available at cost from the Superintendent of Documents, U.S. Government Printing Office, Washington, D.C. 20402.

NUTRIENT DENSITY

What is meant by "nutrient density" and why is it important?

The term "nutrient density" relates the concentration of important nutrients in a food (vitamins, minerals, protein) to the caloric value of that food. Meat and milk are good examples of foods which provide important quantities of nutrients along with calories.

Rather complicated systems have been developed in order to rate foods in terms of their nutrient density. The well-known four food-grouping was devised through the use of one such rating system. The grouping of foods, the amounts of each food recommended, and the suggested frequency of consumption were chosen to assure that adherence to the plan would more or less guarantee an adequate diet.

The enrichment and fortification of selected foods (e.g., cereals, flour, bread, and milk) represent efforts to provide a good nutrient density in popular foods. Perhaps someday a coding system will be worked out to assist individuals in their selection of foods to assure nutritious meals.

In the case of packaged meals, including convenience packaged meals (popularly called TV dinners) and liquid meals, the responsibility falls directly on the producer to provide appropriate nutrient densities. The AMA Council on Foods and Nutrition has suggested that a packaged meal, supplying, say, 25 percent of the total daily caloric intake should also provide at least 25 percent of the nutrients needed for the day.

KILOCALORIES

What is the meaning of the phrase "nutrients per 100 kcal" in infant formulas?

Kcal is an abbreviation of kilocalories. This expression of the energy value of foods is used to refer to large calories, the amount of heat required to raise the temperature of 1 kg of water 1° centigrade (C). The small calorie refers to the amount of heat required to raise the temperature of 1 gm of water 1°C. The kilocalorie, therefore, is 1,000 times the small calorie. The calorie used in nutrition is the kilocalorie although the prefix (kilo) is usually dropped. The small calorie is used in physics.

Pediatricians have begun to express nutrient requirements and formula concentrations in units per 100 kcal because it gives them more latitude in planning an infant's diet. As the age and weight of the infant increase, so do his protein and calorie requirements. The pediatrician can conveniently relate formula and supplementary food needs to calorie requirements with 100 kcal as the basis for calculation. Example: An infant needs about 5 ounces of water per 100 kcal. If the infant needs 700 calories (kcal) per day, the water intake should be 7 x 5, or 35 ounces of water per day.

CALORIC CHECKING ACCOUNT

What is a person's basal metabolic requirement, and how does this relate to his total caloric requirement?

A person's basal metabolic requirement refers to the calories he needs to maintain his involuntary body functions and proper body temperature. In other words, it is the metabolic cost of living.

A woman 25 years old, 5 feet 6 inches tall, weighing 133 pounds, has a basal metabolic requirement of about 1,460 calories. Her recommended (total) caloric allowance for moderate activity, however, is 2,320 calories per day. The difference—860 calories—between her basal metabolic requirement and recommended caloric allowance represents the number of calories she must expend for voluntary activities. It is her caloric "checking account." If all 860 calories are not used during the day's activity, those remaining are transferred from the "checking account" to a "savings account" and thus accumulate in the form of fat. On the other hand if she overdraws her checking account, the savings are called on and weight loss results. A relatively small savings account in the form of body fat is usually desirable.

The energy needed for all voluntary activity increases with the intensity of the exercise. An hour of light housework requires about 70 calories above the basal requirement, while an hour of walking requires 110 calories. Participation in sports, of course, involves greater caloric expenditures. Playing touch football may require as much as 400 calories an hour. This may be contrasted with the amount of energy needed for an hour of driving (36 calories), or for sitting and thinking (only 5 calories per hour). If you are considering losing weight, it should be apparent that nothing will happen if you just "sits and thinks" about it!

FOOD STANDARDS

What is a legal standard of identity for a food?

The food standards or legal standards of identity for food provided for in the Federal Food, Drug and Cosmetic Act are designed to promote honesty and fair dealing in the interest of consumers.

A standard of identity names and defines a particular food and specifies the amounts (usually in minimums) of the ingredients it must contain. Foods which have standards of identity may contain only those ingredients listed in the regulatory specifications; however, many food standards also provide for the use of certain optional ingredients. Foods with legal standards of identity and with no optional ingredients need not carry lists of ingredients on their labels. In most instances when an optional ingredient is used, such an ingredient must be noted on the label. Thus, the standards serve to assure the consumer that the food he buys will be the kind he expects.

Standards of identity have been established for a great many foods—chiefly for canned food, enriched bread and flour, jams and jellies, salad dressing and mayonnaise, syrup, oils, and macaroni products. When a standard of identity exists and a food product is manufactured which does not meet these standards, its label may not carry the standard name. For example, if a jam deviates from the prescribed ratio of sugar to fruit, it must then be labeled as an imitation.

Foods for which there are no standards of identity must clearly state the ingredients on the label. The ingredients are listed in descending order of predominance by weight. The list includes any functional additives used in the product. The name of the product and net contents or net weight must be stated on all food labels along with the name and place of business of the manufacturer.

Consumer information on food standards is available from the Food and Drug Administration.

BALANCE

The word "balance" is used in so many ways in nutrition. What does it mean? There is the balanced diet, caloric balance, nitrogen balance, calcium balance, and vitamin and mineral balance.

"Balanced diet" is simply the practical expression of the interrelationships among various nutrients in an adequate diet.

In the very early days of the science of nutrition and with the relatively few foods available 75 years ago, much emphasis was placed on balancing the carbohydrate, fat, and protein in the diet. Research has since shown that the functions of all the nutrients —vitamins, minerals, amino acids, fats, carbohydrates, and water—are closely related, a concept that is important as more knowledge is gained about cellular metabolism.

The term "balanced diet" probably should not be used anymore. A better one would be "adequate diet." The most noteworthy efforts to simplify the achievement of an adequate diet have been the development of the Recommended Dietary Allowances and the grouping of foods which provide significant amounts of the important nutrients. Foods are grouped into the Basic Four: (1) milk and milk products; (2) meat, fish, and poultry with nuts and legumes as alternates; (3) fruits and vegetables; and (4) breads and cereals. A wise selection of foods from each group, as recommended, will provide an adequate diet.

When the word balance is used in terms like "caloric balance," "nitrogen balance" and "calcium balance," it refers to the equation of intake versus output. A person is in caloric balance when the number of calories consumed equals the number expended. The nutritionist speaks of positive and negative balance when studying calcium and nitrogen metabolism. A person is in positive calcium balance when calcium intake is greater than calcium excretion. Nitrogen balance is related to protein; a person is in negative nitrogen balance when less protein nitrogen is consumed than is excreted.

The food scientist frequently refers to balanced protein, an expression of the nutritive value of protein. When a protein is composed of all the essential amino acids in useful amounts, it is a balanced (or complete) protein. Egg, milk, meat, and some seeds and whole-grain cereals are sources of well-balanced protein.

STAYING QUALITY

What is meant by the "staying quality" of a food?

A food of high staying quality is one that "sticks with you" for a few hours; that is, one that gives a sense of satisfaction and delays the onset of hunger. This is not necessarily related to the amount of food eaten, but rather the rate at which the food is digested and the length of time it remains in the stomach.

"Satiety value" is synonymous with "staying quality" and is now the phrase commonly used. Foods that are high in fat content have the greatest satiety value as fat remains in the stomach longer than protein or carbohydrate. Protein is second on the list and carbohydrates come in last.

-2-
adequate diet

"**A**n adequate diet? Who wants just an adequate diet? I want a superb diet." So say many who hear the term adequate. By definition, adequate diet means sufficient to meet all nutrient (and caloric) requirements. Again, by way of definition, requirements refer to an intake to meet all needs plus a reasonable, safe excess of those nutrients (e.g., vitamin C) which slip away quickly during the day. We use the term "adequate," then, to infer all the nutrients in amounts to meet growth and maintenance requirements.

Is there a simple way to tell if one is well-nourished? How is the nutritional status of a person determined?

Usually, a good look in a full-length mirror gives a person a general idea of nutritional health. If one finds himself either too fat or too thin in appearance, he may be improperly nourished and wish to do something about it.

Most of the time, one should have a general appearance of vitality and well-being. He should feel alert and have the energy needed to perform normal physical activities and to react to and recover from stressful situations, such as disease and infection. Fatigue caused by lack of sufficient rest should not, however, be confused with that caused by poor nutrition. A person's appetite should be reasonably good and he should have a cheerful, rather than irritable, outlook on life's situations. Growth in height and weight should be normal for his inherited body build when compared with other persons of the same age and sex. All of the previous factors are involved in the "total picture" of his nutritional status.

There are, however, several other ways of assessing nutritional status which are more scientific in their analysis. Any one or all of these can be used by a trained observer, such as a physician, in assessing individual nutritional status. They are observation and analysis of:

1. Clinical signs which are characteristic of a well-nourished person: (a) a general appearance of vitality and well-being; (b) a sturdy, well-shaped skeletal frame; (c) well-formed teeth and healthy gums; (d) a muscular structure which is strong, well developed, and properly balanced so that posture is generally erect; (e) a well-rounded body contour suggestive of sufficient, but not excessive, subcutaneous fat which provides moderate padding for protection of the muscles and skeleton; (f) adequate bodily functions, such as a good appetite, digestion, elimination, physical endurance, nervous stability, and prompt and adequate recovery from fatigue or other stress, and (g) clear, smooth skin and mucous membranes.

2. Physical measurements of height, weight, and body composition, followed by comparison of these measurements with standards of growth and development; the latter standards are

important in the evaluation of growing children. These measurements insure that a person is growing and maturing adequately in relationship to his age, sex, and physical activity.

3. Laboratory tests of blood, urine, and body composition. For example, chemical determinations are made of the composition of the blood and urine to demonstrate the presence of necessary nutrients within the body. Laboratory techniques, however, are usually not used as routinely as the other methods in determining nutritional status unless it is felt that exacting nutritional information is necessary.

Questions concerning the history of food intake and other dietary habits will also be asked, as they help in the evaluation of the total nutritional picture. For example, "What, how much, when, and how often do you eat?" and "How are your foods prepared?"

Now let's look at the other side of the coin; what about malnutrition? We have it in this country. What is it, really?

Malnutrition may be classified as primary or secondary. Primary malnutrition is defined as an inadequate (or excessive, e.g., calories) intake of nutrients for the normal body requirement. This condition may be caused by faulty selection of foods, by lack of money to purchase adequate food, or by actual food shortages.

Secondary malnutrition results from factors that interfere with ingestion, absorption, or utilization of essential nutrients or from stress factors that increase their requirement, destruction, or excretion. Two common examples are anemia associated with heavy intestinal infestations (parasites in the intestinal tract) in children, and malnutrition resulting from chronic diarrhea.

In all likelihood, malnutrition is much more prevalent than hunger, *per se,* but it is not as politically dramatic. Malnutrition producing physiological impairment is probably common. Conditions such as iron deficiency, growth impairment, and obesity are widespread. While such classical deficiency diseases as scurvy, beri beri, and pellagra are rare, several cases of goiter and rickets have been reported recently.

The effects of malnutrition on the infant and young child can be devastating. In its severest forms, as with kwashiorkor or marasmus, it can lead to death. Overt malnutrition can produce physical impairment marking the individual for life. The poorly nourished child, the hungry child, will have a shortened attention span which interferes with learning even though there may be no mental impairment. Malnutrition in early childhood has obvious implications for future manpower and economic progress. It adds a fearful urgency to the whole problem.

Human and animal studies have provided evidence that the nutritional state of the mother is an important factor in maternal illness, fetal deaths, premature deaths, neonatal deaths (within four weeks after birth), and morbidity of infants. The high infant mortality rates in certain sections of the country and among certain ethnic groups are in large measure related to poor nutritional status of mothers. Death rates of infants are vastly greater among the malnourished than among the well-nourished.

There you have it: adequate nutrition on the one hand, malnutrition on the other. Which will it be? You judge for yourself.

Why not start your own evaluation? Check your daily food intake and compare it with this daily food guide.

Daily Food Guide

	Child	Preteen & Teen	Adult	Aging Adult	Your Score
milk or milk products (in cups)	2-3	3-4 or more	2 or more	2 or more	
meat, fish, poultry, eggs (in servings)	1-2	3 or more	2 or more	2 or more	
green & yellow vegetables (in servings)	1-2	2	2	at least 1	
citrus fruits & tomatoes (in servings)	1	1-2	1	1-2	
potatoes, other fruits, & vegetables (in servings)	1	1	1	0-1	
bread, flour, & cereal (in servings)	3-4	4 or more	3-4	2-3	
butter or margarine (in tablespoons)	2	2-4	2-3	1-2	

1. The need for the nutrients in 1 or 2 cups of milk daily can be satisfied by cheeses or ice cream. (1 cup of milk is approximately equivalent to 1½ cups of cottage cheese or 2-3 large scoops of ice cream.)

2. It is important to drink enough fluid. The equivalent of 3-5 cups daily is recommended.

3. The recommended daily serving of meat, fish, and poultry (3 oz) may be alternated with eggs or cheese, dried peas, beans, or lentils.

4. Iron-rich foods should be selected as frequently as possible by teen-age and adult females to help meet their high requirement for this mineral: liver, heart, lean meats, shellfish, egg yolks, legumes, green leafy vegetables, and whole-grain and enriched cereal products.

AVERAGE AMERICAN'S DIET

Does the average individual in this country receive an adequate diet?

A 1965 survey performed by the USDA indicated that foods used by households were sufficient, on the average, to provide diets meeting the RDA for calories and the seven nutrients evaluated: protein; calcium; iron; vitamin A value; thiamin; riboflavin; and ascorbic acid. However, great variations were found among the 7,500 households sampled. The USDA reported that:

> Half of the households had diets that met the Allowances for all nutrients. The other half of the households had diets that failed to meet the Allowances for one or more nutrients. Calcium, vitamin A value, and ascorbic acid were the nutrients most often found to be below Allowances.
> About one-fifth of the diets provided less than two-thirds of the RDA for one or more nutrients and were rated as poor.

The RDA were not established to reflect degrees of achievement; they were not intended to represent a nutritional ceiling nor to relate to a nutritional floor. Thus, it may be a distortion of the RDA if a diet is rated poor because it provides less than two-thirds of the Allowance for one or more nutrients. For example, at the time of the survey, the RDA of ascorbic acid for an adult male was 60 mg per day. A safe standard may be in the order of 30 mg. An intake of 30 to 40 mg could hardly be called "poor."

Whether the USDA survey reflects "Nutrition USA" is a moot question. Undoubtedly, plenty of food is available year-round to provide all Americans with adequate nutrition. The survey shows, however, that some households are not making wise food choices.

In 1972, the U.S. Department of Health, Education, and Welfare completed a 10-state nutrition survey in which the problems most frequently found were with the following nutrients: iron, vitamin A, riboflavin, and protein (among pregnant and lactating women). Generally, the incidence of poor nutrition was highest among low-income groups.

When we get down to specifics, average intake means little unless information is available defining the spread of values on both sides of the average value. In nutrition there is reason to be concerned for those on the lowest side of the average because they may experience nutrient deficiencies. Those on the high side will have a surplus of nutrients. When the issue is calories, you can tell who is on the high side of intake simply by looking at him.

We must agree, m re malnutrition exists in this country than we have any right to expect. Correction calls for concerted action by all as the main cause of malnutrition seems to be indifference. Americans must once again be taught to care—to care enough about themselves to take corrective action when personal health is at stake.

Subtle changes are taking place in food habits that suggest different problems for the future. The trends in use of dairy products serve as illustrations. Already, the annual consumption per person of dairy products, excluding butter, has dropped 102.4 pounds from what it was 10 years ago—671.8 pounds. It is expected that by 1980, annual consumption may be 447 pounds, a further reduction of 122.4 pounds. This means that annual consumption would be 33 percent less than in 1958.

The major change has been in fluid whole milk—an excellent source of calcium and phosphorus and a good source of protein and riboflavin. Increased consumption of meats and poultry which has occurred should offset the loss of dairy protein and riboflavin. But what about the minerals calcium and phosphorus? How do we compensate for this loss, particularly during adolescence, when needs are higher than at any other time of life?

The recommendations of a White House Conference Panel make sense: "In view of the declining trend in fluid milk consumption, research should be undertaken to develop substitutes for fluid milk that will provide all the nutritive qualities of milk." The Panel also urged consideration of the fortification of other foods with calcium should it be determined that large groups of people do not receive enough of this essential nutrient. The problem with this staple food commodity clearly illustrates the need for national policies on food and nutrition.

CALORIES PER MEAL

What proportion of the daily caloric need should be consumed with each meal?

There is no general agreement on the proportion of calories that should be consumed at the three conventional meals. The usual pattern for most people is a light breakfast, a moderate lunch, and a heavy evening meal. Custom, work schedule, and personal preference dictate meal patterns.

One school of thought suggests that the evening meal should not be a heavy, high-fat dinner if it is to be followed by hours of sedentary relaxation before sleep. Another recommendation has been that frequent small meals (say, six) are better than three larger ones. These latter two recommendations reflect concern for elevated blood fat concentrations which occur several hours after eating.

Many overweight persons follow a pattern of eating little or nothing during the day and then packing away truly prodigious quantities of food throughout the evening. The night-eating syndrome is far from a perfect pattern . . . unless you consider 300 pounds an ideal weight.

There is general agreement that a three- or four-meal pattern with a reasonable quantity of calories, protein, and the other nutrients at each meal is desirable. A poor or nonexistent breakfast plus a midmorning snack of coffee and a roll followed by a poor lunch is not a profitable meal pattern. It places too much responsibility on the evening meal to provide all the required nutrients. Nutrients probably will not be available when needed by the body.

Perhaps the best advice is to space nourishing meals at appropriate intervals so that neither a gnawing hunger nor a drowsy, overfed feeling results.

NUTRIENT REQUIREMENTS OF ADULTS

Do all adults have the same nutrient requirements?

Individuals do not have identical nutrient requirements and, in fact, one's nutrient requirements can change from day to day. This change, however, is quite small—as is the variation between individuals. Available information permits reasonably accurate estimates of an individual's nutrient requirements based on age, sex, body size, and physical activity. Other factors determining specific nutrient requirements include: growth, pregnancy, illness, food digestion, nutrient absorption, and the environmental temperature. When evaluating nutrient requirements, the AMA generally utilizes the concept of the Recommended Dietary Allowances (described earlier in this book).

DIET AND WEIGHT GAIN IN PREGNANCY

What is a proper amount of weight gain during pregnancy? Are vitamin and mineral supplements necessary for all pregnant women?

The Committee on Maternal Nutrition of the National Research Council indicates that an average weight gain during pregnancy of 24 pounds (or a range of 20-25 pounds) corresponds with a "better than average course and outcome of pregnancy."

The gain during pregnancy consists of the weight of the infant plus the following average gains: placenta and amniotic fluid, over 3 pounds; increased size of uterus, 2 pounds; mammary glands, $^4/_5$ pound; and an increase in the mother's blood volume, 2 $^4/_5$ pounds. This additional weight of the mother (about nine pounds) plus the weight of the child (about seven pounds) still leaves a few pounds unaccounted for. The unspecified weight comes from a built-in safety factor: Evidence shows that during pregnancy the hormone, progesterone, stimulates a certain amount of extra fat storage, and even women who are assured by their physicians that they are not gaining too much weight may notice a little extra fat on the hips, upper thighs, and back because of the hormone action. This extra weight is readily lost after pregnancy.

There appears to be no reason for limiting weight gain to less than 20-25 pounds for the normal, healthy woman. Ideally, the gain may occur as one to three pounds during the first three months with the remainder accumulating rather evenly and consistently during the last six months. Remember, however, that the physician treats individuals, not groups of average or "normal" people; therefore, he makes his recommendations for the individual pregnant woman. Generally, nutrient requirements increase significantly after the first few weeks of pregnancy. The physician may recommend vitamin and mineral supplements, but these cannot be substituted for (or in any way decrease the need for) good food habits. Basically, the diet of a pregnant woman is a conventional one, modified to emphasize foods high in protein, vitamins, and minerals.

Some obstetricians believe that *most* women will require supplemental iron and folic acid (one of the B vitamins). Beyond that, a woman who eats properly may need no supplements at all.

NUTRITION AND PHYSICAL FITNESS

Will any specific foods help in attaining physical fitness?

Good nutrition is an integral part of any physical fitness program. An adequate intake of a variety of foods, along with a rational program of useful exercise, adds immeasurably to a zestful life. No single food assures good nutrition, just as no single physical activity assures physical fitness or increases muscle tone. A variety of foods and activities is the best formula. Meals including meat, dairy products, fruits and vegetables, and bread and cereals should provide a feeling of physical well-being. Foods well prepared and attractively presented also add much to this sense of well-being.

The young boy or girl interested in physical fitness is usually concerned about nutrition. Parents can capitalize on this interest by helping their youngsters form good food habits. A person can be well-nourished and still not be physically fit, but he can never be physically fit without being well-nourished.

A good program of fitness includes careful attention to diet as proper weight maintenance can contribute to a sense of well-being. Adherence to a schedule of physical activity is also necessary. Physical activity should be commensurate with a person's ability and age. Gradual cardiovascular endurance is achieved with a continuous rhythmic exercise program of 20 to 30 minutes' duration at least three times per week. Rhythmic activities which are very conducive to endurance fitness are jogging, swimming, and bicycling. Resistance conditioning most conducive to strength development is isotonic conditioning in which the weight lifted is moved through a range of motion. Whatever the activity suitable for the person, it should be continuous.

ATHLETES' APPETITES

High school athletes have tremendous appetites and often consume everything put on the table at mealtime, then demand more. Is it necessary to serve them great quantities of meat? Such demands place hardships on food budgeting.

Athletic teens have prodigious appetites. The energy requirements for boys can be more than 4,000 calories per day because of the combined demands of great physical activity and rapid growth rate. Meat not only provides protein and calories, but also vitamins and minerals. Just because one is an athlete, however, is no reason to demand an unusual amount of meat. Athletes *do* place great reliance on meat, but their demand of it is more psychological than physiological. Frequently, meat and protein are unduly associated with strength and power. The fact is that the athlete and the heavy laborer have no greater protein needs than do their less active counterparts once their muscle mass has been fixed. Using one's muscles in increased physical activity increases caloric requirements, not protein requirements.

When budgeting for and buying meat, however, keep in mind that less expensive cuts of meat are as nourishing as the most expensive cuts. Remember also that eggs, milk, beans, nuts, and cereal products also are good sources of protein and available energy.

UNDERWEIGHT ATHLETE?

How is it possible for a healthy, teenage boy to gain about twenty pounds in order to be more effective in sports?

During training, the total muscle mass of an athlete may increase significantly. This increase may appear in the form of weight gain for some, while others may replace body fat with muscle mass and, thus, show little weight change.

In determining the optimum physical condition of an individual athlete, body composition is a more important factor than weight. Unfortunately, a scale can't tell the difference between fat and muscle. In the long run, genetic endowment will determine the size and weight of the athlete, unless he "overrides" his potential either by excess fat or muscle accumulation.

VITAMIN SUPPLEMENTS FOR ATHLETES

Do high school athletes need vitamin supplements? Some people think they do, while others say such supplements are useless.

There is no doubt that an individual cannot perform in the most efficient manner unless he is well-nourished. It has *not* been shown, however, that vitamin supplements are useful in improving the performance of a healthy athlete. Foods are the preferred source of nutrients, and vitamin supplementation is completely unnecessary for the athlete who eats properly—meaning one who eats larger servings of the same good foods that are recommended for everyone.

"SPORTS DRINKS"

Is there any merit in the "sports drinks" being promoted for athletes?

"Sports drinks" are dilute solutions of glucose (a simple sugar), sodium chloride and other salts, citric acid, and an artificial sweetener. Commercially available "sports drinks" differ considerably in composition of these components; however, each product is a convenient and consistent supply of the fluid and salts which athletes need for replacing sweat loss.

Thus the "sports drinks" being promoted have considerable merit but no more merit than homemade saltwater solutions can claim. Basically, a simple homemade solution of 1 teaspoon of salt to 6 quarts of water prevents heat exhaustion and heat stroke. There is some evidence to suggest that potassium should also be added in minute amounts.

Athletes will require replacement of greater amounts of water until they are acclimated. A recommended procedure is to regularly weigh athletes before and after games to assess the fluid replacement necessary. The athlete should consume weight-for-weight of fluid—1 pint of fluid for each pound of weight lost.

SALT IN HOT WEATHER

What is a good guide to the amount of salt required during hot weather? Should salt tablets be taken routinely?

Extra salt need not be taken during hot weather except under conditions which cause profuse sweating. Copious sweating associated with hard physical labor or prolonged and vigorous exercise in hot weather may cause sufficient sodium loss to produce illness. The body is able to compensate partially in a few days so that the daily loss of sodium is less as one becomes accustomed or acclimated.

It has been suggested that if the water intake exceeds four quarts per day, one gram of salt should be taken with each additional quart. These are recommendations for continuous and prodigious sweating which might result from participation in a strenuous sport as opposed to, say, being pulled around for an hour or so by a power lawn mower, which barely raises a sweat.

The normal individual in his usual environment is not in danger of sodium depletion. More than enough of this mineral is provided by the usual diet, even without the addition of salt in cooking or at the table. Sodium is found in foods, water, and in a number of condiments and food-flavor enhancers such as monosodium glutamate. The ingestion of sodium in addition to that commonly found in foods is unnecessary and any excess above the body's needs must be excreted. There is evidence that excessive sodium may aggravate hypertension and certain forms of heart diseases so that moderation in use of table salt is advisable.

HOT MEALS, WARM WEATHER

When children come to the table hot and tired in the summer, is it necessary to serve warm meals?

Hot food is usually more appetizing to most people than cold food. Heat enhances flavor and aroma, which can stimulate sagging summer appetites and provide satisfaction. There will be days, however, when it is just too hot to face the prospect of preparing a hot meal. On those days the whole family will appreciate a cool meal such as a "hearty" salad made from tuna, chicken, shrimp, egg, or beans. A single hot dish or bowl of soup also makes an excellent addition to a cold meal.

Children need as much or more food during the summer than they do during cooler weather. In order to keep their bodies at the proper temperatures, they also need more fluids when playing actively outdoors. Children frequently lose weight during hot weather because of inadequate fluid intake, undesirable reduction in food consumption, and insufficient rest.

COLD WEATHER

Do cold weather and the increased exercise often associated with winter activities make greater demands on the body for vitamins and minerals? If so, is it advisable to take a multivitamin-mineral preparation?

The basic need for nutrients is no different in the winter than in the summer. Depending upon the weight of clothing worn, more energy may be needed to keep the body warm when exposure to the cold is extensive, but the average difference between energy needs in warm and cold climates is not great.

Supplementing an adequate diet with vitamins and minerals during the winter is not necessary. It has been claimed that large amounts of vitamin C will help protect against flu and the common cold, but there is little solid evidence to support the theory. Evidence that exercise or heavy work increases vitamin requirements is also lacking. Increased activity, however, increases caloric requirements and, thus, requirements for some of the B vitamins.

TAKING VITAMINS

If vitamins are so important, why are people advised not to take vitamin pills?

Foods properly selected and prepared provide all the nutrients necessary for good nutrition. Usually, the people who advise that supplemental vitamins are needed by all are the very ones who sell vitamins; their motives are based on financial self-interest, not on benefiting public health. Supplements are useful when a person is unable or unwilling to consume an adequate diet, as during illness, allergy, or emotional upsets. The vitamin and mineral preparations used, however, should be *reasonable* amounts. Supplements, by definition, cannot contain more than 150 percent of the U. S. RDA of the various nutrients. In our estimation, larger amounts are unreasonable.

VITAMINS AND WEIGHT GAIN

Can supplemental vitamins cause weight gain?

Not for a well-nourished person. One of the effects of a vitamin deficiency, however, is a reduced appetite. Therefore, a vitamin supplement for a person with a vitamin deficiency may bring about a weight gain as the deficiency is corrected.

SNACKS

Should children be permitted to snack between meals?

A child's weight, energy, and mealtime appetite are the best indicators of the need for snacks. The same criteria can be used to determine the size of snack offered. Children frequently need extra food to help them keep up their energy.

Snacks should contribute their share of nutrients during the day. There is little to be gained by between-meal snacks of candy and soft drinks because most furnish nothing but calories. There are, however, an almost unlimited number of wholesome snacks that can be easily prepared and stored until needed—small sandwiches, milk, cheese, ice cream, celery, carrots, cookies, and fruit. Snacks should not be offered too close to mealtime for fear of reducing appetite. A recent study found that children who enjoyed snacks in the middle of the afternoon actually ate larger evening meals than usual. The snacks probably prevented fatigue, which tends to reduce appetite. Dentists frequently express concern over the increased possibilities of cavities occurring when the wrong kind of snacks are eaten. Avoid sticky sweets and always make certain that the teeth are cleaned after snacks just as after regular meals.

If children are allowed to enjoy an occasional snack, such as a few cookies and a glass of milk, before bedtime it could be a relaxing experience, allowing them to unwind from the day's exciting and demanding activities. Be sure they brush their teeth before crawling into bed. A bedtime snack is of no benefit, though, if it provides too many calories and contributes to a weight problem. The idea that foods can disturb sleep is found in folk tales with many variations. Little evidence supports such beliefs. Give children the opportunity to enjoy a few requested snacks and you will learn if they can tolerate and enjoy them.

TEENAGE EATING HABITS

When teenagers do not eat the right foods, is it good to give them vitamins?

The Council on Foods and Nutrition of the American Medical Association has suggested that vitamin supplementation may be useful during those times when, for one reason or another, desirable food patterns are not being followed. Vitamin supplementation, however, ought to be used only until such time as faulty food habits have been corrected. It is extremely important that teenagers be taught the importance of proper nutrition. Do not use vitamin supplementation in an effort to justify or excuse laziness. Every teenager should learn and practice good nutrition. A proper amount of rest, an adequate amount of physical activity, and proper nutrition are vital to a healthful adolescence.

Since *active* adolescents require 2,500 or more calories a day, allowances can be made for some "junk" foods by careful planning of the basic meals. If the teenager is sedentary and/or overweight, snack foods should be low-calorie items.

TALLER CHILDREN

Does the use of vitamins account for the fact that children are now taller than their parents?

Much as the nutritionist would like to give full credit for the increase in height of our children to improved nutrition over the years, other factors deserve credit as well. Without a doubt, the elimination of most serious childhood diseases and the ability to limit the devastating effects of other infectious diseases have permitted children to enjoy an almost uninterrupted growth period. Children of today are more likely to achieve their genetic potential than were their parents.

SCHOOL LUNCH

What responsibility do parents have in the school lunch?

It is the responsibility of parents to learn whether the school is indeed providing nutritious meals and whether their children are eating the food provided or spending their lunch money on other, less desirable foods. Further, parents must recognize that one good meal a day, be it the school lunch or the home dinner, is not sufficient for children. (A survey conducted a few years ago by one of the large food companies indicated that many homemakers are satisfied that they are balancing the diet when they offer a good dinner that includes the four food groups.) Children deserve to be sent to school with a good beakfast inside them and welcomed home with a warm, appetizing, and nutritious dinner.

Most school lunch supervisors make a sincere effort to prepare menus that provide about one-third of the nutrient requirements for growing children per day. Many schools also publish these menus in the local newspaper in advance, utilizing this opportunity to teach parents about meal planning and nutrition.

SOFT DRINKS, HOT DRINKS, AND CANDY

Our children's school refuses to serve hot beverages on even the coldest of days. Yet they sell case after case of soft drinks every day (not to mention all the candy, cookies, and other sweets). Since when is a soft drink better for my kids than hot tea?

Actually, a beverage's temperature affects its flavor but little else. The rest is psychology. Tea and coffee are no more nourishing than soft drinks and, like cola, contain caffeine, which isn't recommended for children.

The AMA Council on Foods and Nutrition published the following statement on confections and soft drinks in schools:

> One of the functions of a school lunch program is to provide training in sound food habits. The sale of foods, confections, and beverages in lunchrooms, recreation rooms, and other school facilities influences directly the food habits of the students. Every effort should be extended to encourage students to adopt and enjoy good food habits. The availability of confections and carbonated beverages on school premises may tempt children to spend lunch money for them and lead to poor food habits. Their high energy value and continual availability are likely to affect children's appetites for regular meals.
>
> Expenditures for carbonated beverages and most confections yield a nutritional return greatly inferior to that from milk, fruit, and other foods included in the basic food groups. When given a choice between carbonated beverages and milk, or between candy and fruit, a child may choose the less nutritious. In view of these considerations, the Council on Foods and Nutrition is particularly opposed to the sale and distribution of confections and carbonated beverages in school lunchrooms.

BABY FOODS

Are commercial baby foods nutritious?

Baby foods have become one of the most popular of all processed foods. Young families spend between $100 and $200 a year on more than 115 varieties and forms of prepared strained and junior foods.

The baby food industry is employing several new methods of processing which help foods retain greater quantities of original nutrients plus better flavor, color, and consistency. Most of these are based on quick heating to sterilizing temperatures, followed by rapid cooling. However, even with the more careful method, there is some loss of vitamin C (found in orange juice and other fruit and vegetable products). Some of these products are fortified with vitamin C so it is wise to check the label first.

Baby cereals are highly recommended as a source of iron. Babies begin to exhaust their natural stores of iron as early as three months of age, and it is usually at this time that cereals are introduced into the diet. Six tablespoons of fortified cereal will furnish 133 percent of a baby's iron needs if he is younger than two months of age, or 80 percent if he is older. Family cereals such as Cream of Wheat can be a good iron source, but beware of any cereals that are not fortified with iron.

Strained meats are not quite as good an iron source as cereals and they are also more expensive. Since a baby cannot meet his total iron needs from strained meats alone, cereals should remain an important part of the baby's diet even after a wide variety of foods has been introduced in the diet. Strained meats are an excellent source of protein, however.

The protein content varies considerably among baby foods. Compare the following 4 3/4 oz dinners: "High Meat Dinners" (9.5 gm protein); pure strained (100 percent) meats (19 gm); junior meats (25 gm); soups and one-dish meals (3 gm); and cottage cheese mixtures (9.5 gm).

On the average, a 15-pound baby needs 14 gm of protein a day. Of course, when comparing these foods for their nutritive value, you need to consider your baby's likes and, possibly, the price.

Proper warming and storage of baby food leftovers can help to retain nutrients. It is best to remove from the container only the amount you intend to serve your baby. Why not heat the entire contents in the original container? If your baby eats part of the food, the repeated heating of the leftover portion will decrease nutrients and flavor and, in some cases, it may liquefy the food. Leftovers will keep well in the original covered container when refrigerated.

IMPORTANCE OF BREADS AND CEREALS

How important are breads and cereals in supplying nutrients?

Cereal foods—including bread, cereals, flour, and macaroni products—are important for body growth and repair. Whole grain or enriched cereal products offer a relatively inexpensive supply of important amounts of protein, thiamin, riboflavin, niacin, and iron as well as other vitamins and minerals; they are also excellent sources of food energy. Government authorities state that the importance of grain foods in the diet rests on their many-sided nutritional contributions at relatively low cost rather than on large contributions of one or two nutrients. As a source of thiamin, whole grain or enriched cereal products are especially important because there are only a few other foods which contain appreciable amounts of this vitamin. The proteins in cereal grains join those in milk and meat to help in building body tissue and promoting tissue repair, while iron provided by cereals is an important component of hemoglobin in red blood cells.

Cereal grains (wheat, rye, oats, rice, corn, and barley) offer interesting variety in the diet. They appear on the consumer market in many forms—for example, flours, breads, crackers, rolls, cakes, cookies, and other bakery goods; macaroni, noodles, and spaghetti; grits; and many types of cereals. This great variety in types, textures, flavors, and shapes can do wonders in appealing to the appetite and in stimulating the creative homemaker to use cereal foods in new combinations with other foods. Today's consumer can also purchase cereal foods in convenience forms which save endless hours of preparation time; however, these are more expensive.

Remember that not all cereal foods on today's grocery shelves have been made with whole grain or enriched flour nor are they restored to their original food value. Total nutrient value of cereal food can only be determined by careful reading of package labels. Unless the product label carries a statement of enrichment, one cannot be certain it was made with enriched flour. In fact, it is safe to assume that ordinary flour is used in most of the commercial pastries, cakes, and other specialty baked products. Ask the baker or market manager. If enriched flour is not used, indicate a preference for products made from enriched flour. The difference in cost between ordinary and enriched flour is so slight all bakers can afford to use the preferred flour. When food budgets are limited, make sure the cereal foods purchased are labeled "whole-grain" or "enriched" and use the nonenriched products only when variety or extra calories are desired.

IMPORTANCE OF BREAKFAST

Is there really good reason for all the emphasis on eating breakfast?

Breakfast is an important meal since it marks the end of an overnight fast. Studies made on the value of breakfast have shown

31

that performance during the late morning hours is impaired in individuals who skip breakfast.

In many instances, the coffee break or midmorning snack have replaced breakfast. A study was made to determine if there was any discernible difference in the performance of workers who ate breakfast and those who only had a midmorning snack. The observation was that a snack in the middle of the morning did not adequately replace a good breakfast in approximately half of the subjects who participated in the study. This fact was determined by work productivity. Individuals who ate breakfast did considerably more work in the late morning hours than those who omitted breakfast completely.

Deciding what to eat may require more time than the actual preparation! Breakfast today can vary from the few seconds needed to gulp an instant liquid meal to hours for a leisurely Sunday brunch. The food industry is valiantly trying to prevent breakfast from becoming an obsolete meal.

The size of the breakfast depends upon the individual's calorie and protein requirements, although a breakfast which supplies 25 percent of the day's nutrient needs is often recommended. Breakfast ought to be a family meal, with each member adjusting his morning schedule to accomplish this. The morning and evening meals may be the only times the family is together in one place. The crunch of crisp cereal may interfere with conversation but it can be harmonious.

EGGNOG BREAKFAST

Would an eggnog prepared from one egg, one tablespoon of sugar, three tablespoons of powdered whole milk, and eight ounces of whole milk constitute an adequate breakfast?

The breakfast described is not bad nutritionally. It is, of course, impossible to evaluate its true worth without knowing more about the nature of a person's other meals during the day and the spacing of them. The eggnog contains significant amounts of many important nutrients—approximately 20 gm of protein, 510 mg of calcium, 1,150 I.U. vitamin A, and 400 calories. With a breakfast of this nature, however, one would need to make sure that the other meals of the day contained foods with vitamin C and iron, as well as the B vitamins. It is also advisable to avoid the possibility of contaminated eggs by using only eggs which are uncracked and clean.

DANISH PASTRY AND COFFEE BREAKFAST

Isn't a breakfast of danish pastry (or doughnuts) and coffee adequate for some people?

Such a breakfast could hardly be expected to get you through the morning. A couple of small danish pastries would total about 300 calories; two pats of butter would provide an additional 100 calories. The amount of protein is far too little to be considered adequate—approximately 5 gm. Near absence of protein in a meal providing 300-400 calories could result in symptoms of hypoglycemia in two or three hours, a real midmorning letdown.

Doughnuts have even less protein than danish pastries on an equal weight basis. Two plain or raised doughnuts will provide 3 or 4 gm of protein, respectively, and 250 calories. On both counts, this would fall short of a good breakfast.

INSTANT BREAKFASTS

What do you think of the instant breakfasts?

The so-called instant breakfasts supply reasonable quantities of most of the nutrients needed by man. These breakfasts may be either a cake-like square, a powder to be mixed with milk, or a can of ready-mixed product. A portion—one can or the contents of an envelope mixed with eight fluid ounces of whole milk—will provide about 300 calories and 17 to 18 gm of protein. While the vitamin and mineral contents vary somewhat among products, they are designed to provide from 25 to 33 percent of the day's need for nutrients except calories.

There is always concern that foods designed for special use may lack those nutrients needed in minute amounts (trace nutrients). A mixed diet consisting of a variety of foods assures that the important major and minor nutrients are obtained. Since the liquid breakfasts are consumed as only one meal of the day and in many instances are used when otherwise no breakfast would be eaten, we probably shouldn't worry too much about their trace-nutrient content.

NUTRITION AND DENTAL HEALTH

How important is nutrition in the prevention of tooth decay? Particularly, are there any special foods which protect against cavities?

Of great importance is optimal nutrition, beginning early in life, that provides for the development of good quality teeth with some innate resistance to decay. Adequate amounts of calcium, magnesium, vitamin D, and protein are essential in development of such quality. Other food factors found to have a protective effect against cavities include fluoride, phosphates, and trace elements.

Fluoride is one of the most effective nutritional agents used in the fight against tooth decay. Fluoride seems to operate by making tooth enamel more resistant to action of acids in the mouth. Thus far, the best method for providing fluoride to the general population has been through the community water supply.

Dental decay results from destruction of the enamel and dentin of the tooth. Organic acids are formed from the action of bacterial enzymes upon fermentable carbohydrates in the mouth, and these acids attack tooth enamel.

Sucrose (table sugar) is regarded as the carbohydrate most threatening to the teeth. The *frequency* of sucrose intake is partly responsible. Sucrose between meals, particularly in sticky foods, increases the risk of cavities more so than does eating the same sweet, sticky foods at mealtime. There is little doubt about the correlation between the amounts of sweet, sticky foods eaten (and frequency of eating such foods) and the development of cavities.

FOOD FOR THE AGING

Are certain nutrients especially important for elderly people?

The general principles governing the planning of a diet for the older person do not differ much from those for other age groups. Basically, the older person needs the same nutrients required by the young adult, with possibly one exception—calories. In the older age group, the declines in metabolic rate and physical activity indicate a need for a decrease in caloric intake. Unfortunately, the decreased demand for calories by the body is not always accompanied by a decrease in appetite and as a result, overweight or obesity in the older person is commonly observed. Just eating less of everything is not the solution in this case. Thought must be given to the choices of food so that all the essential nutrients will be obtained—the necessary proteins, vitamins, and minerals. The best idea is to use the most nourishing foods and to avoid those that do not provide adequate nutritional value. Plenty of fluids and daily exercise are also important

Some stumbling blocks, however, may prevent the older person from getting an adequate diet. The senses of taste and smell become less acute in later years, and frequently the appetite is affected. More attention may have to be given to flavor and seasoning when preparing foods, as eye appeal and taste appeal are important. Many older people also have difficulty with faulty teeth or dentures. The type of food need not be changed, but the preparation of the food should be modified. Foods that are difficult to chew should be cubed, chopped, or ground.

Finally, the restricted income of many elderly persons means that each food dollar must be spent carefully, allowing little leeway for foods low in nutritive value.

ALCOHOLISM

Is it true that almost all alcoholics suffer from malnutrition?

It is believed that a great many are malnourished. Obviously, the calories from alcohol can replace a good portion of the calories that should be obtained from foods which supply important nutrients. Appetite for "normal" foods may be quite poor, frequently because of gastritis produced by the alcohol.

As the alcoholism progresses, the small intestine's ability to absorb nutrients decreases seriously. Thus, fats, fat-soluble vitamins, B vitamins, and proteins may not be effectively used. Also alcohol increases the urinary loss of some minerals and amino acids.

Alcoholics who do not have severe liver damage (i.e., cirrhosis) frequently recover their health very quickly when they return to an adequate diet and discontinue the use of alcohol.

DISLIKES MILK

If a person dislikes milk, is it possible to obtain a balanced diet without it?

The nutrients that present problems when milk is absent from the diet are calcium, vitamin D, and riboflavin. Calcium and riboflavin are present in cheese, ice cream, legumes, and green leafy vegetables and, of course, calcium can be taken in the form of tablets. Vitamin D is more difficult to obtain. If fortified milk is refused by children, supplements of vitamin D should be employed as advised by a physician. Other nutrients present in milk—vitamin A, thiamin, riboflavin, niacin, and phosphorus—are easily obtained from other sources such as meats, fruits, and vegetables.

Hopefully, the person who dislikes milk will experiment with different flavorings to disguise the taste before giving up milk altogether.

TWO-PERCENT MILK

Is it all right to give children two-percent milk?

It certainly is. Two-percent milk is simply milk with 2 percent milk fat instead of the usual 3.5 percent fat of whole milk. Some producers add an extra amount of nonfat milk solids to two-percent milk to give it more body. The additional milk solids and intermediate amount of fat make two-percent milk only slightly lower in calories than whole milk. Two-percent milk provides about 142 calories per glass (eight ounces) compared with 159 calories per glass of whole milk with 3.5 percent fat.

DISLIKES VEGETABLES

It is difficult to get children (and some adults) to eat vegetables. Is the effort justified? Wouldn't it be simpler to forget vegetables and use vitamin supplements?

Youngsters who are not exposed early in life to a variety of vegetables enticingly prepared will probably never learn to enjoy them. They should not be browbeaten into eating vegetables but should be asked to cooperate in attempting to develop an interest in all foods. With the variety of vegetables on the market today and the many ways of preparing them, it is difficult to dislike all vegetables. If vegetables are prepared in creative ways, youngsters will soon catch on. Of course, it is not necessary to cook vegetables; many of them are most appetizing when served raw. Try tomato juice, too!

Vegetables contribute not only important quantities of vitamins and minerals but roughage as well, important in the digestion of foods and the absorption of nutrients. Roughage is not provided in vitamin supplements. Fruits and vegetables, particularly the dark green and deep yellow vegetables, provide at least 50 percent of the vitamin A (as carotene) in the usual diet. Because they are significant sources of this vitamin, the green and yellow vegetables should be included in the meal plan at least every other day. When properly cooked in a minimum of water, the dark green vegetables also contain important quantities of vitamin C. In general, from 10 to 20 percent of the B vitamins, iron, magnesium, and calcium in the usual diet, come from vegetables and fruits.

MEAT COSTS AND PROTEIN

Are not high meat costs forcing some people to have diets too low in protein?

Recognizing that not all Americans have an easy time obtaining enough of the right kinds of food, we can still make the statement that protein availability is not a serious problem here. Elsewhere in the world, protein shortage for growing children is a problem. In the U.S., the protein available for consumption is equal to 120 gm per person per day. This is roughly twice our needs.

Several possibilities exist to help contend with the high cost of meat. Study the weekly food specials in the newspaper. Use the best bargains for meat, poultry, and fish. Compare prices in shopping for other good protein sources: whole-grain cereals, cheese, milk (especially powdered), legumes, and peanut butter. With a little more time and care, the least expensive foods can be selected to provide more than enough protein.

We probably eat too much protein anyway. Nutritionists are concerned that high-protein diets may have an adverse effect on calcium metabolism—a potential problem for followers of high-protein, high-fat, reducing diets since protein intake is many times the requirement.

LIVER SUBSTITUTE

What's a good liver substitute for a family that simply won't eat liver?

A number of years ago much emphasis was placed on the so-called "protective foods"—selected foods that provided nutrients needed to protect against nutritional inadequacy. Liver as a "protective food" was given much acclaim as an important source of a number of vitamins and minerals. Nutritionists advised people to eat liver frequently, once a week or so.

Now, with the number of foods abundantly available throughout the year, emphasis on the "protective foods" has declined. Proper selection from the variety of nutritious food available is now advised. This approach lends more variability in food choice and, therefore, more variety in meals.

For those not fond of liver, substitution of foods which provide food value similar to liver will still do the trick: (1) other meats, poultry, fish, eggs, milk and milk products provide the protein; (2) other meats, egg yolks, dried fruits, green leafy vegetables, and enriched and whole-grain cereals provide iron; (3) other meats, poultry, milk, and whole-grain or enriched cereals contribute B vitamins; and (4) deep yellow and green vegetables, milk, butter, and margarine provide vitamin A.

If you like neither to cook nor to eat liver—but still think you should—try to get over any squeamishness by finding some gourmet techniques for preparation. Why not experiment? Try cutting liver (membrane removed) in strips, adding flour and seasoning, and deep-frying it for a change.

IRON IN FOODS

Is it possible for the average person to get enough iron without using a supplement?

Not always. Nutritionists and hematologists have been concerned about reports that young girls and women consume diets that provide approximately half of their iron requirements. The RDA of iron for females between ages 11 and 50 is 18 mg a day. The amount of iron available for consumption in the total array of foods on the market is about 10 mg for every 2,000 calories. Since not all iron eaten is absorbed, it is apparent that only about half of the necessary iron is available. This has been confirmed by studies of the dietary habits of women. Women, who have a greater need for iron than do men, consume on the average only 8 to 12 mg per day.

In general, 50 to 60 percent of the iron in the usual diet is supplied by cereals and meats, with nearly equal contributions from each. The proportion of cereals and meats consumed by women varies widely. Whenever weight is a problem, the general tendency is to reduce the amount of cereal products consumed. Cereal consumption decreases as the consumer's affluence increases. Thus, that group of foods which provides additional iron through enrichment often is slighted by women.

Several simple recommendations can be made to increase the amount of iron available. None of these can assure relief, however, if the foods are not eaten by those who need the most iron. Increasing the amount of iron in cereal and flour is one step recently proposed by the FDA; regulations on the enrichment formulas may be revised. If women would eat cereals, this alone would suffice. A number of prepared breakfast foods are fortified at levels higher than that called for in the standard enrichment formula. Some of these foods provide 8 to 10 mg in a one-ounce serving.

Education programs to encourage women to consume a greater variety of foods rich in iron would help. Meat, eggs, green vegetables, beans, nuts, and whole-grain and enriched cereals are the best sources of iron. The inactive, calorie-conscious female probably still would not obtain sufficient iron in her limited food supply.

A third recommendation which has merit is that females with high iron requirements—e.g., those with abnormal menstrual losses, or pregnant women—use supplemental iron preparations as recommended by their physicians. Women who are thinking about starting a family should take steps to build up adequate body stores of iron to see them through their pregnancies.

VEGANS AND OTHER VEGETARIANS

So many different questions have been asked about vegetarianism. We try to answer most of them in the following paragraphs.

A vegan is considered to be a strict vegetarian—that is, one who eats *no* animal products. The term "vegetarian" is used rather loosely and may apply to a person who eats eggs and dairy products but avoids animal flesh. Those persons who refer to themselves as vegetarians differ greatly in both dietary habits and motivations for such habits.

To obtain all the necessary nutrients via a vegetarian diet is possible, although it does require more than a sketchy knowledge of nutritive values of foods. Special care should be taken to include a variety of whole-grain cereals, legumes, nuts and nut-like seeds, as well as a good variety of fruits and vegetables. A vegan will require a supplemental source of vitamin B_{12}, since this vitamin is found almost exclusively in foods of animal origin. By including eggs and dairy products, the more liberal vegetarian will find it less difficult than the vegan to meet requirements for calories, B vitamins, and calcium. Apparently, most vegetarians are able to obtain enough protein from vegetable sources to meet their daily needs. The amino acids from a number of plant foods do add up to complete protein.

Scientists are trying to learn more about the long-term effects of vegan diets for many reasons. First, vegetable foods may become increasingly important as a protein source throughout the world. Also, several studies with vegans have shown that they have lower serum cholesterol levels than their nonvegetarian counterparts. This is undoubtedly partly due to the substitution of vegetable oils for animal fats. However, there have also been studies suggesting that a diet high in fiber (a characteristic of a vegan diet) can bring about a decrease in serum cholesterol.

It certainly would be premature to rave about health benefits from vegetarianism. Some vegetarians will live to an impressive old age, but, then, so will some meat-eaters.

FOOD FIT FOR A DOG

Aren't the nutrient requirements of cats and dogs similar to man's requirements? Why are table scraps not recommended for pets, and why is pet food not recommended for human consumption?

According to an old wives' tale, feeding a dog a lot of meat, especially if it's raw, will make the dog vicious. Most people have learned that cats and dogs are primarily carnivores, or flesh-eaters, but many pet owners have forgotten this or are wondering if perhaps there isn't some truth in the old wives' tale.

"Wolfing" aptly describes the eating pattern of the carnivore, whose teeth are designed for tearing rather than chewing and whose stomach has as a chief function the digestion of proteins. Meats, canned pet foods, milk, and eggs are good sources of protein and supply the other nutrients necessary, including some fat and carbohydrate.

The amount of carbohydrate needed by cats and dogs has not been determined. All-cereal pet foods are inexpensive sources of energy but should be used in moderate amounts—never to the exclusion of major protein foods. When a pet is fed table scraps, the diet may consist of too little protein, too much carbohydrate, and a great deal of unnecessary bulk. Canned pet foods may be designed to be "nutritionally complete" for pets. It is doubtful that these products contain enough of all the nutrients necessary for man, particularly not vitamin C. (Vitamin C is synthesized by dogs and cats.)

Government regulations regarding packaging and processing are similar to those for any canned food. From a bacteriological and nutritional standpoint, these products should be safe for human consumption. There is, however, considerable variation among brands as to content and nutritional value. Some may be lower in protein than others. Overcoming any problems of nutritional acceptability for human consumption would be much less difficult than overcoming the problem of psychological unacceptability.

-3-
weight control

The editor of a leading magazine once stated that the best way to sell magazines was to feature articles on sex, weight reduction, or Billy Graham. What ever happened to Billy Graham? So many articles and books have been written on weight control as to create a serious threat to our nation's resources of paper pulp. If the paper could be recycled at the same rate as people recycle their body fat (the ups and downs of weight) there would be enough to go around. Obesity is a serious situation; we should not make light of it.

A conference we attended many years ago concluded that obesity was a public health problem with no known applicable public health means to correct it. The solution, it was suggested, was to apply every effort to help the public avoid overweight in the first place. Prevention promises more in the long run than does treatment. This grave conclusion still seems to apply, more than fifteen years later.

Public health records suggest that from 25 to 40 percent of our population is overweight, with perhaps 20 percent of us being truly obese, i.e., more than 20 percent over best weight. There is no simple explanation for obesity. Ever so many factors must be taken into consideration—genetics, emotional stability, body chemistry, physical inactivity, overeating, infant feeding practices, family health attitudes, and many more. In a sense, obesity is an energy crisis in reverse: too much fuel stored in the form of fat.

This section answers a few questions about dieting, foods, and calories in weight control. It even tells you how to gain weight.

The section can be criticized for not sufficiently emphasizing the importance of exercise in weight control. Adequate exercise is the most neglected aspect of the maintenance of health and fitness. Americans pay dearly for convenience—in money and ill health. It is quite unlikely that any kind of medical or dietary treatment will be found to compensate for or correct the problems created by physical inactivity. This holds true for both underweight and overweight people. Nutrition and exercise should not be treated as separate entities, particularly in the prevention of overweight. To put this into perspective, this is what Dr. Jean Mayer of Harvard University has discovered: The physically active man of today is less active than the sedentary man of 100 years ago—yet he eats like the moderately active man of a century ago. Think about that—then start walking, riding a bike, doing something!

SUCCESSFUL WEIGHT REDUCTION

If most of the popular reducing diets have been tried without success, is there any hope?

The fact that none of the reducing diets has worked suggests that perhaps not enough time has been taken to become acquainted with some fundamental concepts of weight control. Perhaps the most important of these concepts is that any increase in weight, regardless of how insignificant it may seem, should be reversed immediately. One ounce of fat not gained in the first place is better than the pound which must be removed later.

Second, the reason why unwanted weight has been gained must also be understood. Professional help may well be necessary since there are many causes of the "imbalance between caloric intake and caloric expenditure" which results in overweight. Sometimes, weight gain follows when a sedentary way of life is adopted without having made proportionate adjustment in food intake. Physiologically, however, rapid weight gain seems to occur at rather predictable intervals in the life of the female: (1) during early infancy and at the beginning of puberty; and (2) after maturation at about age 20 to 21, during pregnancy, and at menopause. The mature male, however (except for the tendency to gain weight during early infancy and at puberty), apparently has no specific physiological or chronological periods when there is danger of weight gain. He just slowly gains weight unless he takes steps to reverse the trend.

Third, unless a person truly wants to lose weight and is properly motivated to do so, failure is almost certain. Assuming that a person *wants* to lose weight and is willing to make the necessary adjustments in his way of life, he is ready for the following steps which constitute an adequate dietary regimen.

Check eating habits to determine that a wide variety of foods with all the nutrients needed for good health is being consumed. Is this variety being chosen from each of the following groups: milk and milk products; meat, fish, poultry, eggs, and dried beans or peas; fruits and vegetables; and whole-grain or enriched breads and cereals? Reducing diets need not be nutritionally imbalanced in any nutrient, except for a decrease in calories. Make whatever adjustments are required in food choices to assure that the basic diet is a good one. Now, adjust the *amount* of each food item without eliminating any one food from the diet. The key to weight reduction is to eat less food without haphazardly eliminating any one food completely. Let quality and flavor be a guide; enjoy a little bit of all foods, but not an inordinate quantity of any one.

Reducing diets also should be based on foods normally consumed if they are to lead to a lifetime of successful weight maintenance. If good eating habits are not instituted during the period of weight reduction, continuing maintenance of "ideal" weight will be most difficult, if not impossible. Important as they are, however, careful selection of food and reduction of food intake are not enough—a person must also indulge in regular physical activity commensurate with his physical condition.

Programs of proper weight maintenance ultimately should replace the current preoccupation with weight loss. The change from the "reducing" diet to that for weight "maintenance" is very subtle, with only minor adjustments in the amount of food eaten. Experience gained during the initial weight reduction, however, should make it possible to make whatever adjustments are needed later to reverse temporary weight-gain setbacks.

The inability of bizarre reduction diets to provide adequate weight control because of their radical departure from the normal daily diet is what contributes to their downfall. A successful weight-reduction diet is one which, with minor caloric adjustments, becomes an enjoyable way of life and provides for desirable weight maintenance.

COUNTING CALORIES

If a person wants to lose weight, can he simply count calories without using any particular dietary regimen?

Generally, the use of a table of caloric values as the sole means of selecting foods for a weight-reduction diet should not be encouraged. Foods should never be evaluated strictly on the basis of their caloric value. The inclination of the dieter is to exclude foods which appear to be of high caloric value and to choose only those which are low. The result is frequently a low-calorie diet that is limited in important nutrients.

Foods have been classified into four food groups according to their common content of nutrients: meat, fish, poultry, eggs, and dried peas and beans; milk and other dairy products; fruits and vegetables; and whole-grain or enriched breads and cereals. The selection of foods from these various groups in amounts recommended will provide the nutrients needed and will permit a reasonable management of calories.

LOW-CARBOHYDRATE DIET

Is a diet containing little, if any, carbohydrate suitable for weight reduction?

The case for a reducing diet that is unusually low in carbohydrate is not at all convincing. In the last decade, it has been well-demonstrated that carbohydrates (which include starches and sugars) are important in the diet. The adult who is accustomed to a normal diet probably needs at least 100 gm of carbohydrate a day in order to avoid the undesirable metabolic changes that are representative of carbohydrate deficiency.

What happens when a person is deprived of carbohydrate? Some of the problems are fatigue; low blood pressure resulting from changes in posture; losses of nitrogen, fluid, sodium, and other minerals, which puts the acid-base balance out of kilter; ketosis (an incomplete breakdown of fats, with an accumulation of ketone bodies in the blood stream). In addition, the diet may not contain sufficient roughage for good gastrointestinal functioning.

While some may view with delight the prospect of rapid weight loss on a carbohydrate-free diet, the accompanying physiological changes are certainly undesirable and potentially hazardous. Also, the initial rapid weight loss is largely due to water loss and does not represent an increased breakdown of body fat. When carbohydrate intake is below, say, 50 gm, the amounts of meats and fats in the diet are necessarily greater, and undoubtedly produce a reduced appetite because of their satiety value. The ketones in the blood stream also contribute to suppression of appetite. Weight loss continues, then, because the dieter is consuming fewer calories. Claims that weight loss occurs even with high-caloric intake, but no carbohydrate, are absurd. Although authors of popular diet books frequently say that loss of body fat can occur regardless of high-calorie intake, this is not supported by evidence and, in fact, is refuted by laws of thermodynamics.

Carbohydrates are important in themselves, and the foods which supply them supply other nutrients as well. This also holds true for fats and protein. Claims made for the benefits of any intentionally unbalanced reducing diet not only lack scientific support but also tend to divert attention from the need to maintain and promote good health—the major medical reason for reducing the weight!

THE "PREGNANCY HORMONE"

There is a new reducing plan that requires injections of some hormone produced by pregnant women. Has this method been proved successful?

The hormone used in this method is human chorionic gonado-tropin (HCG) which is prepared from the urine of pregnant women.

Dr. A.T.W. Simeons, a physician who practiced in Rome, first suggested the method about 20 years ago. He reported great success in weight reduction among patients who followed a 500-calorie diet and had daily injections of HCG. Normally, 500 calories a day is not enough to maintain good health, but the physician argued that HCG made it possible for an obese person to get along on 500 calories a day without discomfort. He reported that his patients lost an average of one pound per day, but some lost as much as two pounds per day.

However, the American Medical Association, in its book, AMA *Drug Evaluations*, states: "The claim that daily injections of chori-onic gonadotropin cause weight loss and redistribution of body weight has not been substantiated." Researchers are attempting to learn more about the hormone, but, as yet, no one has answered these questions:

1. Does the combination of HCG and a 500-calorie diet bring about a weight loss not possible with a 500-calorie diet alone?

2. Is HCG useful in long-range (lifelong) treatment of obesity? (If not, an individual undertaking the program is courting great disappointment—at considerable expense!) How many people maintain their weight loss one year after therapy? Two years?

3. If HCG works, *how* does it work? At any risk to health?

As one physician puts it, HCG will more likely continue to be of theoretical interest rather than a practical tool for treating obesity.

WEIGHT GAIN ON LOW-CALORIE DIET

Overweight people seem to continue to gain weight on a very low-caloric intake. Are some overweight people different from others who are over-weight?

Medical scientists are exploring the possibility that some metabolic abnormalities may make people fat; however, the re-search is far from conclusive. In the meantime, there are two con-siderations to bear in mind.

First, what a person ate while becoming overweight may not resemble what he eats while maintaining the extra weight. For ex-ample, the excessive caloric intake which led to the obesity might be replaced by an actual decrease in caloric intake, but not enough of a decrease to cause weight loss. Thus, the obesity level is maintained. The obese person is generally very inactive, and this greatly reduces his caloric requirement so that the obese state can be maintained on fewer calories per day than were required to cause the initial weight gain.

Second, a person's true dietary habit is usually a closely guarded secret or is unrealistically appraised so that caloric intake is frequently underestimated. Accurate dietary histories are difficult to obtain under the best of conditions, as concepts of serving sizes differ and people conveniently forget what they actually ate. This was illustrated in a report of six obese patients who were interviewed to obtain information about their caloric intakes. The initial dietary histories indicated caloric intakes under 2,000 calories per day even though some of the subjects were gaining weight. According to the report, the dietitians, after gaining better rapport with the subjects, recorded dietary intakes of 3,000 to 5,000 calories per day for some of the subjects. It was reported that some patients actually consumed 3,000 to 4,000 calories in a single evening. There have been reports that other obese patients have food intakes equivalent to about 1,800 calories. This number of calories could maintain a state of obesity, but probably could not lead to further weight gain.

Maintain a healthy skepticism about estimates of caloric intake and disbelieve testimonials; they are usually misleading.

MORE GAINED THAN EATEN?

Is it possible to gain more weight than the actual weight of the food eaten? Can a pound of peanuts add more than one pound of body weight?

Persons baffled by this teaser have not learned to think of foods as fuel. The energy-potential (calories) of a food is the crux of the matter, not the weight of the food, because the food is metabolized. One pound of peanuts placed in the stomach will temporarily increase weight by one pound; so will a pound of tomatoes. When metabolized, the pound of peanuts produces 2,600 calories and the pound of tomatoes about 95 calories.

One pound of body fat is equivalent to approximately 3,500 calories if called upon to provide energy. Does this mean that one and a third pounds of peanuts (3,500 calories) can form a pound of body fat (3,500 calories)? No, not unless all 3,500 calories from the peanuts are *excess* calories, that is, calories in excess of the number needed for the day.

There is a temporary, apparent weight gain from the weight of food and liquids consumed, but this is cancelled by excretion, respiration, and the general cost of living. Weight is never stationary; it is constantly fluctuating around a mean value.

Now, as for the possibility that a pound of food could have greater calorie potential than a pound of body fat, yes, this is the case with pure fats and oils. One pound of salad oil, for example, supplies over 4,000 calories.

OVERWEIGHT CHILDREN

When young children are overweight, what type of diet should they follow to lose weight but still maintain good health and needed energy?

When young children enter the growth spurt of adolescence, hopefully, the energy demands of growth may automatically take care of any overweight problem. In all probability, the family physician will prefer to see a weight reduction occur in this manner, rather than attempting to reduce a child's body weight by way of a stringent diet.

However, as most children form eating habits and develop food attitudes by imitating others in the family, it might be well to evaluate the food attitudes and patterns of the entire family, particularly those of the parents. Parental habits often inadvertently contribute to overweight. Check the family on the following: Does the family enjoy nutritious meals including milk and other dairy products, vegetables and fruits, meats, and breads and cereals? If these foods are carefully chosen and attractively presented to normally active and healthy children, they rarely lead to excessive weight gain. Rapid weight gain more often results from poor choice of foods—too little milk, meat, vegetables, fruits, etc., as well as an over-supply of candy, soft drinks, and fatty foods. Too many second and third servings of foods, even though nutritious, also may cause youngsters to gain weight. Do individuals in the family also:

1. Snack between meals on high-calorie sweets rather than on more nutritious foods? This may not only add extra pounds, but may also dull the appetite for the next square meal.

2. Try fad dieting to achieve a ten-pound weight loss in only a few weeks? This is usually of little help. Weight that is lost on a dieting binge is usually regained because correct eating habits are not formed at the beginning and the individual resumes the same faulty eating pattern as before.

3. Nibble constantly? This may be a sign of unhappiness or lack of interesting activities.

Does the family also realize the importance of regular, unhurried, and pleasant mealtimes; early and regular bedtimes; suitable amounts of outdoor play or other exercise; and interesting activities alone and with other people? Physical exercise for healthy children is an excellent way to help use extra food calories, develop good muscle tone, and give children an interest other than food! Aiding the normal growth and development of children is a great challenge for parents and requires their encouragement and calm guidance in many facets of fitness—physical as well as mental, emotional, and social.

A weight-reduction diet for a child should be used only at the suggestion and under the guidance of a physician. Discuss the family's dietary pattern with the physician; he may then offer additional suggestions.

FASTING

Is fasting an acceptable method for reducing weight?

Starvation as a means of inducing weight loss has been practiced for ages. Despite such previous experience, overweight persists. Starvation cannot constitute an entire program for weight control. A number of physicians, however, have prescribed periods of short-term starvation but have incorporated them into their over-all programs of weight reduction. Reports from these physicians indicate that desire for food subsides after a short time so that hunger is not acute.

There is probably no harm for the normal individual in abstaining from food for a day or two. However, nutrition authorities have pointed out that the desire of the starving, but unhungry, patient is to effect a drastic weight loss quickly and that this may induce him to extend the period of starvation unwisely. Starvation, in addition to causing a depletion of body fat and protein, can induce other hazardous effects not readily recognized. A form of gouty arthritis, low blood pressure, and anemia have been reported in some patients after relatively short periods of food privation. Some individuals with certain diseases should never attempt a starvation regimen.

It has been stated that about the only advantage of obesity is that fat people can withstand starvation better than lean ones. Nevertheless, starvation, even for short periods, should not be attempted without medical supervision. We consider fasting to be a method reserved for those very obese persons for whom other methods of treatment have failed repeatedly.

HYPNOSIS

Can hypnosis help a person lose weight?

In special instances, hypnosis has been used to treat obesity, but physicians are only lukewarm about using it. So far, there's no agreement on just how hypnosis works or whether it's even medically suited for such applications. Presumably, hypnosis may help alter eating habits and reinforce basic feelings about food. But, it's doubtful that someone who is poorly motivated could be helped, since the motivation to succeed is of prime importance in dietary change. A physician can advise whether hypnosis might be a practical approach for the particular person, and he should be able to suggest a competent practitioner.

BURNING UP CALORIES

Is it true that some foods "burn up" faster than others? Are there some catabolic foods that can help in losing weight?

The rapidity with which food is digested or absorbed does not affect the caloric value of the diet. Regardless of the time required for digestion and absorption, calories will be converted to fatty tissue if their total intake exceeds energy expenditure.

There are also no foods designated as catabolic. "Catabolic" refers to the catabolic process wherein proteins, fats, and carbohydrates are broken down to provide the body with utilizable energy and, ultimately, excretable end products. In a sense, the body goes through a catabolic process when caloric restriction (through weight reduction or appetite loss) is imposed, as the body is forced to utilize energy stored in the form of fat. Any diet which provides insufficient calories will cause such a catabolic shift toward utilization of stored fat.

Knowledge of the satiety value (feeling of satisfaction or fullness) of certain foods may be helpful when trying to achieve weight reduction. When food intake is limited, the low-caloric diet should be as satisfying as possible; therefore, foods containing protein and moderate amounts of fats must be included. Both protein and fat have a "staying power" in the stomach, whereas foods predominantly high in carbohydrate leave the stomach rather quickly. As fat is the most concentrated source of calories, fat-containing foods should be used in moderation or in accord with the prescribed diet. When a weight-reduction diet is not relatively satisfying, but gives that "empty" feeling, dieters are tempted to overstep the prescribed diet.

RICE DIET

People using a diet consisting of rice, fruit, and sugar have lost about twelve pounds in three weeks. Would it be harmful to follow such a diet?

Many diets advocated as producing a weight loss are nutritionally inadequate. The "rice diet" is a good example; it is grossly imbalanced nutritionally and not recommended for general use.

A diet consisting mainly of rice was introduced by Dr. W. Kempner in 1944 for treatment of hypertension and kidney disease. The daily diet consisted of rice (7 to 12 ounces dry), sugar, and fruit. The rice could be steamed or cooked but no additional salt, milk, or fat was permitted. The diet provided approximately 2,000 calories, 15 to 30 gm protein, 4 to 6 gm fat, and 450 gm carbohydrate. The diet is extremely low in sodium—about 100 to 150 mg daily.

In recent years the Kempner diet has been resurrected as the basis for a weight-reduction diet. Certain modifications allow the inclusion of nonfat milk or butter in addition to the rice, fruit, and sugar. The modified diet averages approximately 1,300 calories and contains more sodium (about 425 mg). This diet is very limited in the type of foods allowed and, therefore, lacks certain nutrients essential to health, specifically iron, protein, niacin, and perhaps vitamin A. There is no doubt that considerable weight would be lost on this diet because of the curtailed caloric intake. The restricted sodium intake also would induce diuresis (increased excretion of urine) which could show up on the scale as a sudden weight loss. This, however, is not a loss of adipose (fatty) tissue but a loss of body water. As soon as the sodium intake returns to the usual level of consumption, an immediate weight gain would probably occur until fluid equilibrium is attained.

A more adequate diet would be one selected from a variety of "everyday" foods which will later help maintain a person's desirable weight. The diet will have built-in permanence since it can be continued on a lifelong basis; such is not the case with the rice diet.

DIETING WITH FISH

Is it true that the consumption of fish four times a week causes a reduction in the caloric content of other foods? Can fish perform such miracles?

Although fish is nutritious and used in most diets, it has no magical properties. There is no food which renders other food calories unavailable. Fish is frequently featured in weight-reduction diets because many varieties are low in fat and, consequently, are lower in calories than many cuts of meat. Fish can be broiled and served with sauces that furnish few additional calories. Fish is also featured in diets designed to regulate blood cholesterol, since the fat of fish contains more of the polyunsaturated fatty acids than does the fat of most meats.

DIETING WITH GRAPEFRUIT

Is it true that grapefruit has a component which oxidizes fat and thus would be beneficial in a reducing diet?

This is reminiscent of other claims for so-called catabolic foods said to mobilize or burn up stored fat. If so, how is it done? With enzymes?

Most fresh foods contain enzymes which can digest fats. The concentration and activity of the enzymes are generally small except in such plants as the castor bean. Food enzymes are inactivated by cooking and digestion and thus could not have any effect on metabolism. Plant enzymes would be of no importance in human nutrition.

The processes of mobilization of stored fat and subsequent metabolism of the fatty acids are very complicated and in part under hormonal control. Even if there were ways to preferentially mobilize and oxidize fat, they would be of limited benefit since the energy released would have to be accounted for.

The body cannot excrete fatty acids, nor can it pass off partially oxidized intermediates of fat metabolism to any significant degree. The oxidation or catabolism of fat yields nine calories per gram of fat utilized. Of course, during caloric deficiency, stored fat is utilized, but fanciful claims for mobilization imply more than this.

The body cannot keep moving fat around; it has to do something with it and there are only two possibilities. The body can store the fat somewhere else, or it can oxidize it as demanded by metabolic needs. Fat cannot be eliminated from the body except after oxidation to carbon dioxide and water.

ICE MILK AND DIETETIC BRANDS

In trying to keep their weight down, some people substitute ice milk for ice cream. Is there any difference in caloric value between the two? How does regular ice milk differ from dietetic ice milk?

Many ice milks are low-fat mixtures made from milk, sugar, and flavoring, usually with added nonfat-milk solids. Generally, an average serving of vanilla ice milk ($^1/_6$ quart) will contain about 137 calories, compared to an equal serving of vanilla ice cream which contains about 174 calories—a difference of 37 calories. (Calories would vary slightly with different brands; the high-fat ice creams may contain 200 calories per $^1/_6$ quart.) The difference in calories might seem insignificant, however, a person on a weight-control program should select nutritious foods providing the least number of calories. If you have been enjoying ice milk as a dessert, by all means continue doing so. However, also remember that eating extra-large amounts of ice milk will easily offset any caloric advantage.

Dietetic ice milk is only slightly lower in calories than regular ice milk. It is designated as "dietetic" not because it is significantly lower in calories, but because it contains an artificial sweetener in place of sugar. Dietetic ice milks are used in diets restricted in the most concentrated source of carbohydrate, i.e., sugar. Persons with diabetes should use caution with serving sizes of any of the products described here and, above all, check with a physician about the use of such foods.

DISLIKE SKIM MILK

When overweight members of the family dislike skim milk and don't like the way it looks, what can be done about it?

Serve all the milk in opaque tumblers, such as aluminum tumblers, and do not put milk on the table in a pitcher. This way the difference in appearance of the milk will be less noticeable. As for overcoming taste prejudices, try using first the two-percent milks (with 2 percent of the fat remaining) and then gradually, over the days or weeks, replace this milk by mixing it with the skim milk. This *may* help in developing tolerance for the taste of skim milk. When preparing fluid skim milk from the nonfat powdered product, make the milk the day before and allow it to stand in the refrigerator at least overnight; this greatly improves its flavor. The powdered milk already mixed with water can also be combined with two-percent milk for better flavor.

"FATTENING FOODS"

Some low-calorie diets include fattening foods such as potatoes, bread, and other starches. Shouldn't such foods be eliminated completely?

It is very unfair to label any food as "fattening." The total calories in a day make the difference, not the presence of any particular food. If an individual ate 3 cups of mashed potatoes (about 600 calories) every day and excluded all other foods, he would lose weight. Why? The total number of calories consumed would be less than the calories expended. Rather than fearing starchy or "fattening" foods, concentrate on using the proper amounts of all foods that are important to the diet.

EATING SLOWLY

Will a person consume less food if he eats slowly than if he eats very quickly?

Possibly a person who is eating slowly is more likely to be aware of the early signals of approaching "fullness" (or the gradual dwindling of the desire for food) than if he were eating rapidly. On the other hand, the fast eater presumably would swallow more air than usual, which could contribute to a feeling of fullness. But a "yes" or "no" answer to the question is not possible. Since the process of digestion begins in the mouth, it does make sense to refrain from bolting food.

Important psychological factors are behind recommendations for slow eating given to persons trying to lose weight. Smaller servings may seem adequate if an individual slowly savors and reluctantly swallows each bite. Also, regulating the speed of eating is an exercise in self-control, a virtue essential to long-term success in weight control.

OVEREATING DURING HOLIDAYS

Are there any suggestions for avoiding the weight problem that always follows the Christmas and New Year's holidays?

The temptation is to suggest that one simply eat less than in years past or exercise more during the holidays. Understandably, when the Christmas dinner is on the table or bowls of fruits, nuts, and candy are at the elbow, it seems impossible to eat less than usual.

If a person is serious about not wanting to gain weight, however, he can take certain measures. Make certain to taste the holiday fare, but not to eat very much of any one item. A person knows by now approximately how much food he can eat every day without gaining weight—use that as a bench mark. Also, deliberately eat less during the few days before the holiday feast. This is preferable to going without after the holidays, as it salves the conscience enough to enable full enjoyment of holiday eating. As holiday treats are usually rich, a great many calories can be avoided by special efforts to prepare low-caloric goodies. Most modern cookbooks include sections devoted to cookies and candies with lower than usual caloric content. Try some of these recipes; it may be possible to eat the cake and not have so many calories too! There is probably no harm in brief periods of dietary indiscretion. It is when the indiscretion extends from Thanksgiving to New Year's that trouble may begin. Use good judgment; avoid having to make a new diet a New Year's resolution.

PERIOD OF RAPID WEIGHT GAIN

When college students graduate, they often tend to gain weight rapidly. Why is this so?

Many times graduation from school or college marks the end of *regular* physical activity. For one thing, athletic facilities are never again as conveniently accessible to most people. In some areas, community sports centers are excellent, but often these are not used regularly by the young people who are beginning careers and perhaps marriage and child-rearing. The once-active student may enter a sedentary occupation. The period of child-bearing is a time when women are especially vulnerable to becoming overweight. Finally, after marriage both partners may find that there are increasingly more demands on their time; an hour set aside for swimming or tennis may seem an impossibility.

All people should count on reducing caloric intake in their early 20's if their total activity has lessened. If each day an individual expends only 100 calories fewer than he or she consumes, a weight gain of 10 pounds will accumulate within a year.

SODIUM AND WEIGHT GAIN

Is it possible to gain weight (as water) because of too much salt in the diet?

The use of larger than necessary amounts of sodium may cause some weight gain because of fluid retention if the sodium is retained by the body; this occurs when a person has a kidney abnormality. In a normal person, however, the fluid retention from large amounts of sodium is temporary and has little effect on weight gain.

WANT TO GAIN WEIGHT

How can one gain weight if he has always been underweight?

It is refreshing to learn that there is at least one adult in this country who is not trying to lose weight. Without knowing whether the person in question is *really* underweight or whether he is just 25 or 30 pounds under what his friends weigh, it should be recalled that certain advantages lie in being somewhat under the so-called average weight for one's age and height. The person who is slightly under average weight has a lower probability of contracting certain diseases and apparently enjoys a longer life than those who are overweight.

True, being underweight is considered a manifestation of malnutrition, or undernutrition. A person is diagnosed as under-nourished when he is losing weight continuously or when he is significantly under his desirable weight for his age, sex, body build, and activity. Continual weight loss or a stabilized lower weight may be the only sign of nutritive deficiency that ever appears in the undernourished adult. Other internal and external manifestations of malnutrition may appear, however, if the condition is allowed to continue, and these may be followed by the more classical signs of grave deficiency disease during the most severe stages of under-nutrition.

The correct treatment for adult undernutrition cannot be insti-tuted until its cause is known. If it can be established that a person is considerably under his ideal weight but has not been losing weight continuously, how did he get this way, and what can be done? Frequent causes of inadequate food intake or loss of appe-tite are social factors, organic disease, and emotional upsets. A physician should certainly be consulted to determine the cause and the best course of treatment. If, for example, organic disease, chronic diarrhea, malabsorption, and hormonal imbalance can be ruled out as causes of undernutrition, faulty nutritional habits them-selves may be the cause. If the appetite does not return slowly and naturally when an adequate diet is reinstated, it can be stimulated artificially by the physician. Eating frequent small meals may also be helpful. Evaluation of one's food and eating habits also will reveal whether the diet is adequate in calories and other nutrients; such an evaluation will be helpful when planning for any dietary modifications that seem necessary.

-4-
special diets

Special diets often differ measurably from the usual bill of fare, serving special functions and taking many forms—low-sodium, low-fat, low-cholesterol, low-calorie, high-protein, gluten-free, and low-fiber. Many variations of each of these special or modified diets exist. As much as possible, these diets are designed to resemble the usual diet familiar and acceptable to the person receiving therapy.

Special diets are forms of therapy—therapy which is indicated for a particular illness and a particular person. Before therapy can begin, however, the physician must learn the individual's medical status and, if possible, determine the cause of the illness. Diet therapy may play an important role in the treatment.

There is no *one* proper low-sodium diet, for example. Perhaps the physician will recommend nothing more than "hands off" the salt shaker when eating. On the other hand, the prescription given may be specific as to the number of grams of sodium allowed daily and may prohibit the use of many foods. The diet must also be adequate in nutrients and adjusted to contain the appropriate number of calories. One low-sodium diet, therefore, cannot meet the needs of all individuals who must reduce their sodium intake.

Therapeutic diets often are prescribed in correlation with special medications, exercises, or other forms of therapy. For a diabetic, the diet, the dosage of insulin (or other agent), and the physical activity of the individual all work together to create a "balance" or state of good control. When a therapeutic diet of any type is prescribed, the best source of information regarding the adjustment of the diet to one's own needs is the physician who prescribed it and realizes its significance.

This chapter does not resemble a hospital diet manual; it does not provide detailed diets. Rather, its contents provide additional understanding for individuals on special diets and for their families. Here and there, some questions and answers deal with what could best be described as deviations from the usual food and diet.

ACNE AND DIET

Teenagers have been encouraged in some articles to eliminate all dairy products from their diet because a hormone in milk is supposed to cause acne. They are also told to avoid chocolate, nuts, and all fried foods. Are these recommendations reasonable?

These recommendations are quite unreasonable and may be detrimental to the health and development of children and adolescents. Milk and dairy products contribute significant amounts of calcium, phosphorus, protein, vitamin A, vitamin D, riboflavin, and other B vitamins. Once such accustomed foods are eliminated from the diet, the nutrients they supply must be replaced. Whoever suggested this elimination will be hard pressed to provide these important nutrients in other ways, especially calcium, vitamin D, and riboflavin. In any event, no evidence exists to prove that milk contains a hormone causing acne.

According to the AMA's Committee on Cutaneous Health and Cosmetics, acne occurs primarily during adolescence when hormonal secretions cause the oil glands in the skin to enlarge. The skin of the acne-prone individual (this is undoubtedly genetically determined to some extent) reacts abnormally to these changes. The oil glands become plugged, producing blackheads and whiteheads. If the oily material penetrates the wall of the oil duct, pimples will result and may become infected. Although acne usually begins with the hormonal changes of adolescence and clears up after a few years, some adults, particularly women in their 20's, have problems with acne.

Acne is not caused by diet, and it cannot be eliminated by merely following the strictest diet. A poor diet may indeed worsen the acne; overuse of sweets and fats may contribute to the problem; and some people may find that they react adversely to particular foods. Chocolate *seems* to be a common offender, but this is still somewhat debatable. Certainly a food that seems to add to the problem should be avoided when this is feasible (as with chocolate or nuts). An association is frequently drawn between the oiliness of skin and the fattiness of foods. The hypothetical association has not been proven, however, and a blanket condemnation of nuts and fried foods is not reasonable.

The AMA recommends frequent, thorough (but not abrasive) cleansing of the skin with soap and hot water. There are many other measures which can help control acne, and a physician's guidance is recommended. It is often a mistake simply to lecture the unhappy adolescent that he or she will outgrow the problem.

DIETS FOR DIABETICS

My mother recently was diagnosed as diabetic. Her doctor did not pre-scribe medication and her diet seems to be an ordinary reducing diet (1,500 calories). Does this seem reasonable?

In many instances, weight reduction will cause the abnormal glucose tolerance of an overweight diabetic to return to normal. Approximately 80 percent of diabetics are overweight and should be aware of the fact that the most important objective in their dietary treatment is attaining ideal weight.

Proper diet, perhaps including weight-reduction measures, is the preferred therapy for diabetics. No hypoglycemic drugs (insu-lin or oral agent) are indicated when the diabetic can be ade-quately treated by diet. Many persons, of course, require medica-tions for good control of the condition; such requirements, how-ever, do not change the emphasis given to dietary treatment.

The diet for a person with diabetes should be individually pre-scribed; it should be as "normal" or easy to follow as possible and somewhat flexible. While many diabetics find it helpful and conve-nient to use dietetic products, such as water-pack fruits, a com-pletely satisfactory diet can be planned from ordinary foods. Avoid-ance of concentrated sweets is a must, whether to assist in the weight reduction or keep good balance between the glucose (blood sugar) and insulin levels. Only the physician can judge the necessity for other modifications—for example, lowering the cholesterol, fat, or carbohydrate content of the "normal" diabetic diet. The usual diet includes an appropriate number of calories, 10 to 15 percent of which are derived from protein, 35 to 40 percent from fat, and 40 to 50 percent from carbohydrate.

FAT CONSUMPTION AND HEART DISEASE

Should an effort be made to change the type and amount of fat in the diet?

The concern over dietary fat is related to its possible role as a factor, among others, in certain forms of heart disease. Regardless of whether dietary fats are associated directly with heart disease, they do appear to be related to the composition of fat circulating in the blood stream and stored in tissues. The composition and amount of circulating and stored fat can be changed to some extent by the diet. The association between certain forms of circulating fats and heart disease is rather significant. Persons with high levels of cholesterol and with certain other characteristics, such as hypertension, heavy smoking, or overweight, are found to have a greater than usual incidence of atherosclerotic heart disease.

An effort to influence concentrations of cholesterol and other blood fats by dietary management is one form of prevention or treatment employed by the physician. The lowering of circulating cholesterol is achieved with some difficulty and requires expert counseling and evaluation. There is no assurance that a casual change in diet will be of any benefit.

The AMA's Council on Foods and Nutrition has recommended that the measurement of plasma cholesterol and other fat-like substances become a routine part of physical examinations. Beginning in early adulthood, the various risk factors should be evaluated at regular intervals. Those persons falling into "risk categories" need professional dietary advice. Changing the type and/or amount of fat in the diet may be of primary importance. On the other hand, a dramatic decrease in circulating fats may be brought about in some individuals by reducing weight to ideal level. A need exists for individualized therapy. There are several different abnormalities of plasma cholesterol and other fat-like substances, having different causes and requiring different forms of therapy.

POLYUNSATURATED MARGARINES

Aren't all margarines really similar? I don't know how to buy one that is polyunsaturated.

Almost all margarines available today are made from vegetable fat, but the fatty acid composition differs greatly among the various brands.

The first ingredient listed on the label is the clue to follow. Look for a margarine that lists a *liquid* oil as the major ingredient. Liquid safflower, corn, soybean, and cottonseed oils contain high percentages of polyunsaturated fatty acids.

If the first item on the list of ingredients is "partially hydrogenated oil," the product will not contain as much polyunsaturated fat as does a product made from liquid oil. This is because hydrogen has been used to saturate the unsaturated acids (i.e., the hydrogen fills the double bonds that are characteristic of the chemical structure of the unsaturated fatty acids). When the first ingredient is "hydrogenated" vegetable oil, the number of polyunsaturated acids is even fewer.

The "special" margarines with their high ratio of polyunsaturated to saturated fatty acids are now an accepted part of diets prescribed to control the kind and amount of dietary fat. In such diets, the physician is interested in all sources of fat and, even though a relatively small amount of margarine is used, the availability of the newer "special" margarines makes his job a little easier. However, one should not be lulled into thinking that the use of the highly advertised margarines or oils is the only step in dietary modification of fat.

In the future, many margarine manufacturers will undoubtedly declare the fatty acid contents of their products on the labels, making it easier for the consumer to learn more about precise composition and suitability of products.

SHELLFISH IN A LOW-CHOLESTEROL DIET

Should people on low-cholesterol diets eat shellfish?

Occasionally. Shellfish and some other seafoods contain a wide variety of sterols—cholesterol-like compounds—which make the analysis of cholesterol *per se* quite difficult. The various sterols react similarly to cholesterol in analytical procedures, resulting in rather significant variation among published reports. Sterols which are not, in fact, cholesterol may be reported in the final results as cholesterol. Some of these sterols may have effects on serum fats and the walls of arteries similar to the effects of cholesterol.

In a recent report from the USDA, the following amounts of cholesterol were reported as milligrams in approximately 3 $1/2$ ounces of seafood: oyster 50, shrimp 150, lobster 85, clam 50, scallop 53, and crab 100.

Liver and egg yolks are considered very high in cholesterol. For the sake of comparison with shellfish, three ounces of liver contain about 438 mg and one large egg yolk contains 252 mg (or 1,480 mg in 3 $1/2$ ounces of yolk).

CHOLESTEROL IN EGGS

Do hard-boiled eggs contain less cholesterol than raw or soft-boiled eggs?

Each egg has approximately 250 mg of cholesterol, and the length of boiling time in no way affects its cholesterol content.

EGG SUBSTITUTES

Are the low-cholesterol egg products also lower in fat than eggs?

The three brands of low-cholesterol egg products (or imitation eggs) that we have compared differ somewhat in fat content. One brand has a little more fat than eggs, but it is largely polyunsaturated fat. Another brand has 80 percent less fat than eggs, while a third has about the same amount of fat as eggs but the fat is polyunsaturated oil. Thus, a good effort has been made either to reduce the total fat or to increase significantly the ratio of polyunsaturated to saturated fat.

FAT IN CHOCOLATE

Is chocolate high in fat or cholesterol?

Chocolate has a relatively high fat content but contains no cholesterol, since the latter is found only in animal products. Chocolate is made from the cocoa bean, dried and roasted. The process of roasting dries out the shell so that the nibs or kernels of the bean can be easily removed. The shell contains very little fat but the kernels contain approximately 50 percent to 55 percent fat, referred to as cocoa butter. These kernels are then ground, producing a chocolate liquor which can be combined with the needed ingredients to form the various types of chocolate. The percentage of fat varies with the type of chocolate. Bitter chocolate, for example, contains approximately 50 percent to 56 percent fat, whereas sweet milk chocolate contains 28 percent to 39 percent fat.

DIETETIC FOODS

Are dietetic foods only for diabetics? How beneficial is their use in general?

Dietetic foods are those intended for special dietary purposes. Earlier, dietetic foods were almost exclusively intended for use by those with diabetes and were foods to which sugar was not added. Often a sugar substitute was used. Today dietetic foods are prepared for use by those on many special diets: low-sodium, low-fat, low-carbohydrate, low-cholesterol, allergic, and diabetic diets.

New FDA regulations are in effect making it easier to ascertain special properties claimed for the food product. The label should now be easy to read, facilitating comparisons with conventional foods. When making the comparison, one may find that the conventional food is, in fact, a better buy. If the amount of the significant nutrient is not much different from that in the dietetic food, buy the conventional product; conventional foods are usually less expensive.

Occasionally, a misunderstanding arises that dietetic foods marketed for use by the diabetic are free of carbohydrates or can be consumed in unlimited amounts. This may not be the case; the type of sweetener used in processing should be considered. Saccharin has no nutritive value. Other sweeteners, such as mannitol or sorbitol, are related to sugars and must be considered to be sources of calories. Mannitol and sorbitol are slowly absorbed and thus do not adversely affect blood sugar concentrations. Their ultimate usefulness in diabetic diets is still being debated.

The diabetic should be wary of soft drinks that do not state caloric content clearly on the label. The low-caloric beverages may not be truly low or zero calorie. A soft drink labeled "sugar free" can be accepted as such and most probably will have negligible calories. The reading of labels is important for the diabetic since total caloric intake as well as carbohydrate consumption are key factors in dietary control.

SALT SUBSTITUTES

May garlic, onion, or celery salt be used in place of table salt for a person on a low-sodium diet?

None of these salts should be used as substitutes for table salt. Garlic salt, for example, is a mixture of salt (sodium chloride) and dehydrated garlic. These products contain approximately the same amount of sodium ions as table salt. Onion and celery salts are prepared in the same way and therefore are of no value as salt substitutes.

You will find salt substitutes in grocery stores or drugstores with the special diet foods. These substitutes are prepared by mixing potassium salts—such as potassium chloride, monopotassium glutamate and glutamic acid—or are simple mixtures of sodium and potassium chloride. Other salt substitutes are available as well—garlic salt substitute, onion salt substitute, seasoned salt substitute, and low-sodium meat tenderizers. It is wise, however, to check with the physician before substituting as there may also be reason to restrict their consumption.

CHEESE IN A SODIUM-RESTRICTED DIET

Can cheese be included in a sodium-restricted diet?

All cheeses are high in sodium except unsalted cottage cheese and cheeses especially processed to be low in sodium. Low-sodium cheeses are available with as little as 3 mg sodium per ounce; dry cottage cheeses, unsalted, will have about 15 mg per ounce. The degree of sodium restriction in your diet would determine the type of cheese allowed. Generally speaking, on strict or moderately restricted diets, only the low-sodium dietetic cheese and unsalted cottage cheese are permitted.

Sodium compounds are used in cheese making for flavor, as emulsifiers, to retard the growth of undesirable organisms, to control acidity, and to assist in the separation of the whey from the curd. Thus, there are many ways sodium can sneak into cheeses.

One ounce of American Cheddar cheese will contain about 216 mg of sodium. Pasteurized processed cheeses can have as much as 490 mg per ounce. Disodium phosphate is frequently used as an emulsifier in cheese spreads. The same type of cheese prepared with a nonsodium emulsifier will have about one-half as much sodium in the final product. For example, one ounce of processed Swiss cheese with disodium phosphate will contain about 350 mg of sodium whereas the same product made without sodium in the emulsifier will contain 200 mg. Read the label to determine what kind of emulsifier was used.

Large-curd dry cottage cheeses can be washed to remove much of the sodium. If the curds are moistened with milk, take note of the fact that milk itself contains about 15 mg of sodium in two tablespoons.

SODIUM IN TUNA FISH

Will rinsing canned tuna reduce its sodium content?

Rinsing canned fish will not reduce its sodium content significantly. If one is on a restricted-sodium diet, it is wise to use the dietetic, water-packed tuna. Dietetic-pack tuna and salmon are prepared without added salt and oil. Diets that are to provide no more than 1,000 mg of sodium per day usually permit only fresh and dietetic-packed fish. Less restrictive diets permit frozen or canned fish, but no salty, specialty products such as anchovies or caviar.

LOW SODIUM VEGETABLES?

Is celery too high in sodium to be included on a low-calorie, low-sodium diet?

While most vegetables are relatively low in sodium, celery and some of the greens, such as beet greens and kale, contain over 100 mg of sodium per 100 gm. Replace celery with some of the other raw vegetables; raw cauliflower, green pepper, and radishes can be kept available as between-meal snacks.

SODIUM IN DRINKING WATER

Should the sodium content of drinking water be considered when a person is on a sodium-restricted diet? How can one find out how much sodium is in the water?

Sodium may get into our water supply in various ways. The type of soil can affect the sodium level, and, in the coastal areas, seawater intrusion can be a significant factor. Aside from the natural phenomenon, artificial methods may increase sodium content. If the water is hard in certain areas, a compound such as sodium chloride may be used to soften the water. Sodium hypochlorite may be added for purification and bacterial control purposes.

A national survey of drinking water to determine sodium levels was carried out from 1963 through 1966 in 2,100 municipalities. The highest sodium content was found in the Midwest and Far West, although there were certain other areas of the country that also had high levels of sodium in the water. This survey revealed that approximately 40 percent of the municipal water supplies would be unsuitable for individuals on 500 mg sodium diets.

The sodium consumed in softened drinking water by an individual who, for medical reasons, is on a low-sodium diet, could use up a large portion of his daily sodium allotment. The amount of sodium added in the softening process is proportional to the extent of hardness of the water, with very hard water often containing, after softening, as much as 70 to 90 mg of sodium for every two quarts. The use of such water may be restricted by the physician. The wisest course is to seek the physician's opinion concerning the use of softened water for a person on a sodium-restricted diet, as the physician best knows the medical history of the patient. Many state health departments, sometimes in conjunction with state heart associations, have determined the sodium content of the drinking water in their respective states. This information should be available to the physician, or in some states it may be directly available from state health departments to individuals on prescribed sodium-restricted diets.

Diets restricted in various levels of sodium may be prescribed by a doctor for a number of reasons, depending upon the type of disease present and the condition of the patient. Typical conditions in which sodium restriction is recommended include severe hypertension or high blood pressure, some renal (kidney) diseases, congestive heart failure, cirrhosis of the liver with accompanying edema, edema of pregnancy, and diseases in which certain medications such as cortisone are given. The mildest form of restriction is the elimination of salt for table use, highly salted or salt-preserved foods, and approximately half of the salt normally used in cooking. Severe restriction, on the other hand, may allow a patient only 250 mg of sodium daily, a diet very difficult for a patient to accept and follow, as taste appeal and food variety are limited. It is estimated that the average American's daily diet contains 10 to 15 gm of salt, equivalent to about 4 to 6 gm (4,000 to 6,000 mg) of sodium daily.

MILK ALLERGY

Some children cannot tolerate cow's milk. What can they be given to make sure they will receive the nutrients ordinarily supplied by milk?

Discuss the matter with the child's physician to determine the reason for the child's intolerance to milk. Frequently, apparent intolerance can be overcome by feeding a very dilute solution of milk and slowly increasing the concentration day by day. Sometimes boiling the milk to make milk protein more digestible will help. Occasionally evaporated or powdered milk may be tolerated, even when fresh cow's milk is not. A number of other products also can be used—goat's milk, milk made from soybeans, and special hypo-allergenic milks; the physician will be aware of these.

Although milk nutrients can be replaced, it is often rather difficult. If milk is not consumed, other dietary sources of calcium, vitamin A, riboflavin, and vitamin D should be used. A physician would probably recommend a vitamin D preparation, since fortified milk is about the only significant source of this vitamin.

SUGARLESS GUM

How do sugarless chewing gums differ from regular chewing gums?

Regular chewing gum consists of sugar, corn syrup, and gum base chicle. The carbohydrates—sugar and corn syrup—are absorbed by the body, with each stick of gum yielding approximately eight calories. An individual who rarely chews gum need not worry about its contribution to his daily caloric intake; however, a person chewing a large number of sticks could accumulate a considerable number of calories. A diabetic who is very sensitive to sugar above his or her allotted intake might also need to restrict his gum chewing.

Gums which are labeled "sugarless" vary slightly in content according to the brand purchased. One typical brand contains mostly sorbitol and mannitol instead of the carbohydrates found in regular chewing gums. Although sorbitol and mannitol are metabolized more slowly than sugar, they yield the same product as does sugar. The difference, therefore, in total value of carbohydrate calories from sugarless gum as compared with regular gum is very slight—with each stick of "sugarless" gum containing about five calories.

DIET BREADS

Is whole wheat bread more suitable for a weight-reducing diet than white bread? What about gluten breads?

The different breads generally available—whole wheat, rye, white, gluten (high protein), French, Italian—are so similar in caloric content that it is not worth quibbling over the matter. One may contain more fat or milk solids whereas another contains more starch or cereal protein, but a slice of each provides about 55 to 60 calories.

ADULT INTOLERANCE TO MILK

Can adults develop an intolerance to milk?

Some persons who consumed milk without distress during childhood develop intolerance to it later in life. The symptoms range from abdominal distention and mild discomfort to cramps and diarrhea.

Although small amounts of milk or cream frequently are well tolerated, larger amounts may cause discomfort. Discomfort usually occurs 30 to 90 minutes after ingestion. However, milk products such as yogurt or buttermilk, in which some of the lactose (milk sugar) has been broken down by bacterial fermentation, can frequently be consumed without discomfort.

In adult-onset intolerance to milk, the enzyme, lactase, which digests lactose in the small intestine, is either absent or present in insufficient quantities. Thus, the undigested lactose causes a problem.

A number of races have an absence of—or inadequate ability to produce—the enzyme, lactase. For such people, lactose can cause great discomfort and they soon learn to avoid milk altogether. When the problem is one of lactase insufficiency, small amounts of milk can be tolerated reasonably well but large amounts of milk overwhelm the lactase available.

CHOCOLATE SUBSTITUTES

What is carob powder? I've heard that it can be used to replace chocolate. Is this true?

The pods of the carob tree, native to the countries bordering the Mediterranean Sea, are ground, producing the carob powder or flour with a flavor similar to that of chocolate. Carob powder, also known as St. John's Bread, is about 75 percent carbohydrate, two-thirds of which is natural sugar. It is low in fat and a relatively good source of protein.

Traditionally, the carob pod has been primarily used for feeding livestock. But in the United States, carob gum (extracted from the seeds in the pod) has long been imported as a stabilizer for ice creams, sauces, and salad dressings. Today, however, many people who are not able to use chocolate (often because of allergies) have found that carob powder is an acceptable substitute. You can use it in baking (use less sugar if substituting carob flour for chocolate) or buy a "chocolate" carob flour candy bar.

There are a number of other substitutes for chocolate. Peas roasted under vacuum, lentils roasted to a dark brown color, chestnuts, and beechnuts are used to substitute for milk chocolate. Palm or coconut oil is substituted for cocoa butter to make a white confection similar to white chocolate. None of these substitutes contain theobromine or other xanthine-like stimulants found in chocolate.

OSTEOPOROSIS

Can a person recover from osteoporosis with an adequate diet that includes extra calcium?

Although osteoporosis is considered to be a deficiency disease, a deficit of calcium is not the only factor causing this condition. Osteoporosis occurs more frequently in women who have had a long history of low calcium intake, but endocrine disorders, immobilization, rheumatoid arthritis, sickle-cell anemia, and nutritional deficiencies such as protein and ascorbic acid may cause osteoporosis.

To initiate effective therapy, a physician should be consulted and the contributing factors determined. Sometimes the use of the hormones estrogen and/or androgen is advantageous for patients because of their anabolic effect on proteins and assistance in the retention of minerals in bone. Treatment with fluoride compounds is gaining favor with the medical profession.

Usually a diet liberal in calcium is recommended. This includes at least one quart of milk, hard cheeses, and the normal allowance of other foods daily. This will provide a daily calcium intake of approximately 1.5 gm which is well above the RDA of 800 mg for the normal adult. A calcium supplement may be required in the form of calcium lactate or calcium gluconate to increase the daily intake. In some cases, vitamin D supplementation has improved the absorption of calcium and mineralization of bone. An adequate diet should be stressed during the early stages of life in order to prevent bone loss. Sufficient amounts of calcium and protein are important for maintenance of bone structure. Current methods of treatment may be helpful in preventing progression of the disease, but until more is known about the causes, it is unlikely that diet and other forms of treatment will bring about total recovery.

ABNORMAL APPETITE FOR STARCH AND CLAY

Why do some people have an abnormal appetite for starch or clay?

The strange craving for nonfood items such as clay, starch, dirt, and plaster is called "pica." A similar craving for ice has been termed "pagophagia" (or ice eating—averaging at least a tray of ice daily over a period of two months or longer). Some scientists who have studied this problem believe that pica and pagophagia are almost always associated with iron deficiency.

A study of women in the southern states, many of whom were pregnant, revealed that tradition and superstition were strongly associated with the practice of pica. The mothers of these women who practiced pica had eaten clay themselves. In some studies, a number of women with the strange cravings of pica were also found to be anemic. When the anemia was corrected, the craving stopped. Others have indicated that the practice of pica is an attention-getting mechanism or an expression of frustration, or that it is due to "nervousness" or "stomach trouble" and the like.

In cases of pica, or even unusual, persistent cravings for specific foods, the possibility of anemia should be considered. Regardless of the source of the problem, each person needs individual therapy, as the practice of pica is often hazardous.

GASTROINTESTINAL DISORDERS

I recently saw a newspaper article describing ulcer diets and low-fiber diets as useless. Please comment.

Little solid evidence exists to show that the common gastrointestinal (GI) disorders are better controlled with special diets than with normal diets. Ulcers have traditionally called for "bland" diets, but there is no reason to think that a bland consistency, color, taste, or odor of a food (as it enters the mouth) is directly related to the action that food *may* have on the GI tract. Many physicians now advise persons with peptic ulcers to avoid caffeine and alcohol but otherwise to eat anything they want that does not seem to cause distress.

Similarly, there is little evidence that special diets are helpful for gallbladder disorders, regional enteritis, ulcerative colitis, diverticulitis, or other colonic disorders. In fact, there is recent evidence that some patients with diverticulitis may benefit more from a normal diet plus extra roughage or bulk than from the traditional low-residue or low-fiber diet.

This is not to say that there may not be temporary, acute flare-ups of a disorder that calls for special attention to diet until the episode diminishes. A physician should certainly be consulted during such periods.

In celiac disease and in certain defects in sugar digestion and absorption, diet is all-important in controlling the disease; diet is directly related to the symptoms, and there are scientific rationale for the dietary prescriptions. There is, for example, a sensitivity to gluten in cases of celiac disease. Eliminating wheat, barley, rye, and oats from the diet thereby eliminates the gluten, or antagonist.

To sum up the situation, the person with GI distress is often the best judge of what he can or cannot eat for reason of comfort.

-5-
nutrients

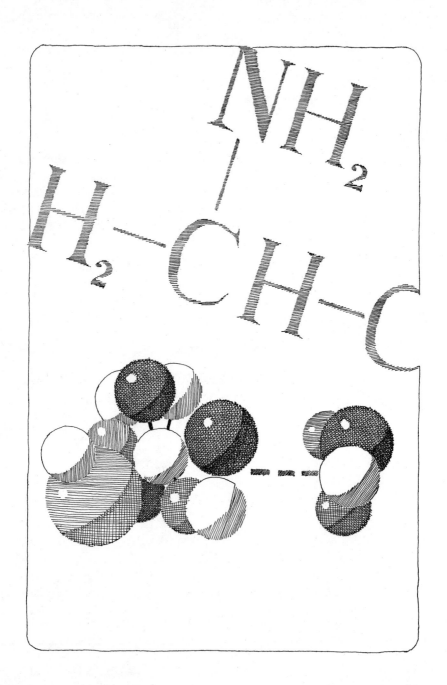

Foods and drink have complex personal and social significance for all of us, but their ultimate purpose is to nourish—to provide our bodies with the nutrients necessary for cell function and the energy resources to make all of the systems go. Our bodies are always busy building complex structures like blood cells and hemoglobin, hormones, hair—all sorts of things—and for this its cells need a constant source of nutrients.

Nutrients are metabolic components that must be provided in food. This means that all of the chemical compounds the body cannot make in sufficient quantities to meet its needs must be obtained from food and drink. The body is a fantastic chemistry laboratory capable of manufacturing the most wondrous of chemical compounds from the very simple raw materials it absorbs. For all practical purposes, the raw materials are amino acids, simple sugars, fatty acids, minerals, water, and oxygen. The catalysts (enzymes) that make the reactions in our chemistry laboratory go in the proper way require the help of vitamins (coenzymes) that also must be supplied in our diets. Nutrients are the food components that nourish our bodies; they may be classified as essential or non-essential nutrients.

The essential nutrients are the minerals and compounds the body is unable to make at all or is unable to make in sufficient quantities to meet cellular needs. Therefore, they must be provided in the food we eat and are really dietary essential nutrients. The non-essential nutrients are those the body can use directly in its chemical laboratory but, in addition to using them from food sources, it can make them from other compounds or nutrients. As long as there are plenty of the starting materials around, the non-essential nutrients can be manufactured in the body. They are not needed in the diet and are dietary non-essential nutrients.

Perhaps an illustration will help. Proteins are the dietary components that yield the amino acid nutrients after digestion. Our personal chemical laboratory needs about twenty-two different amino acids to synthesize the complex proteins in our body. Only eight of the amino acids *must* be obtained from food; the other fourteen can be synthesized in our personal chemical laboratory. The body is glad to get them from food and can use them, but if enough of the essential ones are available, the fourteen can be made from them. In addition, some of the non-essential amino acids can be made from appropriate carbon skeletons by tacking amino groups onto them. The body cannot make the essential amino acids in this way.

The essential nutrients are presented in the table of Recommended Dietary Allowances (inside front cover). There you find protein, the vitamins, minerals, and calories but no specific mention of carbohydrates and fats. Why not? Aren't carbohydrates and fats nutrients? Yes, they are nutrients all right, but their chief function is to provide energy (measured in calories) to make the chemical reactions go inside of our chemistry laboratory and to keep us warm. We discuss essential fatty acids later on (p. 86). In all, the carbohydrates (starches and sugars) provide about 45 percent of the total energy represented in the usual diet. Fats are the other major source of food energy, providing from 30 to 45 percent of our total energy needs. The remaining energy needs are derived from the chemical breakdown of unused amino acids. The sugars and fatty acids do enter into metabolism as intermediates in the syntheses of important compounds, but their main function is in the ultimate production of useful and controlled sources of "chemical" energy.

Looking at the RDA table you will observe something else about the nutrients—the great range in the amounts needed. The RDA for protein is in grams while the RDA for vitamin B_{12} is only three micrograms. There are a million micrograms in one gram! The vitamins are vital (essential) compounds needed in very, very small amounts. With all of the fuss about vitamins we often lose sight of how tiny our requirements for them really are.

Finally, it is our contention that foods are the preferred source of nutrients. With the proper and careful selection of foods there is no need for dietary supplementation with vitamins, minerals, or protein. The selection of foods from a variety of foodstuffs in proper amounts is the wisest way to obtain nutrients at desirable levels. Excessive intake of nutrients and/or calories provides *no* particular advantages.

AMINO ACIDS

What are amino acids and what foods contain them?

Amino acids are the basic building blocks of protein. Every living organism depends upon protein; it is essential for life. Man obtains amino acids from the protein foods he eats. Meats, fish, milk, eggs, and cereals are some rich dietary sources of protein.

Proteins from food cannot be utilized directly by our bodies as the molecules are too big to "pass through" the body's delicate absorptive structures. Thus, proteins are broken down into amino acids by enzymes in the digestive tract. These tiny amino acids are able to pass through the walls of the intestine and are then distributed within the body where they are needed. The amino acids are "put back together" in almost unlimited varieties of combinations to construct the required body proteins (body tissue, enzymes, hormones, etc.).

Proteins in food are made up of different amino acid combinations. At present, twenty-two distinct amino acids have been found, of which all but eight can be synthesized by our bodies from other intermediates as we need them. The other eight must come from foods and are thus known as the "essential amino acids." The body needs a certain balance of essential amino acids to maintain proper protein nutriture.

The nutritive and biological values of a protein are terms used to describe protein quality as it relates to proportions of essential amino acids found in a food. Since animal proteins (from eggs and milk, etc.) have a better balance of essential amino acids than do most vegetable proteins (from corn and rice, etc.), animal proteins are said to have a higher biological value than do vegetable proteins. Poor protein nutriture in the body can result from a deficiency of one or more essential amino acids in the diet. Without a sufficient proportion and distribution within the body of every essential amino acid, a complete body protein cannot be constructed. If the body is called upon to build a necessary protein at a time when one of the essential amino acids is missing, it is much like trying to make a soufflé without egg whites; it just cannot be done.

The best way to assure that the body is provided with all of the essential amino acids is to eat a good variety of protein-rich foods each day. Such foods as meats, milk, poultry, eggs, nuts, cheeses, cereals, and fish should be consumed regularly.

QUALITY PROTEIN

What is meant by high-quality protein? Advertisements are confusing.

Advertisers and educators have talked about "power-packed" proteins, "go-power" proteins, complete and incomplete proteins, animal and vegetable proteins, high-quality and low-quality protein, and balanced and unbalanced protein. What does it all mean?

The nutritional value of a protein depends upon its amino acid composition (explained above). The fact that food, when consumed, is generally mixed with other food proteins is often overlooked when a food is promoted on the basis of its quality or quantity of protein. Proteins provided by combinations of cereals and vegetables or combinations of these foods with foods from animal sources, such as cereal and milk, are usually of high value. A varied diet with reasonable food intake contains many different sources of proteins, and the resulting combinations are more than adequate to meet protein requirements.

ADULT NEED FOR PROTEIN

Is it true that men need more protein than women?

Men and women have about the same need for protein. When the need is expressed as the amount of protein per pound of body weight, however, men, generally being heavier, "need" more protein. The RDA for protein may be used as an illustration, although the RDA represent desirable goals in nutrition, not necessarily need. The allowance for adults is a little more than 0.8 gm of protein per 2.2 pounds of weight. Thus, a 154-pound adult male should have an allowance of 56 gm per day while a 128-pound female would have an allowance of 46 gm. Thirty additional grams per day are recommended for women during pregnancy and 20 additional grams during lactation.

As an approximate guide to the amount of protein in foods, consider that a 3-ounce serving of hamburger contains approximately 21 gm; 3 glasses of milk, 26 gm; 4 slices of bread, 8 gm; 2 eggs, 14 gm; and 1 cup of lima beans, 12 gm of protein.

DIET HIGH IN PROTEIN

Are there any hazards associated with a diet high in protein?

High-protein diets usually contain 100 to 150 gm of protein, from two to three times the suggested allowance. In some instances, this figure may be considerably higher. Generally speaking, the average healthy individual can consume high intakes of protein with no apparent harm. Excess protein is utilized for energy, but this is an expensive way to obtain calories.

Under certain conditions, however, a high-protein intake could pose serious problems. For example, when a person has a kidney disorder in which there is nitrogen retention, or has impaired liver function where protein is not metabolized properly, protein intakes must be restricted.

CARBOHYDRATES

Are the terms "starch" and "carbohydrate" synonymous? Are starches digestible?

These terms are not synonymous. Starches are carbohydrates, but not all carbohydrates are starches. Carbohydrate is a general term used to identify one class of food components. Proteins, fats, vitamins, and minerals are other such general terms. Carbohydrates can be divided into classes: (1) simple sugars, such as grape sugar (monosaccharides) and common table sugar (disaccharides); and (2) the complex carbohydrates, such as starch and cellulose (polysaccharides).

In the plant kingdom, starch can be designated as the storage form of sugar. The sweetness of fruits depends upon the kind and amount of simple sugars produced when starch is broken down by the ripening process or by cooking. In human beings, the energy from starch can be utilized only after it is broken down to simple sugar by digestive enzymes. The most important enzyme in the digestion of starch is found in saliva. Although saliva is thoroughly mixed with food in the mouth by chewing, the major part of starch digestion is carried out by the salivary enzyme after the food reaches the stomach. Food, especially starchy food, must be well chewed to allow time for adequate secretion and mixing of saliva.

FIBER

How important is fiber in the diet?

Fiber or roughage is a most important component that until recently was taken for granted. The foods of our forebearers contained considerably more fiber than do the present-day, highly refined foods. Interest has centered on the complex array of fibrous materials in foods as they may relate to protection against a growing number of bowel disorders.

Fiber assists the proper movement of food mass and products of digestion through the gastrointestinal tract. Optimal digestion of food and absorption of nutrients and the proper fermentation, hydration, and passage of bowel contents relate to the kind and amount of fiber consumed.

The renewed interest in fiber has called attention to many areas open for research. Relatively little is known about the composition of various forms of indigestible fibrous materials from vegetable, fruit, and cereal foodstuffs. Analytical problems of considerable magnitude have arisen. In addition, the bacterial flora of the lower intestinal tract may be influenced by the kinds of complex carbohydrates and fibers that reach there intact. In turn, the kind of bacteria and their end products of digestion may relate to specific diseases. The difficulties of fecal bacteriology and of fiber identification have slowed our understanding of the important interaction of fiber and human health.

ESSENTIAL FATS

Is it necessary to eat fats? Can the body get along without them?

Fats are an essential part of the diet for many reasons. First of all, fats are the most concentrated source of food energy. One ounce of fat, for example, supplies 270 calories, as compared with 120 calories from the same amount of carbohydrate or protein. The importance of this concentrated energy must not be underestimated. A need for calories is as basic as the need for specific nutrients.

Secondly, dietary fat is the source of essential fatty acids. Fats are composed of glycerol and a number of different fatty acids, some of which can be manufactured in adequate amounts by the body. Other fatty acids, particularly linoleic acid, must be provided in the diet. This is easily accomplished, however, as linoleic acid is a very common polyunsaturated fatty acid found in vegetable oils.

As for functions in the body, fats serve as stored energy, protective padding around vital organs and nerves, insulators which prevent sudden changes in body temperature, and carriers of fat-soluble vitamins.

Since fats are almost unavoidable in foods and are manufactured by the body, a fat deficiency is a very rare occurrence.

TERMINOLOGY CONFUSION—FATS AND OILS

Much confusion has occurred over terms such as cholesterol, saturated, unsaturated, polyunsaturated, hydrogenated, and partially hydrogenated, when applied to salad and cooking oils, margarines, and shortening. What do these terms mean?

Cholesterol is a complex fat-like product found in animal tissues. It is not contained in fats and oils made from vegetable sources. The other terms mentioned are descriptive of the chemical nature of fats and oils and can be defined as follows:

Saturated fats have all bonds in their carbon chains filled with hydrogen and are usually solids. Animal fats are generally saturated fats. Unsaturated fats have bonds on the carbon chains which are not filled with hydrogen and which attach themselves to the next carbon atom, forming double bonds. Unsaturated fats are usually liquids and are generally derived from vegetable sources. Some examples are soybean, corn, cottonseed, safflower, and peanut oils. Polyunsaturated fats are unsaturated fats having two or more bonds in the carbon chains which are not filled with hydrogen. Polyunsaturated fats are usually liquids and are produced from vegetables.

Hydrogenated fats or oils are fats that have been subjected to hydrogenation—a process in which hydrogen is added to the fat, filling its "unsaturated" bonds and hardening the fat or oil. Partially hydrogenated fats are fats that have been subjected to just enough hydrogenation to fill some of the bonds; such a partial procedure is especially useful when certain degrees of consistency in the final product are sought.

Edible oils—principally obtained from corn, cottonseed, soybeans, olives, and peanuts—are used for a large variety of food products, ranging from salad and cooking oils to margarines and shortenings. In order for an oil to be used as the basis for margarine or shortening, it must first be hardened, or hydrogenated. An oil can be hydrogenated to obtain about any consistency desired. Oils, especially soybean oil, are often lightly hydrogenated to inhibit rancidity or poor flavor development. Some peanut butters contain a small amount of hydrogenated oil as this prevents the separation of the peanut oil. Several margarine manufacturers have prepared partially hydrogenated products that have all the characteristics of margarine yet contain significant quantities of unaltered vegetable oil. These special margarines have been developed in response to the physician's need for some dietary means to help control abnormally high levels of cholesterol in the blood stream.

MINIMUM WATER REQUIREMENT

What is the minimum requirement for water for an adult?

Water is an important nutrient and a significant component of the body. The body of an adult man contains more than 10 gallons of water. A loss of 15 to 20 percent of body weight as water can be fatal.

The minimum adult requirement under the most favorable conditions is about one quart of water per day. This is a true minimum and does not provide a margin of safety. A practical minimum would be two quarts of water per day. Dehydration, ill health, and, ultimately, death result if water requirements are not met. Under good conditions, man can survive about ten days without water although he can go much longer without food. Water requirements of infants are usually provided in the formula or the breast milk consumed. The pediatrician recommends about five ounces of fluids for each 100 calories fed to the infant. The ratio of water intake to calories for infants is higher than that for adults, which is about three ounces per 100 calories of food.

The requirement for water depends upon water losses in the urine, feces, and sweat and by uncontrolled loss through perspiration and respired air. The loss in the urine is obligatory, since certain waste products can be excreted only by the kidneys with water needed as the solvent. The amount and nature of these waste products and subsequent water requirement depend upon the nature of the diet; the excretion of the end products of protein metabolism requires the most water. (The minimum amount of water loss that will still permit the kidneys to function properly is slightly more than a pint a day, but under conditions of starvation, it may be somewhat less.) Insensible water loss by evaporation from skin and lungs, under the best conditions, amounts to about 1 ½ to 2 pints a day. The amount lost by these routes will vary with the amount of physical activity and the temperature. Water loss by sweating can be enormous, amounting to two or three gallons during a day of hard labor in extremely hot weather. Under these conditions, free access to water and frequent replacement of salt loss is vital. Except under conditions requiring a high salt intake, as in profuse sweating, however, there is no advantage in consuming a great amount of salt.

Sources of water include not only beverages, but also the water in foods and the water produced in the body by oxidation of foods.

Thirst is a fair "rule-of-thumb" indicator of water need. The thirst signal in infants, however, is not a reliable indicator during illness or once dehydration is established. Special care must be taken at these times to assure adequate water intake. Attention to adequate water intake for infants and children during hot weather is also necessary.

The normal kidneys have a remarkable ability to maintain water balance so that excess water is quickly excreted. The kidneys also can help to conserve water as well, but only up to a point. During water privation, less water is excreted by the kidneys and the urine becomes progressively more concentrated. This can lead to serious consequences, since there is a continuing water need for the excretion of waste products. With water privation and continual loss of water through the skin and lungs, dehydration occurs very rapidly. Dehydration can also occur during fever or when large amounts of water are lost by profuse vomiting or severe diarrhea. When severe vomiting and diarrhea occur, both water and minerals must be replaced immediately.

The use of excessive amounts of salt or the ingestion of great quantities of salty foods will produce a thirst or need for water that must be satisfied to maintain the proper fluid and mineral balance in the body. The normal kidneys, if enough water is taken, will in time excrete excessive amounts of salt. If the kidneys are not functioning properly, definite harm can result; salt cannot be excreted, water accumulates, and edema occurs. In such cases of renal insufficiency, the complications of high blood pressure and eventually of heart failure occur.

VITAMIN FUNCTIONS

What do the vitamins do?

Knowledge of what the vitamins do is derived from studies of the pathological changes that occur in cases of vitamin deficiency.

Thus, the functions of vitamins can be described in terms of the deficiency symptoms and pathology they prevent. If, for example, the skin in vitamin A deficiency becomes rough with a condition called perifollicular hyperkeratosis, one could generalize and state that vitamin A helps maintain healthy skin. Night blindness and ultimate loss of sight also occur in gross untreated vitamin A deficiency; one could then state that vitamin A is necessary for good vision. Oversimplification of the case for vitamins serves no useful purpose and suggests that normal health somehow can be further enhanced by extra quantities of the vitamins.

Often we see little paragraphs describing what the vitamins do. Here's one: "Vitamin C promotes healing of wounds and increases resistance to infections; is essential for healthy teeth, gums, and bones; builds strong body cells and blood vessels."

Vitamin C deficiency, scurvy, is a horrible disease that plagued early sailors, settlers, and armies. In scurvy the gums become grossly swollen, red, and bloody, ultimately ending up in terrible condition threatening the firm attachment and integrity of the teeth. One can conclude that vitamin C is necessary for healthy gums! Vitamin C is important in the proper formation of the material that holds together the cells of such tissues as bone, capillaries, teeth, and connective tissues. Collagen is the supporting material for connective tissue. Without vitamin C, collagen is not formed and the connective tissue disintegrates. One can conclude that vitamin C is essential for healthy teeth, bones, blood vessels, and strong body cells.

Certain of the vitamins have reasonably singular functions; vitamin K has an integral role in the mechanisms of blood clotting, and folic acid deficiency results in a particular form of anemia, but most of the vitamins have multiple functions. For detailed descriptions of what vitamins do, we refer you to a nutrition textbook. In the meantime chew on this:

The vitamins are vital substances that function in the utilization and absorption of the other nutrients of food. They play a part in cell formation and neary every biological function in the body. The integrity of all structures, bone, skin, hair, teeth, nerves, cardiovascular system, wound healing—to name a few—depends upon the presence of the appropriate vitamin or vitamins. What do the vitamins do? They make all systems go.

B VITAMINS

What are the vitamins in B-complex?

The expression vitamin B-complex is less frequently used now. As more is learned about the various B vitamins, each one claims individual recognition. For example, vitamin B_{12} must be called to the attention of the strict vegetarian, because B_{12} is not found in plant foods. Also, newer methods of analyzing folic acid levels have revealed in recent years that many pregnant women may require supplements of this vitamin. Generally, however, your knowledge of the vitamins will not need to be extensive if you eat a varied diet. These are the B vitamins:

B Vitamins	Best Food Sources
Thiamin (B_1)	Whole-grain and enriched cereal products, meats (especially liver and pork), dried beans and peas, nuts, eggs, milk, all vegetables
Riboflavin (B_2)	Milk, cheese, meats, whole-grain and enriched products, eggs, green leafy vegetables
Niacin (nicotinamide)	Poultry, meats (especially organ meats), fish, peanuts and peanut butter, grain products, legumes
Pyridoxine (B_6)	Meat, poultry, fish, potatoes and sweet potatoes, whole-grains and seeds
Pantothenic Acid	All animal products, whole-grains, legumes
Folic Acid (Folacin)	Fresh green and leafy vegetables, yeast, meats (especially liver), eggs, whole-grains, and milk; also synthesized in human intestinal tract
Cyanocobalamin (B_{12})	Meats, poultry, fish, dairy foods, and eggs (not found in plant foods)
Biotin	Organ meats, egg yolk, legumes, and nuts

The following are not known to be vitamins, in the strictest sense of the term. Historically, they are grouped with B vitamins.

Choline (generally assumed to be a dietary essential; evidence is not conclusive)	Egg yolk, legumes, meats (especially organ), whole-grains; synthesized in the human body from the amino acid methionine
Inositol (probably not a true vitamin)	Synthesized in human body; found in all the major food groups
Para-aminobenzoic Acid (PABA) (a constituent of the vitamin, folic acid; no evidence that PABA, in itself, is essential to man)	Yeast, liver, molasses, whole-grains

NIACIN EQUIVALENTS

What does "niacin equivalent" mean?

The requirement for niacin (a B vitamin) can be expressed directly in milligrams, but the difficulty is that not all of the niacin ultimately available to the body is preformed. The amino acid, tryptophan, can be converted into niacin. The conversion is such that 1 mg of niacin is derived from each 60 mg of tryptophan. Thus, 1 niacin equivalent is equal to either 1 mg of niacin or 60 mg of tryptophan.

VITAMIN C DAILY

Is it true that vitamin C is the only vitamin that should be added to the diet?

The citrus industry has successfully given the impression that everybody must have citrus juices every day in order to be assured of an adequate amount of vitamin C. However, many foods in addition to citrus fruits contain this vitamin. Tomatoes, melons, berries, broccoli, brussels sprouts, cabbage, asparagus, and cauliflower are examples. One serving per day of one of these foods will provide all the vitamin C needed, and no supplemental source is necessary.

Vitamin C, usually from orange juice, is added to the diets of bottle-fed infants as soon as possible—unless a commercial formula with added vitamin C is used. Human milk from a well-nourished mother supplies enough vitamin C for the infant.

VITAMIN C IN WINTER

Don't most people consume less vitamin C in winter than summer?

This may well be true of many people, but it need not be. The adequacy of vitamin C or other nutrients in the diet nowadays is governed more by individual choice of foods than by season of the year. Canned and frozen fruits, vegetables, and juices are always available. Fall and winter are the *in* seasons for fresh grapefruits, oranges, and tangerines. Early spring brings pineapple, followed by strawberries. During summer, melons, berries, tomatoes, and lettuce are usually abundant and, therefore, are less expensive. Thus, even the individual who scorns all but the fresh fruits and vegetables need not be defeated by the seasons.

SMOKING AND VITAMIN C

What is the relationship between vitamin C requirements and cigarette smoking?

Recent studies have indicated that the blood concentration of vitamin C is lower in smokers than in non-smokers. Smokers were found to retain more vitamin C when large doses were given than nonsmokers. Retention of a high proportion of the test dose suggests low tissue stores of the vitamin. A study of guinea pigs that were exposed to tobacco smoke revealed that the vitamin C content of the adrenal glands had been reduced and that the guinea pigs gained weight less rapidly than another group that had not been exposed to smoke.

More studies will be required, however, before this anomaly can be explained. Whether the increased requirement for vitamin C is due to inefficient utilization, impaired absorption, or multiple causes is not known. In any event, smokers should make certain their diets contain vitamin C-rich foods.

CAROTENOIDS

What are carotenoids?

The carotenoids are a chemically related group of light yellow to dark red pigments which occur widely and abundantly in nature. Fruits, vegetables, dairy products, vegetable oils, leaves, shrimp, and lobster as well as the plumage of exotic birds all contain carotenoids. Estimates indicate that nature annually produces 100 million tons of about one hundred different carotenoids.

Animals, including man, can convert some of the carotenes into vitamin A. Nearly two-thirds of the vitamin A in the diet of Americans is derived in this way. The most important pro-vitamin A pigment, both from the viewpoint of its abundance in nature and the efficiency of conversion to vitamin A, is betacarotene; it is used widely for color improvement and nutritional enrichment of foods.

Prior to the commercial availability of certain of the carotenoids, cooks and the food industry depended for yellow or orange colors upon plant extracts or plants rich in the carotenes. The ready availability of approved pure carotene pigments has largely reduced this practice. When carotene pigments are added to foods, the label will identify them as "artificial colors."

VITAMIN A AND CAROTENE

Are vitamin A and carotene the same?

They are related chemical compounds found in different foods. Vitamin A (retinol) is found in mammals and saltwater fish whereas carotenes are found in plants.

The molecular structure of carotene includes vitamin A in its configuration. Three of the carotenes and another yellow pigment, cryptoxanthin, can be partially converted to vitamin A by the wall of the intestinal tract. By weight, pure vitamin A (retinol) is twice as active as beta-carotene, the most common of the biologically active carotenes.

Because the method of expressing equivalencies of retinol and carotenes is being changed, the 1973 RDA chart lists vitamin A activity as both I.U. (International Units) and R.E. (retinol equivalents). Under the old system, the RDA for an adult male is 5,000 I.U., estimating that half of this vitamin A *activity* is from retinol and half from beta-carotene. Under the new system, the RDA is 1,000 R.E.

What's the difference? First, consider the following:

1 I.U. = 0.3 μg retinol

1 I.U. = 0.6 μg beta-carotene

This adequately explains that retinol is twice as active as beta-carotene. What it does not explain is that only about one-third of the carotene is absorbed, whereas retinol is completely absorbed. The R.E. method takes this into account:

1 R.E. = 1 μg retinol

1 R.E. = 6 μg beta-carotene

Another way of expressing the equivalencies is:

1 R.E. = 3.33 I.U. retinol

1 R.E. = 10 I.U. beta-carotene

If such arithmetic confuses you, make sure you eat a variety of foods, including green and yellow vegetables, and you'll get all the vitamin A you need.

VITAMIN A DEFICIENCY

Much concern is in evidence about protein and calorie malnutrition among infants and young children in developing countries. Isn't vitamin A deficiency also a serious matter?

Vitamin A deficiency in preschool children is a serious problem in many countries. Lack of vitamin A in early childhood is one of the most common causes of blindness. Youngsters under six years of age are most vulnerable.

Vitamin A deficiency often accompanies protein and calorie deprivation. Deficiencies concurrent with infectious diseases take a horrifying toll among infants and young children in underdeveloped countries. The incidence of vitamin A and multiple nutrient deficiencies in the world is known to be very high although precise information is not available. A few cases of severe vitamin A deficiency may exist here. Findings of mild deficiencies have also been reported.

Vitamin A has many functions, an important one being concerned with the perception of light by the eye. One of the first symptoms of deficiency is inability to see well in dim light. This condition is called night blindness and is used as an early diagnosis of deficiency. Youngsters who cannot see well in dim light tend to curb their activity at dusk. Night blindness can occur at any age, but it may be the first sign of impending serious difficulties in young childen.

With continued inadequate intake of vitamin A, the conjunctiva and cornea of the eye begin to show a decided dryness and lack of luster; in addition, the output of tears is reduced. This stage is called xerophthalmia and marks the beginning of eye damage. If not corrected by vitamin A therapy, ulceration of the cornea occurs which can lead to irreversible damage to the eye with partial or total loss of vision. This latter stage is called keratomalacia.

Special efforts are being made by UNICEF and other organizations to provide adequate amounts of vitamin A to impoverished youngsters. Vitamin preparations and foods fortified with vitamin A are being made available, but it is frequently difficult to reach those who need it most.

Parents should make certain that their children receive adequate amounts of vitamin A but should avoid giving them massive doses. Since this vitamin can accumulate in the body, large excesses can be harmful. Supplemental sources are not necessary unless prescribed by a physician.

RECOMMENDED AMOUNTS OF VITAMIN D

What is the recommended amount of vitamin D per day? What are the best sources for this vitamin? Is it possible to obtain too much vitamin D?

The recommended daily amount of vitamin D for infants and children is 400 I.U. This amount of vitamin D will cover growth needs of all infants and children except a very small minority who, because of genetic abnormality, have been shown to require massive doses. Sunlight activates vitamin D precursors in the skin, resulting in a highly dependable, though variable, additional source of the vitamin. The actual dietary need is, therefore, somewhat dependent upon the amount of exposure one has to sunlight. A dietary intake of 400 I.U., regardless of sunlight exposure, is generous and entirely adequate. There is, in fact, no known advantage to a larger intake.

Vitamin D is found in very moderate amounts in a few foods such as eggs, some saltwater fish, and summer milk. As vitamin D does not occur commonly in nature, the standard practice has been to fortify fluid milk with 400 I.U. of vitamin D per quart. Almost all milks (fluid, dry, skim, etc.) on the market are now fortified. Most commercial infant formulas also are fortified with vitamin D.

The Council on Foods and Nutrition of the American Medical Association has recommended that infant diets which do not provide at least 400 I.U. of vitamin D should be supplemented to total an intake of 400 I.U. daily. This does not mean that 400 I.U. should be provided in addition to other sources of vitamin D in the diet, but that the supplement should be adjusted so that the total intake is 400 I.U. Although no harm can come from very moderate excesses of vitamin D, pediatricians have warned against large intakes. Children and adults, including pregnant women, should avoid vitamin D intakes much in excess of 400 I.U. It might be well to examine food labels and to avoid foods, other than milk products, which have been fortified with the vitamin.

Recently, a trend has been for some food manufacturers to add vitamin D, along with other vitamins, to various foods. The Council on Foods and Nutrition, however, recognizes only the fortification of milks with vitamin D and sees no justification for adding this nutrient to other foods such as breakfast cereals, fruit drinks, or candy. Often such an addition of vitamins by the manufacturer is done purely to promote his product's superiority over other similar products, or in the belief that if a little is good, more is better. The American Academy of Pediatrics estimated that it would not be unusual for a child to consume as much as 2,000 I.U. of vitamin D from all possible sources, including vitamin preparations. This amount is more than five times the RDA. A daily intake of 1,800 I.U. over prolonged periods of time might be hazardous to children.

The tolerance for vitamin D varies with the individual, depending on his endocrine system, exposure to ultraviolet light, and his dietary intake of calcium. In certain conditions, such as a type of rickets not responding to the usual therapeutic dose, massive doses of vitamin D might be necessary and well-tolerated. Only a physician, however, can determine whether vitamin preparations containing vitamin D should be taken.

VITAMIN E

What are the functions of vitamin E in the body? What foods are good sources? Can it be harmful in large doses?

It is generally agreed that vitamin E functions primarily as an antioxidant. That is, it seemingly prevents the unwanted oxidation of polyunsaturated fatty acids and fat-soluble compounds in the body and in foods.

Vitamin E has been studied extensively during the last 20 to 25 years, undoubtedly more so than any other vitamin. Still it remains rather obscure scientifically—though it is hardly obscure in the food-supplement market. It is probably involved in certain synthetic activities in the body, such as formation of red blood cells. Deficiencies of the vitamin in human beings are rarely reported.

There are about eight tocopherols that occur naturally in foods and have what is called "vitamin E activity." Thus, vitamin E is measured in International Units (I.U.) representing vitamin E activity, most of which is alpha-tocopherol. For example, one I.U. of vitamin E is equal to one milligram of the synthetic dl-alpha-tocopherol acetate, and one I.U. of vitamin E is equal to 0.74 milligrams of the natural form, d-alpha-tocopherol.

Foods which are considered good sources of the vitamin include salad oils, shortening, margarine, wheat germ oil, green leafy vegetables, legumes, and nuts. Lesser amounts are found in fruits, other vegetables, eggs, and meats.

Toxicity from large doses of vitamin E has not been demonstrated. One should understand, however, that there are no known advantages to large intakes. Apparently, the amount of vitamin E we obtain from foods is quite adequate. For additional information, see p. 116.

VITAMIN K

Why is vitamin K not found in multivitamin-mineral preparations?

Vitamin K, needed for the normal clotting of blood, is not suitable for inclusion in vitamin supplements for a number of reasons. To determine the dietary requirement or a recommended allowance for K is not possible, partly because a deficiency of the vitamin is seldom seen, even among malnourished people. In addition to being synthesized by bacteria in the human intestinal tract, it is available in foods, particularly spinach, kale, cabbage, cauliflower, and pork liver.

Deficiency (hemorrhagic disease) may occur in infants born prematurely or whose mothers have had anticoagulant therapy. Malabsorption in adults may cause deficiency; also, treatment with sulfa drugs and antibiotics may interfere with vitamin K synthesis in the intestine.

Excessive doses of some forms of the vitamin have had adverse effects on infants. Also, K can interfere with the action of coumarin compounds used as anticoagulants.

VITAMIN P

Is vitamin P a new vitamin?

In the late 1930's, a material was isolated from the peels of citrus fruits that was referred to as "citrin" or "vitamin P." Although therapeutic qualities were once attributed to this substance, no significant effects on humans have been discovered or confirmed. To date, there is also no evidence that this nutrient is required by man. In 1950, the Joint Committee on Biochemical Nomenclature of the American Society of Biological Chemists and the American Institute of Nutrition recommended that the term "vitamin P" no longer be used. "Bioflavonoid" has come to replace the original terminology for this nutrient, although it is possible that in some literature the term "vitamin P" is still being used.

VITAMIN TOXICITY

Can't taking a lot of vitamins be dangerous?

Yes, it can. Generally speaking, the water-soluble vitamins B and C are considered nontoxic. A few reports, however, have shown adverse effects from large doses. Niacin may cause flushing, followed by an itching and burning sensation. Vitamin C may cause diarrhea and, under certain circumstances, may contribute to the formation of kidney stones. (The most unusual report of ill effects was the case of a woman who required surgery for an intestinal obstruction. When the surgeon removed several "lumps" and had them analyzed, it was discovered that they were composed of ascorbic acid. The woman had been swallowing several vitamin C tablets each day and had increased her intake when she felt she was getting a cold.)

Vitamins A and D, in particular, are potentially hazardous. Toxicity from their overuse has been diagnosed in humans. What happens is that excessive doses taken over a period of many weeks or months accumulate to toxic levels. These fat-soluble vitamins are stored by the body, in contrast to the water-soluble vitamins that are more easily excreted. As required by an FDA regulation that became effective in 1973, vitamins A and D in amounts above 10,000 I.U. and 400 I.U., respectively, are now available only on prescription.

We do not advise the use of any vitamin supplement of more than 150 percent of the U. S. RDA, except as directed by a physician.

IRON-DEFICIENCY ANEMIA

Is it simply a bad diet that causes iron-deficiency anemia?

Not necessarily. Many physicians believe that the cause among teenage girls and women is more closely related to blood loss than to poor diet. However, many cases of iron-deficiency anemia could be prevented by an iron-rich diet.

Men seldom develop anemia unless they suffer extensive or continuous blood loss—for example, from a bleeding ulcer. Surveys indicate that most adolescent boys consume diets containing adequate iron. Among young children, however, iron-deficiency is more common than we like to admit. The deficiency is most frequently caused by a low-iron intake, beginning during infancy.

Iron is an important constituent of blood hemoglobin. Reserves of iron in the body are important protection against body iron depletion when blood is lost through menses and delivery of a child, and when extra iron is needed during pregnancy and lactation. The amount of dietary iron absorbed from food varies according to need. It is this increased dietary absorption, coupled with adequate body iron reserves, that affords protection against the consequences of iron loss or increased need for iron. If reserves are inadequate or if the iron intake is insufficient, iron-deficiency anemia will develop. Once anemia has developed, therapeutic quantities of iron are given, since the deficit cannot be made up from food iron alone.

IRON FOR INFANTS AND CHILDREN

Do babies need iron supplements? Is it necessary to use a commercial, iron-fortified formula instead of whole milk?

The normal infant is born with enough iron stores to supply his needs for approximately three months if his mother's diet was adequate prior to and during pregnancy. Thereafter, the infant will need a consistently good supply of dietary iron. Growing infants and children have expanding blood volumes which require additional iron.

By age six months, most children have switched from iron-fortified formulas to whole milk, and by the time a child is approaching one year of age, many parents have begun to provide less of the iron-fortified cereals than in earlier months of infancy. Thus, the older infants and preschool children are left particularly vulnerable to iron deficiency.

The iron-fortified, proprietary formulas are very convenient and valuable products. On the other hand, whole milk, although not a source of iron, is just as satisfactory *if* the child is provided with iron-fortified cereals, egg yolk, meats, and green vegetables, all good sources of iron.

The American Academy of Pediatrics has recommended that infants be fed iron-fortified formula (with other foods) throughout the first year of life to assure adequate iron intake.

Following are some of the major sources of iron:

	Mg of Iron (approx.)
Meats (3 ounces)	2.0–3.0
Beef liver (2 ounces)	5.0
Egg (1)	1.0
Oysters, sardines, shrimp (3 ounces)	2.5–5.5
Dry beans, peas and nuts (1 cup)	3.0–5.0
Green vegetables (1 cup)	1.0–4.0

Prunes, dates, and raisins (3 ounces)	2.0–4.0
Enriched bread or whole wheat bread (1 slice)	0.6
Macaroni products, enriched (1 cup)	1.5

CALCIUM-PHOSPHORUS RATIO

What is the significance of the calcium-phosphorus ratio (Ca/P)?

The requirements for dietary calcium and phosphorus are about equal; the RDA for each is 800 mg for adults and 1,200 mg for teenagers. When the calcium-phosphorus ratio is about 1:1, calcium absorption, utilization, and loss are within normal values. However, when the ratio gets far out of kilter (as with all too many diets), calcium metabolism goes awry. The combination of inadequate milk intake (calcium) with grossly excessive intake of phosphorus, from soft drinks (phosphoric acid) and from meat and other animal products, has resulted in from two to four times as much phosphorus in the diet as calcium. The result in the simplest terms is that calcium balance cannot be maintained. More calcium is lost in the urine than can be absorbed from the diet. The calcium needed for its important functions can then come from only one place—the bones. With young children, growth is impaired when the ratio is small (e.g., 1:4). This further underscores the need to regulate children's use of soft drinks, not permitting them to replace milk.

CALCIUM AND THE NERVOUS SYSTEM

What is the value of calcium to the nervous system?

Calcium is directly involved in the orderly transmission of nerve impulses, or nerve messages. Calcium functions in the nerve fibers' acceptance of an impulse, their transmission of it, and a return of the nerves to a receptive state ready for the next impulse. If a nerve is isolated—bathed in a solution that is free of calcium—and then stimulated, the nerves will transmit repetitive and uncontrolled impulses. If too much calcium is added to the solution, the nerve will become depressed and unable to transmit impulses. A calcium deficiency of sufficient severity to affect the health of the nervous system, however, has not been recorded. Calcium is important for normal functioning of nerves, but it does not follow that a person can have a "healthier" nervous system by increasing calcium intake, or an impaired system due to lack of calcium.

TOO MUCH CALCIUM

Is it true that too much calcium in the diet will cause calcium deposits in the joints or arthritis in older people?

Calcium is a vital and necessary mineral in the diet. A lowered calcium intake in adults has been indicated recently as a possible factor in the development of osteoporosis (a diminishing of the bones). Optimal calcium nutrition should be promoted for adults, and one of the best sources of calcium is milk or its products. The recommended amount of milk for adults is one pint per day.

An excessive dietary intake of calcium will not cause calcium deposits in the joints, nor will it have any effect on diseases which affect the joints such as arthritis, gout, and associated conditions. The protective mechanisms in our body regulate the absorption and output of calcium so that the body retains only an amount sufficient to meet its needs.

Medical science has not yet discovered the cause or cure for arthritis. Many self-designated health "experts" would like us to believe that arthritis can be prevented or cured by following a particular dietary regimen; such persons often advise elimination of milk from the diet. At present, there is no scientific knowledge of arthritis that calls for any change in the dietary patterns of adults. (Exception: It is important for overweight, arthritic persons to lose weight!)

A condition known as hypercalcemia, characterized by an excess of calcium in the blood, sometimes does develop in certain individuals. Hypercalcemia can be seen in infants and young children when an excess of vitamin D is present in the diet. Although vitamin D aids in calcium absorption in the body, it is now believed that excessive amounts of vitamin D can cause an excessive absorption of calcium. This condition can be reversed by decreasing dietary amounts of vitamin D. Hypercalcemia is also found in patients being treated for peptic ulcers with both excessive alkali therapy and excessive milk intake; however, hypercalcemia does not occur in cases where alkali therapy is not used, even if large amounts of milk are consumed. Aside from these two conditions, evidence does not support the theory that excessive amounts of calcium are detrimental to the health of an average individual.

MAGNESIUM

I've read that magnesium is very important in the body. Does it reduce cholesterol levels and are any particular foods good sources of magnesium?

Magnesium is one of the major minerals found in body tissue. It activates many of the body's enzymes and may be involved in regulating body heat, muscle contractions, and protein synthesis. Supplements of magnesium, however, have not been shown effective in lowering serum cholesterol levels. Although normal requirements for magnesium have not been precisely determined, most people apparently receive an adequate supply from dairy products, cereal grains, nuts, legumes, meats and, to a lesser extent, from a variety of other foods. Magnesium deficiency is most likely to occur when there is inadequate intake combined with excessive loss through vomiting, malabsorption, or excessive kidney excretion. Surgical patients who have undergone intravenous feedings (without magnesium) for long periods of time, as well as chronic alcoholics and persons suffering from other serious illnesses, have shown symptoms of magnesium deficiency.

ELECTROLYTES

What are electrolytes and what do they do?

The adult body contains about 19 pounds of minerals and roughly 90 percent of this is in the skeleton, largely as calcium phosphate. The remaining 10 percent of the minerals is distributed mainly in solution in the fluids and soft tissues of the body. They are called electrolytes because so much of their function is ionic in nature. The principal electrolytes are: sodium, potassium, calcium, magnesium, chloride, phosphate, bicarbonate, and sulfate. Proteins and organic acids function as electrolytes in certain ways.

In addition to serving as acids and alkalies to assure the proper acidity or alkalinity of blood, urine, and other fluids, electrolytes play vital roles in the transport of fluids and chemicals into and out of cells. These transports require energy and careful control. The principal minerals in the cellular water are potassium and phosphate and, in extracellular fluids, sodium and chloride. The activity of muscle, nerve, and secretory cells is associated with the regulated movement of electrolytes into and out of the cells. Physicians depend upon the measurement of electrolyte imbalances in the diagnosis of disease. Abnormalities and diseases usually result in unwanted excess or inadequacies of certain electrolytes in the body fluids.

NEED FOR FLUORIDE

If fluoride occurs naturally in foods, why is it necessary to fluoridate public water supplies? What happens to fluoride in the human system?

Fluoride is found in most plant and animal tissue. Fish is the most significant food source of fluoride, but tea, milk, eggs, meat, and cheese also supply it. Since different geographical top soils and water supplies vary in fluoride content, the amount of fluoride found in plants and animals of these different areas also varies.

The words fluorine and fluoride are frequently used interchangeably, sometimes causing confusion. Fluorine is the name of the element, which in its free state is a gas, like chlorine. Fluorine is a corrosive gas. Fluorine in combination with other elements, or as a free ion in solutions, is called fluoride. When discussing the fluoridation of water supplies, fluoride is the appropriate term to use. The usual concentration of fluoride used is 1 part per million, which is equal to about 1 mg in each quart of water.

Fluoride is added to water supplies as a public health measure, a simple means of providing adequate fluoride to people in all areas. Fluoride levels in water are measured before the element is added to assure that the resulting fluoride content will be at the most beneficial levels. In some areas it is necessary to reduce the level of naturally occurring fluoride. The use of fluoridated water in those areas needing fluoride supplementation, however, yields a consistent supply of fluoride over a long period. Where the municipal water supplies are not a source of fluoride, the American Dental Association has recommended the application of a fluoride compound to the teeth. Although fluoride has been effective in reducing the incidence of dental caries by approximately 60 percent, fluoride cannot provide complete protection against dental caries. Its use is only part of a preventive program.

When the human being ingests the small amounts of fluoride found in food or water, the major proportion of the fluoride consumed is excreted in the urine. The remaining fluoride is deposited in the hard tissues of the body—the bones and teeth. Some studies have shown that osteoporosis (reduction in the number of bone cells) is less common among elderly people living in areas supplied with fluoridated water. Although several other factors are involved in the development of osteoporosis, fluoride may have some protective effect, similar to the protection given tooth enamel against dental caries. No evidence shows that the fluoride thus accumulated is in any way harmful. If fluoride is to have any effect on the teeth, however, it should be used during the time which the teeth are being formed—from infancy through childhood.

TRACE ELEMENTS

Why do we not have guidelines (or RDA) for nutrients such as copper and selenium?

Trace elements (or micronutrients) are so called because they are found in very small amounts in foods, and those that are known to be essential for man are needed in minute quantities. Determining the essentiality of a trace mineral is difficult; much more research is needed in this area of nutrition. Also, many of these elements are toxic, even in small amounts. The margin between required amounts and toxic amounts may be small. Generally speaking, a diet adequate in the other nutrients will supply sufficient amounts of trace minerals.

Copper is known to be essential—it is a constituent of some enzymes—but even a mediocre diet supplies enough (about 2 mg per day). Selenium is probably essential for man, but not much is known about the requirement; the same holds true for chromium and molybdenum. Manganese and zinc are known to be essential, and recently an RDA was established for zinc (15 mg per day). Diets providing sufficient animal protein will be quite adequate in zinc. Zinc, like copper and most other trace elements, is necessary for some of the body's enzyme functions.

Iodine, iron, and fluorine—discussed elsewhere in this book—are also trace elements. Cobalt *per se* may not be a nutrient, but it is one of the constituents of vitamin B_{12}.

-6-
sense, half-sense, and nonsense

Nutrition is not an exact science nor a science blessed with many absolute measurements. Biochemistry or life chemistry is a complicated but orderly process of all of the reactions that take place in the body. Biochemistry is a study in complexity. The processes of reproduction, growth, activity, maintenance, and repair of tissues, resisting or succumbing to infections, recovery from trauma—all of the things we represent as human beings—relate in one way or another to nutrition and the food we eat or fail to eat. Is it any wonder that, in addition to what little sense one reads or hears, there is one whale of a lot of half-sense and nonsense broadcast about nutrition? It is easy to assume the cap and gown of the pseudo-expert.

When exact measurements upon which to base a true judgment are not available (say, of the human requirement for vitamin D) the scientist must depend upon correlative information from studies with other species and upon what has been called informed judgment. Thus, the scientist, calling upon his past training, his research and that of others, experience, and whatever information he can bring to bear on the issue, derives a judgment; he makes an informed decision. Depending upon the complexity of the subject, only a few scientists have the know-how to provide useful, probable answers. Only a few have the credentials. But, by its nature, the science of nutrition requires the application of informed judgment more often than we would like. We simply can't wait for well documented answers when feeding populations or caring for the ill or nourishing the grossly premature infant.

The point is that too many laymen and not-very-well-informed professionals are confusing issues with utterances of half-sense and nonsense. We hope that our efforts to explain how complicated the science of nutrition can be have also illustrated for you why it is so easy to concoct a plausible explanation for a complicated health issue—and then to sell a book, a health food, or a "supplement" to cure whatever the ailment happens to be. Not infrequently, the research cited to support a cure or to justify the promotion of a non-essential nutrient bears little or no relationship to the subject under discussion. Often the nonsense claimers cite only studies with small animals but neglect to mention that research with human beings failed to yield the same results. This is the case with many of the false claims for the efficacy of vitamin E in treatment of muscular dystrophy, for example.

This section is not very large because we have not set out to make sense out of all the half-sense and nonsense. To do that would require all of the pages available and it would be pretty dull reading. It would be negative. Then, about the time we finished, we'd have to start all over again, simply because there is so much money to be made and so much publicity available to those who profess to have the key to longevity. We hope that the well informed reader will not be misled by half-sense and nonsense and that these pages will help you decide which is which.

The belief of a consumer that superior health and freedom from disease can accrue from the use of "health foods" is strong and not easily dissuaded. Unless the diet contains some exotic seed, bone meal, yeast, or perhaps "organically grown" food, the consumer is convinced that he is nutritionally impoverished. Thus, the consumer loses faith in conventional foods and becomes a nutrition neurotic. The *nutrition neurotic* is characterized by dependence on unusual and esoteric food; the belief that organically grown foods are the only reliable foods; the use of "far-out" food supplements and "natural vitamins"; the willingness to try any new reducing regimen; the loss of faith in modern processing; and the fear that conventional foods cause degenerative diseases.

The true *food faddist,* however, probably is the on-again, off-again dieter who often falls prey to the latest diet craze regardless of his previous failures. Unfortunately, the sciences of nutrition, physiology, and psychology have not yet discovered all of the answers to the problem of obesity. Until such time, many will presumably experience failure after failure in their efforts to reduce; prevention is still the best treatment for obesity.

The promoters of these strange attitudes concerning the food supply are easy to identify. They reap their fortunes while extolling the virtues of "tiger's milk," desiccated liver, wheat germ, brewer's yeast, halibut liver oil, vitamin E, bone meal, and sunflower seeds. Their profits are made through the sale of books and magazines, not to mention popular public lectures or sales of their own brands of "naturized" food supplements. These leaders promote their philosophies by half-sense innuendoes and wild promises of glowing health, making their statements difficult, if not impossible, to combat.

Anyone, however, can contribute directly or indirectly to misinformation, and separating fact from fiction can be difficult. Unfortunately, misinformation on food, nutrition, health, or disease—whether it arises from the misleading statements and untruths of the faddist promoter and nutrition neurotic or the often *misinterpreted* pronouncement of the eminent doctor and scientist—can attract the attention of the lay public. When authoritative, scientific information is prematurely reported or reported out of context, it too can contribute to nutrition nonsense. This is unforgivable. Recent examples of information which has been misused are as follows: high-fat, low-carbohydrate, liquor-a-plenty reducing diets; attachment of the name *Mayo* to an ill-conceived weight-reduction regimen; and the save-your-arteries-with-vitamin-E-saga. The government, the food industry and its associations, educational institutions, the medical professions, and allied professions all have a responsibility to educate the consumer to distinguish fact from fancy. The nutrition neurotics and the food faddists need help—adequate public health information is a must!

NATURAL VITAMINS

A friend of mine has recently become a convert to natural vitamins and health foods. My problem is that she never misses an opportunity to *educate* me, particularly on natural vitamins. I have the impression that most nutritionists think this is a big hoax. Is it?

"There may be some hoax
By those who coax
To try the natural way.
Their claims fool some folks
Who don't know the ropes
Of Nature's natural way."

A pharmacist who recently visited two manufacturers of "natural" vitamins discovered that nature had been given a large "synthetic" boost by nature's helpers (chemists). For example, the natural vitamin C in rose hips had been "adjusted" from the original 2 percent to 50 percent by adding chemical ascorbic acid. The same was true of the B vitamins, which were synthetic chemicals added to yeast and other such products of nature. Labels, nevertheless, stated that the products were "natural" or "organic."

This kind of situation, troublesome for consumers, can be corrected through legal definitions of the terms used on labels. In all fairness, however, the human body makes no protest about the source of a vitamin and doesn't get sidetracked by terminology. The body puts to work a specific chemical compound (e.g., a vitamin) without asking whether it was synthesized by an exotic plant or by a human chemist.

ORGANIC FOOD

Why is there so much objection to organic foods? Some of us appreciate being able to get foods that are not loaded with chemicals.

The objection is to the economic fraud perpetuated by organic food vendors rather than objection to the organic foods as such. Organic foods are invariably higher priced, in short supply, and the buyer has absolutely no assurance that he is getting what he pays for. What he hopes for is a food that (1) was grown in soil fertilized and conditioned by manure and humus; (2) was not treated with pesticides; (3) was minimally processed, and (4) contains no chemical additives. The trouble is, you see, the consumer must trust the proprietor, the proprietor must trust the supplier who, in turn, must trust the grower; and if supplies are short, who is to know if dwindling stocks are reinforced from *any* available source?

Truthfully, no test applied can determine whether a food was grown by organic methods or by conventional methods of agriculture. The nutrient content is the same and the pesticide content may be the same—or it may be higher in "organic foods" as was found by the New York State Department of Agriculture. So, how can you tell which is which? Maybe by appearance.

The serious "organic farmer" uses a seed variety that produces vegetables resembling home grown. But, production is small since hand labor is required, limiting the size of the farm and the amount of crop that can be grown. Unusual marketing requirements dictate air freight to distant cities and immediate merchandising before the produce spoils.

It is unfortunate that the term "organic" was chosen, we guess by the late J. I. Rodale, to describe the products. We understand that "organic" is considered "natural" and, therefore, has a wholesome ring. Actually, "organic" is a misnomer. Plants are able to use only inorganic elements to support their growth. These elements are supplied by fertilizers or by soil in which the microorganisms are consistently transforming organic matter into the inorganic elements that are used by plants.

ZEN MACROBIOTICS

Where did the Zen diet originate and what are its benefits?

One "benefit" is severe malnutrition, having led to death in a few documented cases. The "Zen macrobiotic" diet was originated by a Japanese man named Georges Ohsawa (Yukikazu Sakurazawa). In the literal sense, "Zen" means "meditation" and "macrobiotic" describes that which has longevity or a long life. The diet is often associated with the Zen Buddhist religion, but actually there is no connection between the two.

The diet has ten stages. The first, or lowest level, of the diet is composed of cereals, vegetables, fruits, seafoods, and desserts. The diet progressively diminishes to the highest level, composed completely of cereal. The dieter is encouraged to try the particular level that helps him achieve a state of "well-being." Once he outgrows a certain level, he then promotes himself to a higher level, ultimately to the all-cereal stage. Any undesirable condition resulting from the diet is said to be merely temporary, disappearing with time and continued reliance on the diet. Ohsawa further claimed that by selectively choosing a certain level, a person can be cured of certain diseases, such as cancer and epilepsy.

Frankly, the diet is dangerous. In 1965, an investigation brought before the Passaic grand jury in New Jersey revealed that people had suffered serious deficiency diseases, such as scurvy, and even death after being on the diet for only a few months. Death was attributed to starvation in most cases.

The diet advocates a restriction of fluids as much as possible. This can cause serious kidney malfunction. Ironically, one person suffering from such kidney trouble stated that she felt guilty because she didn't "progress" to the all-cereal level of the diet. Fortunately, she sought the help of a physician.

The Passaic grand jury recommended that the public be warned of the dangers inherent in the diet as outlined by the writings of Ohsawa. The AMA's Council on Foods and Nutrition published a warning and alerted the medical profession to the increasing popularity—which seems to be sporadic—of the diet among young people.

EFFECT OF SOIL ON NUTRIENTS

Have the soils in this country become worn out, resulting in less nutritious crops?

The old assertion about depleted soils should have worn out years ago. For decades, a favorite pitch used by food-supplement salesmen has been: "You need our products to supply the nutrients that you don't get from foods grown on our country's depleted soils."

The major determinant of nutritive value of a food is genetics. A carrot has genes which cause it to develop pro-vitamin A (carotene). If the carrot grows, it will contain a good amount of carotene. If the soil is truly depleted, the carrot simply won't grow.

The farmlands of this country are well cared for, with fertilizers formulated to provide the nutrients for plant growth, and crop yields are very high. Crops grown in various parts of the country may differ in the amounts of certain nutrients they contain, particularly trace elements such as iodine, selenium, fluoride, or zinc. In many instances, fertilizers are designed to compensate for lack of minerals in particular soils. Other factors which influence total nutritive value include geography, season, sunlight, and the maturity of crops at harvest.

MEGAVITAMIN THERAPY

Isn't nutritional therapy (megavitamins) becoming an accepted form of treatment for many problems, especially mental illness?

First of all, use of massive doses of vitamins reaches beyond the realm of nutritional therapy and is probably best regarded as drug therapy.

By definition, a vitamin is a substance vital to the body in small amounts. The proponents of megavitamin therapy are speaking of amounts a thousand times greater than our requirement for the vitamins. At these levels, any effects are considered as pharmacological—drug-like action—not related to vitamin action. But *vitamin* is a magic word, isn't it?

In addition to "megavitamin therapy," the term "orthomolecular vitamin therapy" has crept in to describe what the pied pipers say is providing each cell in the body with the optimum environment of chemicals. To accomplish this, they say, requires amounts of vitamins far in excess of the RDA. Saying it is easy; proving it is something else again.

Initially, megavitamin therapy referred to the use of large doses of niacin to treat schizophrenia. Twenty years later, this method remains highly controversial; in fact, several studies have indicated that the niacin is ineffective. Proponents of the method branched out, began using niacin plus folic acid, ascorbic acid, pyridoxine, B_{12}, and other vitamins and minerals, and alleged that such treatment was helpful for schizophrenia, autism, hyperactive children, alcoholism, geriatric problems, and many others. Usually, the orthomolecular psychiatrists prescribe tranquilizers and other medications in conjunction with the vitamins, depending upon the "biochemical abnormalities" of the person. "Biochemical abnormalities" is in quotes because the prescriber more often than not makes up the "biochemical abnormalities." The additional medications make it nearly impossible to determine whether any beneficial results obtained were due to vitamins or other aspects of the treatment. In either event the vitamins get the credit.

The boosters of megavitamin therapy are omnipresent in the media, gracing our television sets endlessly. Glibly they cite anecdotal "evidence" to support their fanciful claims. They seek support from each other rather than publish evidence for impartial evaluation by their peers.

A Task Force of the American Psychiatric Association reported in 1973 that the credibility of the megavitamin proponents or orthomolecular psychiatrists had diminished because of their consistent refusal to perform controlled experiments and report results in a scientifically acceptable manner, and because their methods and theories—when examined critically—were unconvincing. The Task Force Report ended with the following: "Under these circumstances, this Task Force considers the massive publicity which they promulgate via radio, the lay press and popular books, using catch phrases which are really misnomers like 'megavitamin therapy' and 'orthomolecular treatment' to be deplorable."

VITAMIN E FOR EVERYTHING

Can vitamin E prevent heart disease? Does it cure muscular dystrophy? Aging? Sterility? Emphysema? Wrinkles?

The questions about vitamin E are endless. Health food addicts push it. Athletic coaches swear by it. Late night talk-show guests revel in it. They insist that vitamin E cures everything from heart disease to emphysema, reduces cholesterol, and protects the lungs from the ravages of smog. The only quandary they leave you with is, "Have you had enough?" Even here, they have an answer. "Fifty milligrams didn't help? Here, have a couple of grams."

Let's face facts. It's true that most animals deficient in vitamin E show symptoms of disease. But, although authorities agree that vitamin E also has a role in human health, the importance of that role is not established. It has been termed "an embarrassing vitamin" by some scientists who work with it. To some extent, E is still a vitamin looking for a human disease.

What can we say, for sure? Biologically speaking, we know that E works as an antioxidant; that is, it can prevent stored fats in the body from breaking down, becoming oxidized. Fat that has become oxidized can cause changes in the walls of blood cells. The true significance of these changes is being studied. Monkeys deficient in vitamin E develop an anemia similar to that in some premature infants. And vitamin E deficiencies that cause anemia have been found in children in the Near East. Infants, particularly if premature, are vulnerable to E deficiency if they are fed formulas containing too little of the vitamin. (Human milk is rich enough in vitamin E to protect against anemia.)

Important research now underway on vitamin E and other antioxidants is exploring the aging process, how radiation damages tissues and whether man can be protected from the harshness of his environment by biological intervention. So far, one fact emerges from research speculations. Taking large doses of E to protect yourself against aging or smog is jumping into a mass, unchecked experiment. Reliable studies are underway. Answers are coming. But some of us can't—or won't—wait.

The question often asked about E is, "Will E heighten sexual potency?" What sparked this rumor was the discovery that a deficiency of E makes male rats sterile and interferes with their mate's gestation. But no link between E and human reproduction has ever been found. So, it is true that E does affect male sexuality—but only if the male is a rat.

Reasonably good evidence now shows that vitamin E supplements can give relief from certain types of leg cramps. As for its role in cardiovascular diseases, many researchers studying the action of vitamin E have failed to document claims that E is helpful.

For now, it would be prudent to follow the advice of the Food and Nutrition Board of the National Academy of Sciences: "The apparent absence of vitamin E deficiency in the general population suggests the amount of the vitamin in foods is adequate."

Nearly all the miracles claimed for E can be traced to experiments with tissue damage occurring in vitamin deficient animals; a nutritional muscular dystrophy is one example. Diseases similar to those in E deficient animals have never been found in humans. Nor do these human diseases respond to vitamin therapy. In short, we've probably been handed an overdose of bunk about vitamin E.

VITAMIN C AND THE COMMON COLD

Is there scientific evidence that vitamin C is helpful in preventing or treating the common cold?

The little bit of evidence suggesting that vitamin C may be helpful in treating a cold is unconvincing. At this point, it seems unlikely that use of the vitamin will be a practical method of coping with the ubiquitous cold viruses. Taking as much as 10 gm, in some cases, of ascorbic acid per day in an attempt to turn a giant sniffle into an occasional sniff hardly seems worth the effort.

Laboratory experiments have demonstrated that ascorbic acid does not increase the resistance of tissue culture cells to the strains of viruses known to cause colds. Many different groups of viruses are known to cause colds. In both human and animal studies, scientists have used these viruses to induce colds artificially to study the effects of ascorbic acid when administered both before and after exposure to the viruses. No evidence supporting the benefits of ascorbic acid has been uncovered.

In one study with 91 human volunteers inoculated with a cold virus, 47 persons were given massive doses of ascorbic acid for several days both before and after inoculation, and 44 persons received placebos—a false preparation lacking the active ingredient. Between the two groups, no difference in the number or severity of colds was discovered. Findings on the frequency of sore throats were similar.

On the other hand, a recent Canadian study revealed that persons taking vitamin C supplements had 30 percent fewer days of disability due to colds than did persons receiving placebos. The researchers did not know the relative importance of their findings, and they stated that there was still insufficient information to warrant any recommendations for use of ascorbic acid in treating or preventing colds.

Finally, we have all heard testimonials that go like this: "I take vitamin C every day, and I haven't had a cold for two years." This proves nothing. The possibility always exists that many other factors are involved. For example, the person making the statement may have changed jobs in recent years and has contact with fewer people (and fewer viruses).

To date, no objective, conclusive evidence supports the theory that extra vitamin C is at all helpful.

LECITHIN

Is lecithin useful for lowering blood cholesterol?

Lecithin has not been found effective in lowering serum cholesterol. A diet high in fats can increase the blood levels of both lecithin and cholesterol.

Lecithin is a phospholipid (a fat-like substance) found widely in foods and also synthesized by human beings. It has been touted by some as a heart disease preventative, but evidence does not support this.

A constituent of lecithin is choline, considered to be a vitamin for some animals. It is probably not a dietary essential for man; if the diet is adequate in protein, choline can be synthesized with help from one of the amino acids, methionine.

PROTEIN AND HAIR

Does protein improve the growth and texture of hair?

A true protein deficiency such as kwashiorkor, which is found among children in less well-developed areas of the world, results in striking changes in the hair. The child's hair becomes thin and brittle and loses its pigmentation. Once the minimum protein requirements are met, however, additional protein will not affect hair growth and characteristics. Unless one has a protein deficiency (not very common in this country), it is unlikely that protein, either added to the diet or applied directly on the hair, will be of any help.

VITAMINS FOR GRAYING HAIR

Is there a vitamin that prevents gray hair or restores the original color of gray hair?

No known remedy has yet been discovered to prevent or reverse the graying of hair. When it was found that pantothenic acid, a B vitamin, would prevent gray hair in certain strains of laboratory animals on deficient diets, there was great hope that it would work similarly in humans. Unfortunately, it did not. Neither did para-aminobenzoic acid (PABA), a so-called B vitamin. Recently, PABA has been extolled as a cure for gray hair, infertility, and impotence. Really, now! Some people will say anything to sell a product.

B_1 FOR BUGS

I have heard that vitamin B_1 (thiamin), if taken in a dosage of 100 mg about one-half hour before a hiking, camping, or fishing trip, will keep mosquitos from biting. Is there any truth in this claim?

No. The same goes for vitamin B_6, also claimed to be a mosquito repellent.

24-HOUR CLEANSING

Is it good to have a 24-hour fast every now and then, just drinking liquids, in order to get rid of toxins and wastes?

We have always thought that persons making recommendations such as this must have slept through their biology classes and, therefore, were left with some naive ideas about the functionings of the human body.

An adequate supply of liquids *is* essential for all normal body processes, including elimination of waste products. In the absence of food intake, however, the body does not close down like a toy factory that brings on the cleaning crew after hours. A person is kept alive and alert by the production of fuel, whether from an external source (food) or an internal source (liver glycogen and other fuel reserves, including body tissue). In either case, production of "toxic" materials, e.g., ammonia and urea, continues.

Further, the kidneys are superbly efficient in determining which substances in the blood stream have to *go* and which must stay (and how much). As for the intestinal tract, it needs no "rest" from food but, conversely, is dependent upon bulk for good functioning.

We know of no physiological benefits from fasting. And, as hunger pangs say, nobody wants to fast.

ENZYME-CONTAINING PREPARATIONS

Enzyme-containing preparations are sold by health-food stores as digestive aids for the aging. Are these preparations of any value?

Some very fanciful claims have been made for oral enzyme preparations. Most claims, if not all, are either false or are so exaggerated they are meaningless. Usually, the over-the-counter enzyme product is promoted by claiming or implying that many people suffer from impaired digestion and that this can be improved by using oral enzyme preparations. Advertisements suggest that as people grow older they tend to suffer from progressive deficiencies of digestive enzymes. According to the advertisers, all kinds of terrible things happen when "digestive powers fall off"— bloating, gas, and churning pain. Product promotion of this type, unsupported by significant evidence, promotes self-diagnosis and self-medication by the consumer, usually unqualified and lacking the knowledge to make correct decisions. Such a situation is deplorable.

In fact, no acceptable evidence shows that digestion is improved in the normal person by the use of supplementary enzymes, nor, for that matter, is there evidence that reduction of digestive capacity with age results in impaired digestion. Even if this should happen, therapy by replacement with appropriate, potent enzymes is best handled by the physician.

The first enzyme to come in contact with food is one which digests starches and is found in saliva. Its action continues only a short time after the food reaches the stomach. Pepsin, an enzyme that initiates but does not complete protein digestion, is secreted by the stomach. Relatively little digestion takes place in the stomach, however, as this organ serves to prepare food for digestion in the upper intestinal tract. The most significant digestive enzymes are produced by the small intestine and by the pancreas, which secretes its juices directly into the small intestine. These enzymes break down fats, carbohydrates, and proteins, making possible their absorption into the body. Unless tissues which produce these digestive enzymes are diseased or have been removed surgically, no purpose is served by the ingestion of oral digestive enzymes. The human digestive capacity greatly exceeds the demands put upon it.

-7-
foods and their composition

———

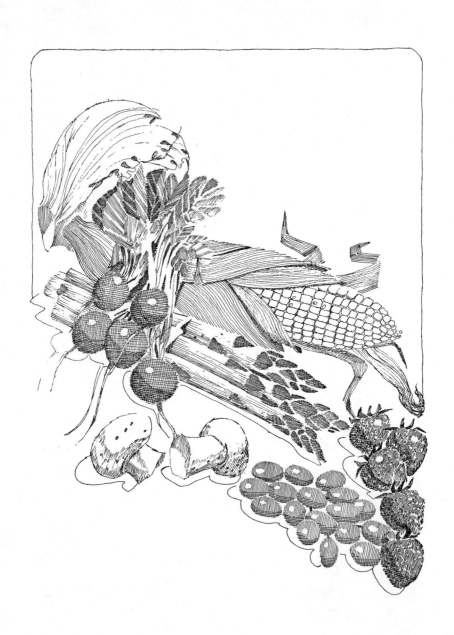

Food too often is taken for granted. Carefully selecting foods to provide attractive, nourishing meals is an often neglected art. Most families observe cyclic menus developed over a period of time around foods the family members will eat. Experimentation with new foods or with new ways to fix old foods doesn't happen very often. This is a shame for there are so many ways to make food fun and attractive.

This section describes foods and their nutritional values. Information is given about changes taking place in the design of manufactured foods. The food industry, in response to consumer demands as well as response to changing raw materials, is continuously developing and changing products. Since the name of the game is profit and consumer satisfaction, change is to be expected. It is easy for the consumer to make nutritional mistakes as there are so many food products and snack items available. There is more opportunity for error than in the olden days of quite limited varieties of food. To avoid mistakes, one should know something about food.

This section could have included tables of food composition reproduced from Government documents, but since people seldom get past the calorie column, we avoided tables. Tables of food composition give answers to questions infrequently asked; they do not tell about the lore of food or ingredient composition. We couldn't use tables. Being cold and impersonal, tables of food composition can't tell about the significance and importance of food to human values and the meaning of the changes that are occurring.

Social and cultural changes are taking place with great rapidity. There is no reason to fear change unless a significant value is lost in the process. An exchange of one value for another can lead to social progress; similarly, elimination of a value which impedes progress can be very desirable. However, when an important social and cultural value is gradually eroded to the point that it loses all significance, then there is reason for concern.

Food may soon become a cultural artifact. This does not mean that food will disappear; it simply means that it will lose its social and ritual importance and become a means of maintaining life and energy. Food and mealtime have occupied prime positions in social and cultural mores since time immemorial. Food is losing its cultural value through loss of identity with the agricultural community, abetted in part by the proliferation in the market of industrially-created foods.

The egg is one of the few staple farm products delivered direct from farm to table, thereby retaining an image of rural life. Fruits and vegetables are derived directly from the farms but these food items have a hazy cultural significance. In most families, the image no longer exists of father producing the food and mother blending her personality with the dishes she prepares.

Fabricated or designed food which looks, tastes, and feels like the real thing is another example of a trend leading to a potential change in the social value of food. Meat-like products, derived essentially from spun soybean protein, are now generally available. Religious groups that avoid meat or certain kinds of meat presumably could use products made entirely from vegetable matter without compromise of their religious vows.

The combination of developments leading to the impersonalization of food and the subsequent loss of social significance may hasten the day when the social value of food becomes a cultural artifact. It can be argued that this loss will have far-reaching effects on the family institution which already has many chinks in its foundation. The problem with gradual permissive erosion of a cultural value is that we seldom know what we should have feared.

SUGAR

Is brown sugar higher in nutrients and lower in calories than white sugar?

While white sugar is a source of calories only, brown sugar retains some of the molasses from which purified sugar crystals are separated and, therefore, is a source of *small* amounts of the minerals found in molasses. If all sugar added to the diet were dark brown, this food could be regarded as a good source of iron (2.6 mg per half-cup). The calcium value is much less significant.

Brown and white sugars are virtually identical in caloric value. A half-cup of brown sugar contains 370 calories; a half-cup of white sugar contains 385 calories. Keep in mind that calories are an important part of total nourishment. Sugar is wholesome; overuse of sugar is not.

HONEY

I've always thought that the darkened color of honey meant that it was old, but I usually see dark honey for sale in the store. Why is this allowed?

Honey may darken somewhat when stored for a long time, but it will still be wholesome. The color and flavor of honey are determined by the floral sources from which the bees collect the nectar. For example, a light colored, mild flavored honey comes from clover. Other popular types of honey include those derived from citrus blossoms, buckwheat, tupelo, sage, and basswood. Most honey on the market is a blend derived from different floral origins. However, if a honey is labeled a single flavor, it must contain at least 51 percent of that flavor.

Honey is usually sold as liquid honey—that is, honey extracted from the wax comb, which is convenient because it is ready to use. Liquid honey may be blended with 10 percent crystallized honey and sold as creamed honey. Creamed honey is fine in texture, spreads easily, and does not drip. Honey marketed in the comb also is available. Comb honey is more expensive as it is difficult and costly to produce.

An important factor in determining quality when buying honey is the grade. The grades are U.S. Grade A or Fancy, U.S. Grade B or Choice, and U.S. Grade C or Standard. These grades are based on clarity, absence of defects, and flavor with respect to the predominating floral source. Color is not a factor in U.S. grades.

Store liquid and comb honey tightly covered in a dry place to retain flavor and aroma. Creamed honey should be stored in the refrigerator. If the stored honey has crystallized, place the container in warm water to melt the crystals.

HONEY VS SUGAR

Is it healthier to use honey instead of sugar?

Practically speaking, it makes little difference. There are small amounts of nutrients in honey, but the ratio of nutrients to calories is very poor. Aside from the carbohydrate, the most significant nutrient in honey is the iron. One would need to eat over 5 tablespoons of honey (310 calories) to obtain 0.9 mg of iron—the amount found in one medium egg yolk.

CALORIES IN ALCOHOL

Are there as many calories in alcohol as in the carbohydrates?

More. Alcohol provides about seven calories per gram, compared with four calories per gram from either carbohydrate or protein. (The other calorie source, fat, provides nine calories per gram.)

The alcoholic beverages highest in calories generally are those containing good amounts of carbohydrate in addition to the alcohol: sweet liqueurs and dessert wines, drinks mixed with ginger-ale or other sweetened soda, and the fancy concoctions made with alcohol plus cream, sugar, chocolate, and coconut.

An ounce and a half of gin, whiskey, rum or vodka, with nothing added, contains about 105 calories. Mixed drinks such as martinis, manhattans, and old fashioneds, have 140 to 180 calories per 3 $1/2$ ounces. Liqueurs average about 65 calories per cordial glass ($2/3$ oz); wines vary from about 85 calories per glass of champagne or sauterne to 160 for port. Beer has about 114 calories per glass (8 oz).

Contrary to popular beliefs, beers and wines are not good sources of vitamins. Most of the nutrients present in the grains, grapes, or other fruits are left behind in the processing.

Alcohol may serve limited medicinal purposes (such as a glass of wine to stimulate a poor appetite or to add a little cheer to the life of an elderly, nursing home patient), but it is a poison when consumed in immoderate amounts.

CELERY CHEWING

Does celery have a negative caloric value because of the energy required to chew and digest it?

An eight-inch stalk of celery will provide about five calories. A 110-pound person will expend about 0.3 calories per minute while eating. That little piece of celery would have to be chewed for 16 minutes to be of no caloric value.

THROWING AWAY VITAMINS

Homemakers are often told by nutritionists to use the liquid from canned vegetables. How much actual nutrient loss is there when the liquid is poured off?

It has been estimated that approximately one-third of the vitamin and mineral content is lost when the vegetable liquid is discarded.

COFFEE WHITENERS

Are coffee whiteners low in fat? Cholesterol?

Coffee whiteners are non-dairy coffee cream substitutes—a convenience food developed to act as cream in coffee. In some instances the coffee whiteners have been developed for those who prefer vegetable fat to dairy fat or who want to avoid cholesterol. The vegetable oils used in coffee whiteners, while free of cholesterol, are usually those oils containing high percentages of saturated fatty acids (i.e., palm oil, coconut oil, partially hydrogenated vegetable oil). In fact, the whiteners may contain more saturated fatty acids than are found in milk fat. Some manufacturers are now beginning to switch to oils containing more of the polyunsaturated fatty acids and will probably give this information on the labels in the future.

The composition of a coffee whitener will depend somewhat on whether it is powdered, frozen, or fluid. Powdered coffee whiteners, on the dry weight basis, contain considerably more fat. Most whiteners contain 10 percent fat, 2 or 3 percent protein, and sufficient sugar to provide desired sweetness. Depending on the type used, natural cream contains 10 to 12 percent fat; "half and half," 12 percent; light cream or coffee cream, 20 percent. The final amount of fat in coffee with cream will be about the same as when liquid whiteners are used.

Some coffee whiteners are promoted for use on cereal or fruits. Users should understand that the mineral and vitamin content of these products is substantially less than that of milk or cream. Such beverages are not recommended for use by children as replacements for milk.

CHICORY

What is chicory, sometimes added to coffee?

Chicory is a member of the endive family. In preparation for coffee mixtures, the root of the plant is dried, roasted, and ground. It is then mixed with coffee, with the average mixture being 35 percent chicory. Chicory is less expensive than coffee and is considered an extender or adulterant when used with coffee. The package label must declare its presence.

In the amounts used, chicory does not contribute anything of nutritional significance to coffee. It does, however, add color and a characteristic bitter taste to coffee which many individuals consider a real treat. Blends of coffee with chicory are popular in Louisiana and in the French section of Canada as well as in several European countries.

DECAFFEINATED COFFEE

Several brands of coffee claim to have 97 percent of their caffeine removed. Is this possible, and, if so, how is the caffeine extracted from the coffee beans?

The most common procedure for decaffeinating coffee is to soften the coffee beans by steaming them under pressure. The caffeine is then extracted with alcohol; the extracting solvents are driven out by resteaming. After treatment, the coffee beans are roasted, packed, and sold like standard coffee. Manufacturers have not yet been able to remove all the caffeine; their best efforts produce coffee containing about 0.05 percent caffeine, or about 3 percent of the original amount. Regular coffee contains from 1.5 percent to 1.9 percent caffeine.

CAFFEINE IN CHOCOLATE

Does hot chocolate contain caffeine?

Hot chocolate contains approximately 50 mg of caffeine per cup—that's about half the amount in a cup of coffee—plus somewhat larger amounts of a similar stimulant, theobromine.

Children love chocolate-flavored beverages, but they are also more sensitive to the effects of stimulants than adults are, so don't go overboard with the chocolate for the children.

WHITE CHOCOLATE

What is white chocolate? Does it contain any stimulants?

The cacao mass that imparts the color to chocolate has been removed from white chocolate. White chocolate contains more nonfat milk products and sugar but about the same amount of fat as milk chocolate. Both kinds of chocolate contain the stimulant theobromine, with milk chocolate usually having the greater amount, 0.2 to 0.4 percent.

VANILLA EXTRACT

What is vanilla extract? What is the difference between it and imitation vanilla?

Natural vanilla, for use in flavorings and perfumes, is derived from the pods of several species of orchids belonging to the genus vanilla. These pods are filled with an oily pulp containing minute seeds called vanilla beans.

Vanillin, a volatile oil that has the characteristic aroma and flavor of vanilla, develops in the beans during the curing process. To make vanilla extract, vanillin is dissolved in alcohol.

Synthetic or artificial flavoring is much more in use now because it is less expensive. Vanillin can be made synthetically. Ethyl vanillin has a more intense vanilla odor and flavor than vanillin and may also be used in artificial flavorings. The actual constituents of such flavorings need not be listed on the label, as the Food and Drug Administration requires only that the product be labelled as an artificial flavoring.

PROTEIN CONCENTRATES

Is it likely that the new protein concentrates developed for feeding hungry children overseas will find their way into commercial channels in the United States?

Protein concentrates are food materials processed to increase materially their protein concentration by removal of fat, carbohydrate, and water. Some examples are soybean concentrate with 90 percent protein and cottonseed meal concentrate with more than 55 percent protein. Protein concentrates may be sold commercially in the United States if wholesome and useful products are developed utilizing them. At present, most protein concentrates are not adapted easily as a primary food source because of poor consumer acceptance and because they have no functional properties which contribute technological advantages to the manufacturer, as does wheat flour. Hopefully, with the solving of many technological problems, protein concentrates can become a significant source of protein for human feeding other than as formula bases or gruels. With the exception of production of soybean flour, little has been accomplished in product design to permit exploitation of the nutritional advantages of these concentrates.

Soybean protein represents perhaps the cheapest source of protein in the world. Soybean technology is now quite well advanced, enabling the addition of nonfat or full-fat soybean flour to many products in commercial channels. A soybean concentrate with about 90 percent protein has been available in large quantities for some time. With or without added vitamins, this concentrate is used as a basis for a beverage and for supplementation of other foods to increase protein intake.

A technique has also been developed for changing the physical nature of soybean protein, producing fibers or strands that can be molded into products similar to the consistency of meat. The spun protein will hold water, flavoring, and coloring agents and, therefore, has technological advantages useful in food-product design. The cost is rather high at the present time, but the development of spun soybean protein is encouraging.

SOYBEANS

What is all the big "to-do" about soybeans?

Soybeans were relatively unknown to consumers in the United States a generation ago. Now soybeans have revolutionized American farming and are a major U.S. cash crop. Soybeans ultimately may revolutionize the food industry as well. Whole soybeans contain about 40 percent protein and 20 percent oil. Soybeans are now our major source of edible oil. The bean itself, or the defatted press cake, also constitutes a rich source of protein.

Whole soybeans have a bitter flavor and some antibiological components which must be removed or destroyed. The protein of soybeans does not possess the "functional properties" of wheat (gluten) or the useful, although limited, properties of corn or rice. Soybeans have a particular flavor, partially due to the treatment necessary for their use as food. Eastern cultures long ago learned to cope with these problems to some extent. Fermented soybean products, fried cakes, soy curds, and soy milks are examples of foods which have been used for centuries in the East. These foods have not enjoyed an enthusiastic reception in this country, however. Soy-based infant foods and a few specialty products derived from soybeans have been on the market.

Soybeans are very plentiful and hold great promise as a base foodstuff to help feed overwhelming populations. A soybean product concentrate which is a granular powder has been available for a number of years and is used as a food supplement in overseas relief programs. A number of soy milk preparations have been developed both here and abroad as part of a program to increase the protein intake of infants.

Food scientists have been studying the protein of soybeans intensively. The protein may be separated by a variety of techniques into fractions which hopefully will combine high nutritive value and useful processing and solubility characteristics. One process of interest is so-called extrusion cooking of full-fat soybeans to produce a flour. The flour can then be used to prepare a variety of products designed to meet the needs of specific age groups and to fit cultural patterns here and abroad. Another promising development has been the perfection of a technique to spin filaments of soy protein. Spun soy protein filaments are a food raw material of amazing versatility with intriguing possibilities. For several years now, they have been used to create imitation foods, particularly imitation meats.

SOY AND BEEF MIXTURES

What are the soy extenders available for use with hamburger and meatloaf?

The extenders contain a protein product (textured vegetable protein) derived from soybeans. They stretch the protein content of ground meat while increasing the number of servings per pound. The soy extenders differ functionally from the old-fashioned bread or cracker crumbs and egg mixes by maintaining the consistency of the beef while stretching the meat.

Some markets sell a premixed combination of ground beef and textured soy protein. Since the meat in the mix is four or five times more expensive than the soy extender, the net result is more servings or a lower cost for each serving.

For palatability, the total fat content must be considered; otherwise a dry patty without characteristic juiciness results. The usual practice is to start with ground beef containing 30 to 33 percent fat. When the beef is mixed with the extender, then cooked, the final product contains around 22 to 24 percent fat—about right for the the best hamburger.

The extended product ideally contains 70 to 80 percent meat. The soy extender provides about half its weight as protein, resulting in a very slight increase in protein in the mix. There is, however, a 20 percent reduction in the other nutrients of meat since the extender presently carries neither vitamins nor minerals. In time, nutrients will probably be added so that it resembles the nutrient composition of meat.

MEATLOAF

How can meatloaf be stretched without dilution of its nutritive values?

A 3 ½ ounce serving of meatloaf, according to food-composition tables, contains 16 gm of protein and 1.8 mg of iron. What this means is that if the serving size remained the same but the actual meat content were reduced by one-third, the protein contribution would still be substantial.

It is possible, however, to add to the nutritive value of the meatloaf while "stretching" it. Along with the usual extenders, such as bread or cracker crumbs, wheat germ or dried-milk powder may be added. Both will add protein, minerals, and vitamins, and the wheat germ will boost the iron content also. (See also question above on soy and beef mixtures.)

GRADES AND USES OF GROUND BEEF

Could you give some guidelines for the practical uses of different grades of ground beef?

Ground beef varies in price and in amount of fat depending upon the portion of beef selected for grinding. In general, four kinds of ground beef are displayed in the market: regular ground beef, lean ground beef, ground chuck, and ground round. Of course, ground sirloin can be prepared, but it probably would not be on display.

Regular ground beef (hamburger) is the least expensive and contains the most fat. Depending on state laws, beef fat may be added to it to yield a total fat content of not more than 30 percent. This is accomplished by adding 15 to 20 percent additional fat. The practice in many areas is to prepare a product with about 25 percent total fat.

Lean ground beef is regular ground beef prepared after careful trimming of border fat. The usual fat content is 10 to 15 percent. Very lean ground beef is quite appropriate for use in calorie-controlled diets.

Ground chuck can be somewhat variable in fat content. It is leaner and more expensive than regular ground beef but may have more fat than lean ground beef. Ground chuck will have from 15 to 20 percent fat.

The most expensive and leanest ground beef is ground round steak. Its general usefulness is somewhat limited.

The characteristics of the ground meat particles and the amount of fat contained in them are important attributes in determining the usefulness of the various kinds of ground beef. Meat that is too lean will not make a good patty. The nutritional quality of the protein will be the same regardless of the price but the amount of protein will vary inversely with the amount of fat. A lean ground beef will perform about as well for most dishes as does ground round or chuck at a lower cost.

The butcher will grind any kind of meat you might desire. Discuss your needs with him; he will recommend the kind and grade of meat that will best serve your needs.

FROZEN MEATS

Is frozen meat as good as fresh?

Within the next decade, 75 percent of all fresh meat will be merchandised frozen. Already many retail outlets are changing over to frozen meats, as a labor- and space-saving device for the grocer; thus, this saving could eventually be passed on to the consumer.

Frozen and fresh meat have similar nutritional value, although fresh meat may lose some of its natural juices when stored at normal refrigeration temperatures. The industry uses fast-freezing methods and packaging that seal in the original quality of the meat. Nevertheless, a majority of shoppers buy fresh meat and freeze it at home, according to a USDA and meat industry sponsored survey of homemakers. Of the women interviewed, 87 percent said they buy fresh meat and freeze it in their home freezers. Seventy-nine percent of the women interviewed said they were not interested in buying meat already frozen.

Market research analysts made spot checks to learn why consumers were hesitant about purchasing frozen meats. They discovered that consumers suspect frozen meat may have something wrong with it. These doubts are unwarranted.

Commercially frozen meats do not require a thawing period but do require additional cooking time. When preparing a roast, approximately one-third to one-half more time should be allowed for cooking.

The extra time required for broiling steaks and chops depends on the surface area and thickness of the cut of meat as well as the temperature used. If a thick cut of meat is used, it is advisable to place the meat farther from the heat so that the surface does not brown too much before the desired degree of doneness is achieved. When braising, there is no basic difference in cooking time between frozen meats and unfrozen meats.

If meat is to be thawed prior to cooking, it should be kept in its original wrapping.

PREPACKAGED MEAT

Meat is usually packaged so that only the top side is visible. Shouldn't one be able to view the entire cut?

When nonleaking packages are designed to permit display of all sides of the meat, the butcher undoubtedly will use them. He wants to display his products in a manner that will fully satisfy the customer. On the other hand, he isn't too happy when his meat is handled, poked, and prodded. A break in the package or a hole punched in the wrapper could cause loss of juice, thus creating an unattractive display. Nonleaking packages are being developed, and some may now be in use. The butcher is in a profit-making venture so he must prepare his meat display as expeditiously as possible. If there is doubt about the meat on display, ask the butcher for an opinion. The store wants each customer's business and the personnel should be as helpful as possible.

There are still some butcher shops where special cuts are prepared. It may, however, be necessary to pay a little more for the meat and service.

AGING MEAT

Is the meat used in fine restaurants aged differently from the meat sold on the retail market?

Most fresh meat available on the retail market has undergone a normal, but minimal, process of aging during the six to ten days required to move it from the meat packer to the home oven. This rather minimal aging permits a considerable amount of tenderizing of the meat to take place.

The aging of meat for fine eating establishments is a different process. Usually, only ribs and loins of the best quality beef, lamb, and mutton are selected for aging. Since these cuts are already rather tender, the major purpose of aging is to permit the development of the characteristic aged flavor, although additional tenderness also is achieved.

According to the National Live Stock and Meat Board, the three most widely used methods for aging meat are dry aging, fast aging, and vacuum packaging. In *dry aging,* the meat is held at temperatures of from 34°F. to 38°F. for three to six weeks. The degree of humidity in the cooler determines the dryness of the aged meat. When low humidity is used, exposed meat surfaces remain dry. With humidities of from 85 percent to 90 percent, less evaporation loss from meat surfaces occurs, and mold growth is permitted on the outside of the meat. The mold one sees growing on the surfaces of meat displayed in restaurants and fine meat markets is intentional.

In the *fast-aging* process, the meat is held at a much higher temperature for up to two days. The humidity is high and the room is especially controlled to reduce bacterial growth. In *vacuum packing,* the meat is held in a moisture-proof vacuum container which protects it from surface spoilage and weight loss during the two or three weeks required for the product to reach the consumer.

Meat produced by the fast-aging process is distributed through retail outlets. If aged meat is preferred, ask the retailer to hold the meat for a longer period of time, as it is difficult to age meat at home because of the special temperature-humidity requirements.

MEAT PROTEIN AND CALORIES

Do certain cuts and varieties of meat contain more protein, vitamins and minerals than others? Which are highest in calories?

Meat in general is an excellent source of protein and also a good source of iron, phosphorus, niacin, riboflavin, and thiamin as well as other nutrients. Liver is an outstanding source of iron and vitamin A.

The protein and fat proportion of meat correspond to the lean and the fat tissue, respectively, and the amount of water present. (Meat, even cooked meat, contains more than half its weight as water.)

Certain varieties and cuts of meat vary considerably in lean and fat content and, therefore, in caloric value. Beef tenderloin, round, or rump, as well as veal and leg of lamb (trimmed of outside fat), are examples of lean meats. Other types of meat are well marbled with fat that cannot be removed—pork and beef cuts such as rib roast, porterhouse steak, and club steak. The amount of fat found in meat depends upon the species, feed, and age of the animal and the extent to which fat has been trimmed from the carcass and the type of meat preparation at home or in a restaurant.

It is important to know the nutritive values of cooked meats, as a considerable amount of fat is lost in the drippings during cooking. A three-ounce serving of extremely lean, cooked meat would provide about 27 gm of protein and 7 gm of fat, while three ounces of cooked meat which was well marbled would provide about 24 gm of protein and 14 gm of fat. The protein value of the two types of cooked meat is, for all practical purposes, quite similar. Should less fat be desired, broiling would greatly reduce the fat content by permitting fat to drip off. Broiling, compared to other cooking methods, yields meat of the lowest fat content.

CORNED BEEF HASH

What is the amount of beef (and protein) found in canned corned beef hash?

Canned corned beef hash is a product for which the USDA has established a standard of identity. The federal standard specifies that corned beef hash must be at least 35 percent (by weight) cooked beef and no more than 15 percent fat. Ingredients such as potatoes, curing agents, and seasoning must be included as specified by the standard. Other ingredients are optional.

A three-ounce serving of corned beef hash contains more than an ounce of beef and supplies about 165 calories, 8 gm of protein, 2 mg of iron, and small amounts of other minerals and vitamins.

HAMS AND MORE HAMS

Why are some hams juicier than others? Which ones need cooking?

The moistness or juiciness of ham depends on the fat and water content. The water content varies according to curing and smoking given the ham. Both processes may produce a drier ham, particularly when salt alone is used in the curing solution. The use of sugar in the curing solution reduces the tendency of salt to produce tissue firmness.

The USDA now requires that additional water retained after curing be removed. However, as much as 10 percent moisture may be added, but then the label must state that water has been added.

Ham containing more than 10 percent extra water must be called "imitation ham." This is a strange approach; maybe "water-logged" would be a better label statement.

The salting or curing of hams is an old process of preservation, but it is still important for product preservation and flavor.

Today, the curing solution is pumped into the vascular system and then the ham is soaked in another curing solution. Smoking of hams imparts flavor and acts as a complementary preservative to the curing process. Country-style hams are dry-cured and are firm in texture with a lower moisture content than other hams. Country-style hams always require relatively long cooking before eating. Smoking and curing make the ham free of harmful trichinae. Thus, these hams need to be cooked to an internal temperature of 160°F., as opposed to a fresh ham which should be cooked to 170°F. (Fresh hams, not cured or smoked, should be treated the same as fresh pork.)

Canned hams have been smoked little, if at all, after curing but have been heat-processed for eating. Canned hams generally retain more moisture than do other forms of ham—in fact, nearly twice as much as the dry, country-style hams. Incidentally, there is very little waste with canned hams, so they are frequently the best buy.

The method of cooking will affect the moistness also. If the label does not state "ready to eat" or "fully cooked," assume it needs cooking. Ham, even canned ham, should be kept cool. Country-style ham is an exception, depending upon what is used in the curing process.

FRANKFURTERS AND LUNCHEON MEATS

Are frankfurters and luncheon meats (bologna, etc.) considered good sources of protein?

Yes, luncheon meats are good sources of high-quality protein, iron, thiamin, riboflavin, and niacin. With more than 200 varieties of luncheon meats and sausages sold in the United States, however, it is rather difficult to be specific about their nutrient composition. Bologna (typical of most luncheon meats), salami (an example of the high-protein sausages), and frankfurters can be used to illustrate general nutrient composition.

Two slices—about two ounces—of bologna provide 9 gm of protein. Two slices or about two ounces of salami provide 14 gm of protein, while two frankfurters provide 14 gm. Such meats can provide from one-third to one-half of the 25 to 30 gm of meat protein considered a reasonable intake per day. The additional protein needed can be obtained from foods such as other meats, poultry, eggs, fish, legumes, cereals, milk, and milk products eaten throughout the day.

Food energy from the same-size servings of bologna, salami, and frankfurters will amount to 130, 260, and 200 calories respectively. A bologna sandwich with a couple of slices of cheese, a thick slice of raw onion, and a dash of horse-radish mustard is not only delicious eating but also a good way to make the onion more nourishing.

COMPOSITION OF HOT DOGS

Is it true that hot dogs contain chicken meat; also, is anything being done about the fat content of hot dogs?

Frankfurters and other cooked sausage products may now contain up to 15 percent poultry meat with a proportionate amount of skin. When poultry is included, it must be named in the list of ingredients on the label. Products labeled, for example, "frankfurters with chicken" contain larger amounts than 15 percent poultry.

Frankfurters are astoundingly popular in the United States. Total annual consumption is 1 1/2 billion pounds, roughly equivalent to 1.14 million miles of hot dogs. The per capita consumption is about 32 feet per year, equivalent to 8 pounds, assuming ten 5-inch franks per pound.

The USDA has placed the maximum fat content of frankfurters and cooked sausage products at 30 percent. There is not sufficient evidence of any health hazard associated with the average of 1 1/2 hot dogs per week per person to justify concern about the total fat content. Children, the major consumers of hot dogs, need the energy provided by fat in their diets. If there is a medical reason why a product containing about one-third its weight in fat should be avoided, the individual would logically be advised by the physician to avoid certain kinds of meats and sausages and in this manner would be adequately protected.

FISH STICKS

Are frozen fish sticks as nutritious as fresh fish?

The nutritive value of frozen fish sticks compares favorably with fresh fish prepared in the same manner. Four breaded fish sticks weighing a little over 3 ounces provide about 16 gm of protein. The values for the other nutrients are essentially the same as found in lean fish.

The fat content, the major determinant of total calories, depends to some extent on the method used to cook the sticks. Heating in the oven will assure the least number of calories. Frying in a little fat or deep-fat frying will increase the fat content since fat will be absorbed from the cooking medium. The total calories will vary from 160 to 200 per serving.

Fish sticks are a dependable source of protein and can be counted on to form the basis of a simple meal with a minimum of inconvenience.

"DRAWN" FISH

What is "drawn" fish?

"Drawn," when it refers to fresh or frozen fish, designates whole fish with their insides removed. These fish are usually scaled before cooking and their heads, tails, and fins removed.

FAT IN FISH

Which kinds of fish are lowest in calories?

Fish can be classified according to their fat and caloric content. Cod, flounder, haddock, halibut, sea bass, yellow perch, and red snapper have low caloric value. They contain 2 gm of fat or less and 80 to 100 calories per 3-ounce serving but also contribute 19 gm of excellent protein—a great nutritional bargain at minimum caloric cost. Herring, mackerel, salmon, trout, and sardines contain almost the same amount of protein but more fat (8 to 10 gm), and thus more calories (170 to 200) per 3-ounce serving. The method of preparing fish, as well as the garnishes and sauces used, also influences the total caloric value of a fish dish. Broiling assures the lowest fat content, as some fat is lost through drippings. Heavy cream sauces and the sour cream dressing used on herring greatly increase caloric value, but a lemon garnish will add zest to the fish with no increase in calories. Fish canned in oil, such as sardines and tuna, contribute even more fat (20 to 24 gm) to the diet, but draining the solids can reduce the fat content to about 8 gm. Sardines also can make very significant contributions of calcium and iron (354 and 3.5 mg respectively) since the bones are included in the canned product.

DARK MEAT VS LIGHT MEAT

Is the dark meat of poultry more nutritious than the light?

Little difference exists between the nutritive values of white and dark meat. White meat is somewhat lower in cholesterol and fat. Dark meat contains a little more riboflavin and iron, although less niacin. Indulge your preference!

ROCK CORNISH GAME HENS

What are Rock Cornish game hens?

A Rock Cornish game hen is produced by breeding a Cornish game hen and another breed of chicken, frequently the White Rock. The Cornish chicken grows rapidly and is a sturdy bird but is not noted for its meatiness. The Rock Cornish game hen, however, develops within six or seven weeks into a plump one-pound hen with a large proportion of meat. At this weight, they are known for flavor, meatiness, and the appearance of a mature bird. Each person is usually served a whole bird either roasted or barbecued.

SWEETBREADS

Sweetbreads are often considered a delicacy. Are they as rich in nutrients as organ meats—liver, for example?

Sweetbreads are usually thymus glands from calf, lamb, or young steer. They may also be a combination of thymus and pancreas. Liver is a much richer source of most of the vitamins and minerals, but sweetbreads, nevertheless, are a good source of protein, the B vitamins, phosphorus, and iron.

PROTEIN FROM PETROLEUM

Is it true that protein can now be derived from petroleum or coal products?

Yes, research scientists are obtaining protein from single-cell bacteria and yeast organisms grown on certain simple petroleum fractions. The petroleum provides the carbon necessary for cell growth. The protein representing a large proportion of the total content, is recovered and purified to produce a protein concentrate. Though work is still in the research and development stage, the results are very promising. Scientists are now willing to forecast that the single-cell protein grown on cultures containing fractions of petroleum or coal products may represent a significant resource in a few years.

The advantage of using hydrocarbons readily available from petroleum makes this process an attractive one for helping meet the future protein needs of the world. It has been estimated that three million tons of protein per year, about equal to the world's present protein deficit, could be produced by microorganisms at the expense of only one percent of the world's annual petroleum production.

Much remains to be accomplished in the perfection of methods of production and in the development of useful products from the derived protein. There is an acute need for protein foods of high biological value to help alleviate present shortages and to meet future requirements. Technological innovations will be required to produce useful protein foods from protein concentrates. This remains a challenge to food scientists.

MILK FAT

Jersey cows are noted for their production of milk with a high-fat content. Is milk with such a high-fat content hard to digest?

In commercial dairying, the trend in herd selection is toward cows which produce high yields of milk rather than milk high in total fat content. Nearly all the whole milk sold in this country contains from 3.25 to 3.8 percent fat. Milk from the Jersey cow, however, contains about 5 percent fat; it is the richest milk available.

Adults and most children usually have no difficulty digesting the fat in milk. However, for very young children and infants who do not tolerate the high fat content, try serving milk with differing amounts of fat. The proportion of fat can be controlled by mixing whole milk and fluid skim milk. Of course, two-percent milk (2% fat) is now available in most areas of the country.

EVAPORATED MILK VS "HALF AND HALF"

Is evaporated milk the same as "half and half"?

No. Evaporated milk is milk from which one-half of the water has been removed by evaporation. Although the milk solids, fat, and water content may be adjusted before or after evaporation, the final product must contain not less than 7.9 percent milk fat and not less than 25.9 percent total milk solids. Evaporated milk diluted with an equal part of water will have essentially the same composition as whole milk although it will not have the fresh milk flavor.

"Half and half" is simply a mixture of equal parts of light cream and whole milk. The mixture contains about 11.5 percent milk fat and possibly nonfat milk solids to give the product more body.

COLOR OF SKIM MILK

Why is skim milk bluish in appearance?

The color of milk depends on the amount of fat and the nonfat solids present. The usual white milk appearance is related to the size and dispersion of the fat globules as well as the calcium and casein. Pigments, such as carotene and riboflavin, impart a yellowish color to milk. Although such cattle breeds as Guernsey and Jersey are able to transfer more of the carotene to the milk fat than can the other breeds, little is gained by attempting to influence the color of milk by changing the nature of the cow's feed. When fat is removed, as with skim milk, the bluish-white color is related to the presence of riboflavin and milk-solid components.

NONFAT DRY MILK

When nonfat dry milk is processed, are any essential nutrients eliminated, making it nutritionally inferior to whole milk?

Nonfat dry milk is produced essentially by removing fat and water. The fat is removed in a conventional manner by centrifuging liquid whole milk; the water is usually removed by processes which employ elevated temperatures and reduced air pressure to facilitate removal without damaging the milk protein.

The removal of fat from the milk also means the removal of fat-soluble vitamins A and D, which are concentrated in the cream fraction. Fortified nonfat dry milk has become available in recent years. The standard of identity for nonfat dry milk adopted by the Food and Drug Administration permits fortification such that one quart reconstituted may contain 2000 I.U. vitamin A and 400 I.U. of vitamin D. The standard of identity does not *require* fortification.

Reconstituted nonfat dry milk is becoming increasingly popular and, in many instances, is replacing fluid whole milk in the diet. A considerable amount of nonfat dry milk also is distributed in relief and school lunch programs. Use of the fortified product should be encouraged. Because milk is counted on to supply nearly all of our vitamin D and much of our vitamin A, it is important that all forms of milk be appropriately fortified. The legal and technological barriers to the fortification of nonfat dry milk have been overcome. Check labels carefully to be certain that vitamin A and D fortified nonfat dry milk is used.

CONDENSED MILK

What is the composition of condensed milk?

Condensed milk (or sweetened, condensed milk, as it is usually called) is made by removing a little more than half of the water from milk which has been previously sweetened. It contains about 8.5 percent fat, 55 percent carbohydrate, and 8 percent protein. Condensed milk is too sweet to be used in place of whole milk after dilution.

SOUR CREAM AND YOGURT

Are there any differences between sour cream and yogurt?

Both products are formed by the action of acid-producing bacteria, but there the resemblance ends. Sour cream is made by treating a specially prepared light cream (18 to 20 percent fat) with a culture starter of the same organisms used to make buttermilk. The cultured cream is allowed to stand until the desired acidity is achieved. Sour cream contains about 18 percent fat. One cup has 454 calories, 43 gm fat, 6.7 gm protein, and 245 mg calcium.

Yogurt may be made by mixing skimmed, whole, or evaporated milk or a combination of any of these with one of three bacterial cultures. Yogurt made from skimmed milk contains less than 2 percent fat. One cup has 122 calories, 4 gm fat, 8.3 gm protein, and 293 mg calcium. Of course, added sugar and fruit will increase the calories. Generally speaking, though, yogurt is much lower than sour cream in calories and fat.

MARGARINE VS BUTTER

Is it true that margarine has fewer calories than butter?

For all practical purposes, butter and margarine are equivalent in calories and nutrient content. Both contain about 100 calories per tablespoon and are at least 80 percent fat. When vitamin A is added to margarines, it is used in the amounts found in butter—15,000 I.U. per pound.

Whipped margarines or butter contain somewhat fewer calories, by volume, than the stick products, but they are all similar when compared by weight.

The "diet margarines" in a sense are imitation margarines, because they do not conform to the standard of identity of regular margarines. These products identify all ingredients on the label in descending order of amounts. If water instead of fat is the major ingredient (which accounts for the lower calorie content), water is first on the list of ingredients.

ICE CREAM AND ICE MILK

What is the difference between ice cream and ice milk?

Ice cream contains more milk solids than does ice milk, and the most important of the solids is the milk fat. The total caloric value of both frozen desserts will depend upon the amounts of fat, sweeteners, and nonfat milk solids used, and these can be varied to some extent. The manufacturing processes are such that ice creams and ice milks can be produced which differ only slightly, if at all, in total calories. This may come as a surprise to those who think of ice milk as a "low-calorie" food.

The minimum amounts of the major ingredients which may be used in the manufacture of ice cream and ice milk are controlled by state and federal standards. Considerable latitude is permitted in the selection of the type of nonfat milk solids and other ingredients used. It should be understood that, for the most part, food standards define the lowest permissible amount of an ingredient which may be used in a food with a generic name.

Ice cream in most states and all ice cream shipped interstate must contain at least ten percent milk fat but may contain more. Some ice cream with as much as 16 percent milk fat is manufactured. When nuts, fruits, or candy are added, the mix is diluted so that bulky, flavored ice creams, for example, may have only 8 percent milk fat. The standards also state that ice cream may weigh no less than 4.6 pounds per gallon. Most quality ice cream weighs more.

Ice milk may contain no less than two percent and no more than seven percent milk fat. This is one of the few foods for which standards establish both the minimum and maximum amounts of any ingredients which may be used.

The distinctiveness of ice cream and ice milk is determined by the proportion of ingredients and the processes employed in mixing and freezing. The important ingredients are milk fat, nonfat milk solids, sugars and syrups, stabilizers, and emulsifiers. The amount of whipping or overrun employed is of paramount importance in the manufacture of such frozen desserts. Without a predetermined amount of whipping, quality cannot be assured. Excessive whipping will produce a frothy product which will freeze too hard.

During the freezing steps, the mix is rapidly agitated or whipped to incorporate just the right amount of air into the structure of the frozen mix. The final freezing steps must be accomplished rapidly to obtain the smallest ice crystals possible. Otherwise, the final product may be coarse. There is nothing sneaky about overrun since the minimum weight of the product per gallon is specified.

Ice cream can be increased in volume 70 to 80 percent or even 90 percent, but ice milk is generally overrun about 60 percent. Thus, even though an ice-milk mix may not be as rich as an ice-cream mix, the amount of overrun (and the amount of sweeteners used) will determine the caloric concentration on a portion basis. In ice creams, as the amount of fat is increased in the mix, the quantity of nonfat milk solids is decreased somewhat, resulting in some reduction in protein and mineral content. These rather complicated reasons make it difficult to compare a finished ice cream and a finished ice milk. The caloric value will not always follow the fat content because of the nature of the mix and the extent of whipping.

Now, all of this means that you may or may not be avoiding calories by using ice milk instead of ice cream. It is possible to obtain a highly whipped, minimum-fat ice cream (10 percent fat) that is not different in caloric value from a quality ice milk. It is possible to find brands of ice cream with 60 calories more per one-sixth quart serving than in an ice milk.

As long as the products conform to the applicable standards of identity, the composition need not be stated on the label. If one wishes to know the fat content of either ice cream or ice milk, he will have to consult the manufacturer. Reasonable average values for the caloric equivalents of one-sixth quart portions of ice cream and ice milk might be 174 and 137, respectively.

SOFT ICE CREAMS

I heard that soft ice cream sold at drive-ins does not contain milk products but is made of vegetable protein and oil, such as soybean. Is this right?

Depending on where you live and the state laws involved, the soft-serve frozen desserts may be ice cream, ice milk, sherbet, mellorine, or parevine that has not been hardened and stored like the usual store-bought frozen dairy products. The first four do contain milk products but parevine does not.

Mellorine is a frozen dessert that combines nonfat milk solids with vegetable fat (such as soybean) or with a combination of vegetable fat and butterfat. Parevine has egg or vegetable protein instead of the milk solids, and the fat is of vegetable origin. Both products are at least three percent protein and six percent fat, by weight. Sherbet and ice milk contain less fat (about two percent) than mellorine or parevine, but ice cream contains more (ten percent or more).

CALORIES IN SHERBET

Is sherbet lower in calories than ice cream?

A serving of ice cream usually provides 50 to 60 calories more than the same amount of sherbet; 174 and 120 calories per three-ounce serving of ice cream and sherbet, respectively. The different brands of both products vary somewhat in caloric content. Ice cream supplies appreciable amounts of calcium, protein, riboflavin, and vitamin A to the diet. Sherbet, however, contains much smaller amounts of these nutrients. Orange ice has the same number of calories as orange sherbet and provides little else than calories. The nutritional return of a serving of ice cream, therefore, is far greater than that of orange sherbet or orange ice.

FATS IN CHEESE

Are there any low-fat cheeses on the market?

Generally speaking, there are very few low-fat cheeses that have a flavor acceptable to consumers.

The fat content of cheese depends upon whether the milk used in its production was skim milk, whole milk, or a combination of these. The composition of cheese also depends on the conditions under which the curd is precipitated and separated. When the whey is discarded, most of the water-soluble nutrients of the milk are also discarded.

The simplest of cheeses is cottage cheese. It is a soft, uncured cheese prepared from a skim milk curd that is not allowed to ripen. A creaming mixture is added, and the finished product, as required by law (the standard of identity), contains at least 4 percent fat. A low-fat (2 percent) cottage cheese is also available in many areas; plain, or dry-curd cottage cheese is not as acceptable in flavor and is not generally available. The percent of milk fat is now stated on the labels, which will be helpful to the consumers concerned about fat intake.

The flavor of natural cheeses that develops during the ripening process depends upon the presence of certain components of milk fat. Low-fat curd cheeses usually do not have the characteristic moistness, texture, or flavor expected of natural cheeses. Technological advances may overcome these handicaps. Most cheeses—e.g., Cheddar, Swiss, and Roquefort—contain 7 to 8 gm of fat per ounce. Processed cheeses are essentially similar to the cheeses or mixtures of cheeses from which they are made. They will contain about 7 gm of fat per ounce. Cheese spreads and cheese foods have 4 or 5 gm of fat per ounce.

Because most U.S. cheeses are made from whole milk, they are, by weight, from 22 to 25 percent fat. Switzerland's *Sapsago,* a hard cheese made from skim milk, is a grating cheese with about two percent fat. It may be available in specialty food stores.

Natural, low-fat cheeses do not develop appropriate flavors; accordingly manufacturers turn to processed cheeses when producing products that are relatively low in fat. The natural cheese texture is accomplished with water, milk ingredients, emulsifiers, and stabilizers. Such products are five to ten percent fat. At the present time a cheese (not a processed product or spread) that is lower in fat or reduced in calories must bear a fanciful name, and it may not be identified as an imitation cheese. The Filled Cheese Act prohibits the marketing of a cheese containing vegetable oil or other non-dairy ingredients unless it bears a fanciful name.

Although cheeses for which there are standards of identity are not required to carry a label statement of ingredients or nutritional information, the industry is voluntarily providing more and more information in both areas.

COTTAGE CHEESE VS MILK

Is cottage cheese as nourishing as milk?

Not quite. The outstanding features of cottage cheese are its good quality protein, relatively low caloric content, and ease of handling. A very versatile cheese, it can form the base of a cheesecake or a salad and is a great snack when topped with apple butter, applesauce, or other fruit. Two ounces of cottage cheese have about the same protein value as a glass of milk, but considerably less calcium, riboflavin, and vitamin A.

ROQUEFORT AND BLUE CHEESES

Aren't Roquefort and blue cheese the same? Are they made from cow's milk?

In accordance with a French law that dates back to 1666, cheese called Roquefort has to be made in the area of Roquefort, France, and must be made from sheep's milk. Thus, cheese of the same type made elsewhere in France is called *bleu* cheese. In other countries, including the United States, similar cheese may be labeled "blue" and, more often than not, is made from cow's milk.

The mold powder used in the preparation of these cheeses is made by inoculating bread with *Penicillium Roqueforti*. The bread, several weeks later, is ground and sprinkled over the cheese. The flavor of the cheese is attributed not only to the mold (blue-green in appearance) but also to heavy salting and milk fatty acids.

151

VEGETABLES: CANNED, FROZEN, FRESH

Are fresh vegetables nutritionally superior to frozen or canned vegetables? When a certain vegetable is grown locally and is in season, is it a better buy fresh?

Scientific methods used today in commercially preserving foods guarantee that processed vegetables, whether canned or frozen, will be safe and wholesome.

In the industrial canning process, the vegetable is harvested at the proper time to assure optimal size, appearance, and nutritive value. The product is cooled immediately after picking and rushed to the factory, washed, and blanched and immediately processed by a short-time, high-temperature process. The cooking process, followed by a very rapid cooling period, is the key to the superiority of industrial procedures over many home procedures. The food is cooked in a closed system with a minimum amount of air and cooking time. When the final product is prepared for home consumption, it is necessary *only* to warm the food prior to serving. Warming, rather than use of extreme heat, assures that once again the vegetables are given minimal treatment.

As for the freezing process, when vegetables are quick-frozen the nutrient values are equal to or perhaps even higher than those of fresh vegetables which may not have been properly handled in the chain of farm to market to consumer.

Home grown, freshly harvested vegetables cooked almost immediately generally will not have greater nutritional value than high-quality processed vegetables. Slow-cooking methods used frequently by homemakers often destroy as many vitamins as are lost during the industrial canning process. Fresh vegetables which have been poorly stored at the market also may be less nutritious than those freshly picked from a home garden. Naturally, fresh vegetables that are locally grown and in season frequently are cheaper than the commercially processed vegetables. But sometimes, even in season, fresh vegetables can be more expensive than canned or frozen ones.

Even though there may be significant loss of nutritive value from vegetables during both industrial and home processing, this loss is more significant to the vegetable than to the consumer. Do not be fooled by reports of 10 to 20 percent nutrient loss; this is not necessarily of major importance. A food which contained 40 mg of vitamin C and lost 20 percent of it would still contain 32 mg—a very good amount!

WINTER SUPPLIES OF FRUITS AND VEGETABLES

In the winter the fresh fruits and vegetables in local markets are not as nice as during the summer. Does this mean they are low in vitamins?

While it is true that fruits and vegetables in the northern markets often are shipped from great distances, they are nevertheless quite nutritious—not so valuable as garden fresh vegetables, perhaps, but still capable of providing their share of vitamins and minerals. The fresh fruits and vegetables available during the winter, along with canned and frozen varieties and along with the other foods that make up a balanced diet, can supply all of the nutrients needed. Thus, a variety of foods, carefully selected and prepared, will provide adequate nutrition winter or summer.

BLENDED VEGETABLE JUICES

Does blenderizing have any effect on the nutrient value of vegetables?

If the juices and pulp are well blended, the nutrient content of the liquified product should reflect that of the vegetables from which it is made—no more, no less. Some might argue that since the cells of the vegetables are ruptured in the homogenizing process, cell contents which might otherwise not be available are released and thus made readily available. The difference in nutrients, if any, would be slight; cell contents are well extracted during digestion.

If you are making your own blend, be sure to throw in some carrots for vitamin A, tomatoes for vitamin C, and onions for zap and sociability.

DRIED VS FRESH PEAS

Are split peas as nourishing as fresh peas?

Curiously, dried and fresh peas are not easily compared. Fresh peas are harvested at the time when their vitamin content is the highest. Peas to be dried are permitted to mature; maturation, in addition to the drying process, results in a reduced vitamin content.

Fresh or frozen green peas can be considered excellent sources of iron and thiamin and good sources of vitamins A and C, and riboflavin. The protein content of two-thirds of a cup of cooked peas is equivalent to that of two slices of whole wheat bread (5 gm). Although the protein content of dried split peas is nearly twice that of fresh peas, the vitamin C content is negligible; and dried split peas have less than a tenth as much vitamin A. The iron and thiamin contents, while reduced, are maintained at good levels. Riboflavin levels are fairly constant in both types of peas.

The nutritive value of the protein of peas is excellent, being one of the best of the vegetable proteins. Cooked dried peas can be substituted occasionally for meat. Baked dried peas or a thick split-pea soup will provide better than 8 gm of protein in a large serving.

VITAMINS IN BROCCOLI

Is broccoli a good source of vitamins?

Broccoli is one of the richest vegetable sources of vitamin C and vitamin A. Three ounces of fresh broccoli contain 90 mg of vitamin C, more than is found in the usual servings of citrus fruits. About a third of vitamin C is lost in the blanching process preparatory to freezing. Frozen cooked broccoli contains 60 mg of vitamin C per serving (3 1/2 oz). This loss is unfortunate, but a serving still provides more than the RDA for the vitamin. There is no significant difference in the vitamin A value (2,500 I.U.) of fresh and frozen broccoli.

SAUERKRAUT

I know that sauerkraut is rather low in calories. Is it also low in nutrients?

Sauerkraut is a reasonably good source of vitamin C. While it doesn't deserve more than one cheer for its nutrient contributions, sauerkraut does add its share of the total day's requirements and adds more than its share of zest.

The USDA reported that sauerkraut consumption has been increasing. It's popular enough that food technologists have spent time devising an acceptable freeze-dried kraut.

YAMS

What is the nutritive value of yams?

In some sections of the country, the soft-fleshed, orange-colored sweet potato is incorrectly called a yam. The yam may be yellow or white and is sweeter and juicier than the sweet potato. Depending on variety, the sweet potato is hard- or soft-fleshed but is characterized by its deep yellow or orange color.

Yams contain only a trace of the yellow carotenoid pigment—from which vitamin A is derived—whereas the sweet potato is one of the richest sources of it. One small sweet potato, cooked in the skin, supplies 8,100 I.U. of vitamin A and 22 mg of vitamin C. The same amount of cooked yams contains only a trace of vitamin A and 9 mg of vitamin C. Both contain significant amounts of the vitamin B-complex.

Those plump, southern "yams" frequently seen in produce sections of stores nowadays are really sweet potatoes, rich in nutrients. When these are cut open, no yellow or faint orange color is found but rather a deep coppery color. The shape—plump in the middle, with tapered ends—is different from that of other sweet potato varieties, but it is most confusing that they should be called yams.

COS (ROMAINE) LETTUCE

What is cos lettuce? How does it compare with head lettuce?

Cos or Romaine lettuce has long, tapered leaves. The outer leaves are heavy and somewhat coarse and are dark green in color. The inner leaves may be a golden yellow and are crisp and tender. The outer leaves taste sweet.

Cos is one of five categories of lettuce, the remaining being: butterhead, looseleaf, stem, and iceberg (head) lettuce.

Cos lettuce has about eight times as much vitamin A value as does head lettuce (2,600 I.U./100 gm) and nearly five times as much vitamin C (24 mg/100 gm). Get acquainted with the varieties of lettuce and enjoy their nutritional and visual benefits.

NUTRIENTS IN MUSHROOMS

Do mushrooms have any nutritive value, or are they merely a decorative item?

Mushrooms, if used in sufficiently large amounts, can be considered a good source of niacin and iron. In proportion to the calories (only 28 in 3 $^1/_2$ ounces), the nutrient level is pretty good. Even if used for merely decorative purposes, mushrooms can transform a simple meal into a gourmet delight.

SPINACH FOR IRON?

Spinach used to be recommended widely for infants and children as a good source of iron. Why is it rarely mentioned now?

Spinach is an excellent source of carotene, which the body converts into vitamin A, but recent studies have shown that, although the iron content of spinach is high, the iron exists in a form not readily absorbed in the digestive tract. More satisfactory food sources of iron are eggs, meats, and whole-grain cereals. There is, however, no reason why the average person who likes spinach should not eat it when the opportunity arises, nor why anyone who dislikes it should eat it, provided other green vegetables are included in the diet.

FRIED GREEN TOMATOES

How do fried green tomatoes compare nutritionally with the ripened red tomatoes?

Tomatoes, as they ripen or mature to a bright red color, increase in vitamin A content; green tomatoes have less than one-third of the vitamin A found in mature red tomatoes. Many people—especially those who grow their own vegetables—have specialty recipes for the immature tomato. If your general diet is adequate in vitamin A, eat the green tomatoes with a clear conscience.

NUTRIENTS IN BEETS

Is there any nutritional value in beets?

Not very much. One cup of cooked, diced beets provides 60 calories, 2 gm of protein, 1.2 mg of iron, and 6 mg of vitamin C.

This is not a particularly impressive list of nutrients, although the iron is significant. Despite their red color, beets contain almost no vitamin A.

FROZEN ONIONS

Are frozen onions really safe to use?

Clean, frozen onions are safe, as nothing can happen during the frozen state that would create a health hazard. Frozen onions and onions in frozen food mixtures are available commercially. The practice of home freezing of onions, however, may not be the preferred nor the most economical method of preservation due to variability of personal skills in vegetable preparation and freezing.

To insure an adequate supply of fresh onions, store them in a cool, dry place. If onions are thoroughly dry and have adequate ventilation, they should remain in good condition for six to eight months. If onions are purchased in an air-tight container, be sure to remove them from that container before storage to insure proper ventilation.

SEA KELP

Why do nutritionists object to sea kelp if it is rich in nutrients?

Nutritionists do not object to the use of sea kelp but, rather, to deceptive claims for "health" foods. Unfortunately, sea kelp is often classified as a "health" food. In fact, it is only one of the many hundreds of foods available for our nourishment and good health. Sea kelp contains many nutrients found in sea water; it's a good source of iodine and other minerals.

EGGPLANT

Is eggplant a nourishing food?

Eggplant is mostly flavor and water. Cooked eggplant consists of 95 percent water and 4 percent carbohydrate, which doesn't leave much room for anything else. Its vitamin and mineral content is negligible. Breaded eggplant is a good example of a dish in which the breading may be more nourishing than the original food. The best that can be said about eggplant is that for many people it can be a delightful accompaniment to a meal.

NUTRIENTS IN PUMPKIN

The pumpkin is a grand symbol of fall as a jack-o-lantern or as the makings of a wonderful pie, but does it also have nutritional value?

The pumpkin itself does not provide much other than vitamin A, for which it is an excellent source. One cup of prepared pumpkin will supply 14,800 I.U. of vitamin A, which is two to three times the RDA for adults. The same amount of pumpkin will also contain about 2.3 gm of protein, 1.4 mg of niacin, and a lot of good eating. The food value of pumpkin pie depends as much upon the eggs and milk as upon the pumpkin.

POWDERED OR MASHED POTATOES

Are "instant" powdered potatoes as nutritious as freshly made home-mashed potatoes?

Recent studies showed that fresh, cooked potatoes contained from two and one-half to five times more vitamin C (ascorbic acid) than any of the brands of dehydrated, cooked potato products tested; they also contained more thiamin. Some brands of dehydrated potatoes contain more vitamin C than others. Since the U.S. population does not rely on the potato as its sole source of vitamin C, there will probably be little concern over the decreased availability of vitamin C in the dehydrated product.

Even though the instant, dehydrated potato products may offer less of some nutrients, this is not particularly significant when one considers that their advantage in the marketplace lies in their long shelf life, their economy of space, and their ease and speed of preparation.

PURPLE POTATOES

Are there really purple potatoes?

Yes. These potatoes are usually grown in small numbers as specialty items and are used by restaurants and hotels to put a dash of color into salads and other food items. They are considered safe to eat.

Color in vegetables may be a manifestation of certain minerals in soil. Iron or manganese in heavy concentration may impart a dark red hue, for example. In most instances, however, color is due to organic pigments. The most common coloring in vegetables is carotene. It is primarily responsible for the yellow coloration in pumpkin, squash, carrots, and most other yellow or orange vegetables. In combination with another pigment, chlorophyll, it provides green color in certain leafy vegetables.

Although purple potatoes have not been investigated to determine the source of their color, it is probable that anthocyanin is the pigment responsible. Anthocyanins are present in many fruits and vegetables. They are responsible for the deep purple of certain varieties of Bermuda onions and for the dark red of cranberries.

While some of the yellow pigment, carotene, can be converted to vitamin A, the other pigments *per se* are not known to provide anything of significance nutritionally. The mineral elements of some vegetable colors, such as the magnesium in chlorophyll, may make important contributions, however. The real value of most plant pigments is making food colorful and attractive.

LETTUCE SALAD

Does a lettuce salad have very much nutritive value?

Crisphead lettuce makes a significant contribution of vitamin A and adds some of that substance too often lacking in our diets—roughage.

There are many ways to increase the value of a green salad. One small tomato more than triples the vitamin C and also boosts the vitamin A considerably. Ingredients such as sliced eggs, cheese strips, and avocados add many nutrients.

The caloric content of lettuce is very low—approximately 15 to 20 calories per serving—but the commonly used salad dressings (other than low-cal) on the average contain nearly 100 calories per tablespoon.

VITAMIN C IN RADISHES

Is it true that radishes are a good source of vitamin C?

Not for those of us who occasionally eat two or three radishes. But, then, it is actually a matter of personal taste. If you eat radishes with great relish, multiply the number of radishes by 2.5 mg to determine the total vitamin C.

ASPARAGUS

Is there a difference in nutrients between green and white asparagus?

Green and white asparagus compare favorably on all counts except vitamin A and iron. Green asparagus contains twice as much iron (1 mg in 3 medium spears) and ten times as much vitamin A (295 I.U.). Both have small amounts of many other nutrients.

White asparagus, by the way, is produced by mounding dirt around the plant so that the stalk, developing underground, never turns green.

FRUITS CANNED IN WATER OR SYRUP

Does the heavy syrup in canned fruits influence their nutritive value?

The total nutritive value of fruit per equal serving, whether in a water or syrup pack, is the same except for calories. Fruits packed in heavy syrup provide more calories because of the added sugar. One cup of water-pack peaches, for example, provides 900 I.U. of vitamin A and 62 calories. The same quantity of syrup-pack peaches contains the same amount of vitamin A but 156 calories. Packing fruits with syrup enhances their flavor and, judging from consumer preference, increases their acceptability. Since more fruit is consequently consumed, this probably justifies the presence of the added calories.

STRAWBERRIES

Does the bright redness of a strawberry indicate its vitamin A content?

The colored pigments in strawberries do not belong to the family of compounds converted in the body to vitamin A. Strawberries are, however, an excellent source of vitamin C, containing 90 mg per cup. They are also a surprisingly good source of iron. Imagine, as much iron (1.5 mg) in a cup of fresh strawberries as in an extra large egg!

NUTRIENTS IN GRAPES

Are grapes a good source of vitamins?

When compared with that of many other fruits, the nutritive value of grapes is not very impressive. One cup of grapes, depending upon the kind used, furnishes 70 to 100 calories and small amounts of most vitamins and minerals. Nevertheless—and all lovers of wine will agree—the grape is a glorious fruit.

MANGOS

What food value is there in a mango?

Mangos are an excellent source of vitamin A and a good source of vitamin C. One-half of a mango (about 3 oz) provides 4,800 I.U. of vitamin A, 35 mg of vitamin C, and a lot of juice.

WHITE VS PINK GRAPEFRUIT

Is there any difference in nutrient value between fresh white grapefruit and pink grapefruit?

Both white and pink grapefruit are rich sources of vitamin C, each containing about 35 to 40 mg in a medium-size half. Pink grapefruit has considerably more vitamin A than white grapefruit, averaging as much as 400 I.U. of vitamin A value in one-half.

APPLE JUICE AND CIDER

Is there a difference between apple juice and cider?

Fresh apple juice not containing a preservative and not treated to prevent fermentation is usually referred to as sweet cider, whereas fermented apple juice is commonly known as hard cider. The product labeled "apple juice" is one subjected to some preservation process to prevent spoilage and is sold in sealed bottles and cans.

One reference, recognizing the possibilities for confusion in terminology, reserves the term "apple juice" for products which contain less than 0.5 percent alcohol by volume, regardless of the method of preservation. Apple juice products containing more than 0.5 percent and less than 8 percent alcohol are considered as cider, whereas wine has more than 8 percent but less than 24 percent alcohol by volume.

In terms of calories, there is no appreciable difference. A six-ounce portion of the canned fresh product provides approximately 87 calories; the same amount of fermented apple cider provides 71 calories.

ORANGE DRINKS

When orange juice is high in price, can a powdered orange drink be used as a substitute? Is there sufficient vitamin C in such a drink?

The label on the orange drink will indicate the amount of vitamin C in a usual serving. The RDA for vitamin C is 40 to 45 mg for children and adults, respectively. A large number of citrus-based beverages and canned or frozen fruit juices can be used at times when fresh fruit is scarce. Experiment with a variety of fruits and beverages. Delightful as orange juice is, it is only one of a large number of products which can be used to assure an adequate intake of vitamin C.

ACEROLA JUICE

Of what value is acerola juice? Why is it added to some commercial infant foods?

Acerola is a fruit related to the cherry that grows in the West Indies. It is one of the richest known sources of vitamin C. One hundred grams (a little less than one-half cup) of acerola juice contain 1,494 mg of vitamin C. This is nearly 30 times the vitamin C present in the same amount of orange juice. Infant food manufacturers who have wished to increase the vitamin C content of juices or fruits have sometimes used acerola juice as a source of vitamin C.

DRIED FRUIT

Packaged dried fruits sometimes darken in color. Are they still safe to use when they become dark brown in color?

Dried fruits are usually considerably darker than the fresh variety, the darker colors being caused by changes in the natural fruit pigments. A browning action, similar to that which takes place on the cut surface of many fruits, may also occur. Fruit is customarily treated with sulfur prior to drying in order to reduce any color changes. The fruit in question may not have been properly treated before drying. The dark appearance of some dried fruits may affect their acceptability; however, the color of the fruit has nothing to do with its wholesomeness.

CALORIES IN DATES

Do dates have too many calories to be allowed on a weight-reduction diet?

Three to four dried pitted dates contain about 85 calories, a significant contribution of calories when added to the total daily caloric intake. Dates do, however, provide small amounts of calcium, potassium, phosphorus, iron, thiamin, and riboflavin. They are a favorite of many, especially in homemade date-nut bread fresh from the oven. Those on weight-reduction diets may prefer to give up other foods to enjoy some dates—*occasionally*.

WATERMELON

Does watermelon contain many vitamins?

Watermelon contains very good amounts of the A, B, and C vitamins and is even a relatively good source of iron. A half slice of melon, not too thick, is a real bargain in calories—about 50.

VITAMIN C IN PINEAPPLE

Is pineapple considered a good source of vitamin C?

Although pineapple contains considerably less vitamin C than the citrus fruits, it could be classified as a good source of this nutrient. An average serving of pineapple will provide about half the RDA for vitamin C. Three-fourths of a cup of fresh pineapple contains about 20 mg of vitamin C; the juice has about 3 mg per fluid ounce.

FIG BARS

My family uses fig bars as a snack food. Are they a nutritious food? How many calories do they contain?

Nutritionally, a fig bar is not much more than a concentrated source of energy. Figs do not provide many nutrients, as their vitamin, protein, and mineral content is very low. A half-ounce fig bar is equivalent to 56 calories, with nearly all of the calories derived from carbohydrate. Carbohydrates in figs are sticky, adhere to the teeth, and could promote the growth of decay-causing bacteria. As snacks, fig bars are far from ideal.

WHOLE-GRAIN AND ENRICHED

What is meant by whole-grain? Enriched? Are the whole-grain breads and flours superior to the enriched?

A whole-grain bread, cereal, or flour contains the three principal parts of the seed (or kernel), i.e., the germ, the endosperm (inner layer), and the bran or covering. Whole wheat or graham flour, for example, is made by grinding the entire kernel. An enriched wheat flour, such as all-purpose flour and cake flour, is milled from wheat that is essentially free of germ and bran and contains added thiamin, niacin, riboflavin, and iron in amounts within limits set by federal standards.

Minerals and vitamins are more concentrated in the germ and bran than in the endosperm from which most flours are made. Whole-grain products contain a wider array of nutrients, including trace minerals, vitamin E, and the lesser-known B vitamins as well as thiamin, riboflavin, niacin, and iron. Since bran is largely indigestible, whole-grain products also provide a good deal of roughage. The nutritional significance of whole-grain products is dependent upon the consumer's use of them, and consumers have long shown a definite preference for white flours and white breads.

The enrichment program began in the 1940's. By that time chemists had developed the ability to prepare some of the vitamins in pure, inexpensive forms. Considerable evidence had accumulated to indicate that many Americans had diets that were deficient in thiamin, riboflavin, niacin, and iron. Thus, the Government, with the support of scientific groups and the cooperation of millers, made it possible to add vitamins and minerals to flour, breads, and cereals. During World War II, such enrichment was compulsory, and subsequent to wartime legislation, several states established laws requiring enrichment of flour and bread.

Because of other improvements in the nutritional quality of foods and increases in family incomes that came about during the same period of time, we shall probably never know precisely how great a role enrichment has played in improving the health of our people. We do know that enrichment was followed by not simply a decline but a virtual disappearance of the classical vitamin deficiency diseases.

FATS IN BREAD

Are commercial breads high in fat?

One could hardly call bread a "high-fat food." Most breads contain less than 1 gm of fat per slice. It is the butter you spread that adds fat to bread.

BLEACHED FLOUR

What is the difference between bleached and unbleached white flour?

Flour that is freshly milled contains certain pigments that naturally oxidize and whiten within two to three months. Flour that is labeled "bleached" has had bleaching agents added in order to remove the pigments more quickly and thus decrease the need for the costly warehouse storage required for the "unbleached" flour. The bleaching agents used are quite harmless substances which have been approved by the Food and Drug Administration.

REGULAR VS "QUICK-COOKING" CEREALS

Does it make any difference whether the regular cooked cereal or the "quick-cooking" type of cereal is used?

The nutritive values of both types of cereal are approximately the same. In some of the quick-cooking varieties, a salt substance is added during manufacturing which brings about a quicker gelatinization of the starch and significantly reduces cooking time. The type of cereal purchased is strictly a matter of personal preference unless one is following a diet restricted in sodium (salt) intake.

NUTRITIONAL VALUE OF GRITS

Is it true that grits are not very nourishing because they are made from white instead of yellow corn?

The only difference, although not significant, is in vitamin A activity. A cup of cooked yellow corn grits would provide about 100 International Units of vitamin A activity, while grits made from white corn contain only a trace. A one-cup serving of cooked, enriched grits provides 120 calories, 3 gm of protein, 0.7 mg of iron, 0.11 mg of thiamin, 0.1 mg of riboflavin, and 1 mg of niacin. The most important concern, nutritionally, is that *enriched* products be used.

CALORIES IN PIE CRUST

Why is pie crust so high in calories?

About one-third of the weight of the finished product consists of fat. Carbohydrate makes up nearly half of the weight. One wedge of a baked pie crust will provide about 93 calories without even considering the pie filling or upper crust.

According to the USDA, an average serving of apple pie may provide 330 calories, just under one-third of which will come from the lower crust.

PASTA

What is pasta?

Pasta is a general name for macaroni products including spaghetti and egg noodles as well as macaroni itself. The name is derived from the dough or paste from which the final products are made.

MACARONI AND EGG NOODLES

Are enriched macaroni and egg noodles as nourishing as mashed potatoes made with milk and butter?

On the basis of equal servings, the similarities in nutrient content are more striking than the differences. Compare half-cup servings: macaroni and egg noodles contain more starch (33 and 50 percent respectively) and less fat, and a little more protein than mashed potatoes. These differences are reflected in the calorie values which are 75 and 100 for macaroni and noodles, respectively, and 95 for mashed potatoes. The vitamin B content for the three is about the same. The potatoes contain small amounts of vitamin C, not found in the pastas.

PANCAKES

Do pancakes make a nutritious meal? How many calories are in an average serving?

Pancakes leave the griddle in many sizes and are doused with varying amounts of butter, syrup, or other ingredients, depending upon individual preferences. Therefore, the nutritional value of a pancake meal may vary considerably. Values can be calculated for standard pancakes and then added to, depending on the variety of pancakes served. As a standard of comparison: four pancakes (4 inches in diameter and 1 ounce each) made from enriched pancake flour, oil, eggs, and milk provide 225 calories, 7.2 gm of protein, 215 mg of calcium, 1.2 mg of iron and about $1/10$ to $1/5$ of the daily need for vitamins.

Almost everyone wants butter on pancakes. One pat of butter is equivalent to 50 calories and, if three pats are used, the total calories (butter plus pancakes) would be 375. Next the syrup is added—who knows how much? Three tablespoons (two ounces) would add 165 more calories to push the total for the pancake meal to 540 calories. As there are only 7 gm of protein in this meal so far, the addition of some sausage is advisable. Three links of pork sausage (3" × $1/2$") will provide 10 gm of protein but also 280 more calories. This brings the total calories from the pancake meal to 820 with only a moderate offering of protein. To reduce calories, use less butter and syrup. Pancakes make a magnificent meal—but only once in a while, as they are very high in calories and low or borderline in protein value.

BAGELS

I'm trying to avoid eggs and am big on bagels. Is the egg bagel the only variety containing eggs?

It would help to know if you are avoiding the whole egg or just the yolk. Plain or water bagels may contain egg white, but not the yolk. Most other varieties, including onion, whole wheat, or butter bagels, are made from a basic egg bagel formula. These would likely contain the whole egg or yolk. Your best bet is to read the label—or make your own.

CLASSIFICATION OF CORN

Is corn considered a cereal or a vegetable?

Corn is a grass and is classified as a cereal. Milled corn products such as corn bread, corn meal, corn-based breakfast foods, and corn grits are classified as cereals. However, sweet corn—on or off the cob—is considered a vegetable and would be found listed among the vegetables in food tables.

POPCORN

As snacks go, is popcorn a pretty good one?

As would be expected, popcorn contains few nutrients. But surprisingly enough, popcorn ranks lower in calories than the other popular "low nutrition" snack foods. One cup of plain, popped corn has 50 calories; with butter, 80 calories; sugar coated, 135 calories. A current novelty is to sprinkle grated cheese on popped corn and broil for a minute. Every tablespoon of cheese adds about 25 calories and minor amounts of protein and calcium.

WILD RICE

How does wild rice compare in nutritive value to ordinary rice?

Although wild rice is classified with conventional rice, the plant and the grain differ considerably from cultivated rice. Wild rice, for all practical purposes, is not cultivated but grown wild in mud flats and shallow lakes in the eastern United States and Canada. The beds reseed themselves even though a large portion of the annual crop is harvested.

Pure wild rice is considered a gourmet item and is relatively expensive. Mixtures of wild rice and other grains, such as long-grain rice, are available at lower cost. The mixture is a fair substitute when the flavor and texture of wild rice are desired.

Wild rice resembles wheat more than rice in its nutrient composition. The vitamin content of wild rice is of the same order as whole wheat but it contains more riboflavin. Both wild rice and hard wheat have about 14 percent protein, twice as much as rice. The protein content of these grains is diluted after cooking due to the increase in water content.

NUTRITIONAL VALUE OF NUTS

Do pecans have a nutrient value similar to peanuts? What is so special about dry roasted peanuts?

Pecans have good nutritional value but somewhat less than peanuts have. Peanuts are generally recommended as a relatively inexpensive source of protein. One ounce of roasted peanuts without skins contains 8.6 gm of protein and approximately 180 calories. By comparison, an ounce of chopped pecans contains 2.8 gm of protein as well as 208 calories. Most nuts supply good amounts of B vitamins and iron.

As a rule, peanuts are oil roasted. Thus, the phrase "dry roasted" simply means that no oil was added during the roasting process. The oil roasted nuts are eight to ten calories richer per ounce, which hardly seems significant considering that the nuts to begin with are 46 percent fat.

SUNFLOWER SEEDS

Are sunflower seeds exceptionally nutritious?

Sunflower seeds contain good amounts of protein, the B vitamins, iron, and, to a lesser extent, calcium. They are also rich in fat and calories—over 13 gm of fat and 160 calories per ounce.

As a snack, sunflower seeds rank with peanuts as one of the best snack foods, but most of us will need to refrain from over-indulgence. For the vegetarian, sunflower seeds and other seeds and nuts assume a more important role in the diet (see p. 39).

PUMPKIN SEEDS

My small son loves dried pumpkin seeds (prefers them to candy). Are they nutritious?

Pumpkin seeds (kernels) certainly are nutritious and are superior to candy as a snack food. The kernels are an excellent source of iron and high-quality protein. One ounce of kernels supplies 160 calories (a large percentage of which is from the fat), 8 gm of protein, 3 mg of iron, and good amounts of the B vitamins. Needless to say, an individual who tends to be overweight should go easy on pumpkin seeds and other dried seeds, such as sunflower and sesame.

A GOOD EGG

How can one tell when an egg is fresh? Should an egg which is not fresh be used?

Generally, a fresh egg—an egg properly stored to retain its high quality—has a large portion of thick white that stands up firmly when the egg is broken onto a flat surface, and not a thin, watery white which is less viscous and spreads out readily. Its yolk is not watery but firm in appearance and does not break easily when the shell is opened. Fresh eggs will not have absorbed off-odors. When a fresh egg is hard-cooked and removed from the shell, a small air space will be observed.

Fresh eggs of high quality are better for poaching, boiling, and frying and will produce thicker, stiffer custard and cakes of high volume. An egg which is not quite as fresh, however, can still be used for scrambling and other types of egg cookery.

Eggs lose freshness quickly in today's commerce; however, they are moved from the farm to the table very rapidly. Commercial egg handling is designed to retard undesirable changes and to retain the egg's fresh qualities as long as possible. To assure freshness, it is best to store eggs at low refrigerator temperatures (35° F. to 45° F.) in their original carton since they should be stored with the large end up and lightly covered. Buy in quantities which will permit a reasonable turnover of eggs in the home.

BLOOD SPOTS IN EGGS

Occasionally there are small blood spots in eggs when they are opened. Should such eggs be discarded?

An occasional blood spot in an egg is attributed to a slight extra pressure on the blood vessel of the ovary of the hen so that a small clot adheres to the yolk of the egg. This does not indicate a diseased state in the hen, and the clot can be easily removed by the homemaker with no fear of its having contaminated the egg in any way.

This clotting phenomenon is entirely unrelated, however, to the presence of large amounts of blood in the white; this latter phenomenon is due to hemorrhage in the oviduct of the hen. An egg with these large areas of reddish coloring is generally heavily infected with bacteria and develops a definite unpleasant odor which is noticeable upon breaking the shell. Eggs of this type very seldom reach the consumer, as they are usually discovered in the candling process and are then discarded.

EGGS EXCEL

Is an egg really high in nutrients?

An egg is an excellent source of protein, vitamin A, and iron and a good source of riboflavin, vitamin D, and other vitamins and minerals. The calcium contained in an egg is in the shell, however, and is thus not usually available to the diet.

PEANUT BUTTER

Is peanut butter a source of protein?

A tablespoon of processed peanut butter contains about 4 gm of protein, indicating that peanut butter is about 25 percent protein. To get the same amount of protein found in a three-ounce hamburger patty, one would have to eat about five or six tablespoons of peanut butter. Unfortunately, this amount of peanut butter would add to the diet 350–450 calories more than a hamburger patty. Such an addition of calories would be extremely undesirable for some, especially those needing to lose weight; therefore, peanut butter is not a complete substitute for meats.

PEANUT BUTTER—CHUNKY OR SMOOTH?

I have heard that chunky peanut butter is more nutritious than the smooth variety. Is this true?

The only difference is peanut particles. Each spread contains 25 percent protein and 50 percent oil, with the remaining 25 percent composed of carbohydrate, fiber, salt, and water. The composition of peanut butter varies somewhat among manufacturers and is dependent upon the proportion of peanuts, oils, and seasoning agents as well as the quality of peanuts used. Most manufacturers use peanuts of the highest quality.

CASSEROLE CALORIES

Can a casserole or stew contain more calories than the ingredients used?

While casseroles and stews can gain intriguing flavors during cooking, they cannot gain calories. A hot dish *will* yield energy to its environment as it cools, but that's a different matter.

The caloric value of a mixture equals the energy of its components. There may be a tendency to overlook some of the ingredients which could yield calories. If the caloric value is estimated on the weight or volume of a serving before and then after cooking, there might be an increase due to concentration of the ingredients by water lost in boiling. This would be a relative increase in calories.

PIZZA

If a family likes pizza, is it all right to give it to them fairly often?

Pizza prepared properly with lots of meat or sausage, cheese, and tomatoes has good food value. Pizza is usually a good source of protein and calcium and also contributes its share of iron, vitamins A and C, and the B complex vitamins to the daily diet. Pizzas make a fine teen snack or party treat and also add variety to family mealtime.

SOUPS

Is there any real nutritional value in soup?

It was the 12th century physician John of Milan who said: "Soup makes the teeth white and the eyes clear, fills the stomach, and assists the digestion." Although no studies support the first two statements, few would argue that soups are an excellent way to "fill the stomach."

The nutritional value of soup depends on the ingredients used in the preparation. For example, one serving of cream of chicken soup made with whole milk will contribute approximately 6 gm of protein, 139 mg calcium, 1.5 mg iron, 640 I.U. vitamin A, as well as other nutrients.

Commercially prepared soups are available in condensed, frozen, and dehydrated states. Storage space need no longer be a problem with keeping soups on hand.

Estimates show that there are approximately 1,000 different soups throughout the world. The imagination of the cook and the variety of ingredients native to each country make soup one of the most versatile foods.

BROTH, BOUILLON, CONSOMME

Are broth, bouillon, and consomme different?

Broth is the liquid obtained from meat or poultry that has simmered in water. Brown stock made from lean beef and bone is used in preparing bouillon and is lightly seasoned. Some of the meat is browned before adding it to water. Consomme is usually made from two or more kinds of meat—veal, chicken, or beef. The liquid is strained and highly seasoned. Nutritionally speaking, all three types of soup have approximately the same value, with one cup providing the following nutrients: 10 calories, 2 mg calcium, 0.05 mg riboflavin, 2 gm protein, 1 mg iron, 0.6 mg niacin. These soups do not provide a substantial amount of nutrients to the diet. They have value primarily as stimuli for the appetite and as sources of liquid in the diet; they can be made more nutritious by the addition of meat, vegetables, or noodles.

SPICES, HERBS, CONDIMENTS

How do spices, herbs, and condiments differ?

Less distinction is now made between the terms spices and herbs; both are covered by the word "spices." Herbs are prepared from the leafy or soft portion of certain plants, while spices are derived from roots, buds, flowers, fruits, barks, and seeds. Since both owe their distinctive aroma and flavor to characteristic volatile oils, the portion of the plant containing the highest concentration of these oils is used—the bud of clove, root of ginger, and leaf of mint are classic examples. More than thirty herbs and spices are in common use in this country, and the demand is growing as more people become interested in gourmet cookery. Condiments are made up of combinations of spices and other ingredients. Catsup, chili sauce, prepared mustard, and steak sauces are examples of common condiments. All of these products are used to enhance or accent natural food flavors or to impart a special taste.

It is best to buy spices in a glass jar which can be closed tightly with a screw top. Small boxes and cans may be less expensive but they cannot be resealed and thus do not protect freshness as effectively as do the glass jar containers. Buying whole spices also will increase the length of time they will be at top freshness. Whole spices will keep for several years, while ground spices decrease in flavor after about one year. Spices can also be protected from flavor loss by being stored in a cool, dry area away from light. It is not necessary to refrigerate spices, but they should not be stored directly over the stove because of heat. However, they often end up there.

HOSPITAL GELATIN

Gelatin is served frequently as a dessert in hospitals. Why is this so?

Gelatin is well accepted, is easily digested, and can be used in just about all dietary regimens. It can be used to make an economical and versatile salad or provide a dessert base that mixes well with fruits to add variety and color to meals. Hospitals can serve gelatin in a variety of ways with assurance that most patients will enjoy it. Gelatin protein, however, is incomplete nutritionally because it is lacking in several important amino acids. Its low nutritive value is of no great significance, however, when it is used in conjunction with an otherwise adequate supply of foods of high-quality protein.

COMMERCIAL MAYONNAISE

What ingredients are used in the preparation of commercial mayonnaise?

Mayonnaise is one of many food products for which there is a federal standard of identity. A food for which there is such a standard need not list the ingredients on the label, except for certain optional ingredients for which a label statement is required. Processors, however, are encouraged to list ingredients voluntarily.

Mayonnaise is an emulsified, semi-solid product consisting of vegetable oil, water, an acidifying agent, and one or more substances containing egg yolks and seasoning. The legal standard of identity for mayonnaise requires that it contain not less than 65 percent by weight of vegetable oil. Most mayonnaise, however, will contain from 75 percent to 80 percent oil, with soybean oil (not hydrogenated) being used by about 85 percent of the manufacturers. The acidifying agent most frequently used is a diluted vinegar, containing not less than 2.5 percent acetic acid. Lime and lemon juice also may be used as part of the acidifying agent. The egg yolk substances may be whole, dried, or frozen eggs or egg yolks. The amount of egg yolk to be used, however, is not stated. No yellow coloring agent may be used because of the possibility of giving the impression that the color is due to egg yolks; thus, turmeric and saffron are prohibited as seasonings. A variety of optional seasoning agents is permitted, however, including sugar, dextrose, corn syrup, honey, salt, and any spice, except the two mentioned above and others imparting a yellow color. Only these optional ingredients may be required to be listed on the label.

KOSHER FOODS

What makes a food kosher?

The word "kosher" means sanctioned by Jewish law as ritually fit and proper for use. The term is commonly used in reference to the Jewish Kashruth laws, which are concerned with the selection, preparation, and service of food.

These Kashruth laws classify foods into three groups:

1. Foods inherently not kosher such as pork and pork products; birds of prey; shellfish such as lobster, crabs, and oysters; and fish without fins and scales such as eel and swordfish.
2. Foods inherently kosher such as breads and cereals, fruits and vegetables.
3. Foods such as meat and poultry which if processed correctly become kosher. Meat must come from quadruped animals that are cloven-hooved, graze, and chew their cud such as cattle, deer, sheep, and goats. Poultry such as turkey, chicken, duck, and pheasant is also allowed. The animal must be healthy and have not died a natural death; it is killed so as to cause the least amount of pain and the maximum amount of blood drainage. The meat is then carefully inspected by a rabbi or religious representative at the slaughterhouse and is again inspected periodically at the meat market. The meat is cleaned by being soaked in cold water, salted, allowed to stand to let the blood drain off, and then rinsed to remove the salt.

Fish with fins and scales are also allowed and include cod, haddock, halibut, salmon, trout, and tuna.

Milk and meat products must not be cooked or eaten together. For example, ice cream cannot be included in a meal containing roast beef. Usually two meals of the day contain dairy products and one meal contains meat and its products.

-8-
food myths, actions, and hazards

Food myths abound; they are as old as man himself. Some myths are charming, others are nonsense; many are dangerous. Can you remember *Folk Medicine* and *Arthritis and Folk Medicine* (Holt, Rinehart & Winston, N.Y., 1960) by D. C. Jarvis, M.D.? These two books neatly illustrate all three characteristics of myth—charm, nonsense, and danger. The gist of the books is that Vermonters in their early folk medicine found vinegar and honey to be useful for about every ailment, but especially useful in the treatment of arthritis. We were concerned when the books first appeared because Dr. Jarvis went a little too far in his translation of folk medicine into contemporary medicine with quite fanciful claims for honey and vinegar. He promised cures for nearly everything. In easy steps he turned Vermont folk medicine into a dangerous practice.

Foods do affect the body but they hold little magic. Foods are packages of nutrients along with other components put there by nature's design or accident or by the tampering of man. Under the wrong circumstances, the components can cause harm. In this enlightened day we needn't worry much about the naturally occurring hazardous materials in our foods, even though less is known about the naturally occurring toxicants in foods than is known about the chemicals man adds to foods. The food and agriculture industry has learned rather well how to cope with the natural compounds that could harm man. Thank goodness for that. We do not suggest nonchalance but would rather direct your attention to other food-borne hazards: bacteria.

Bacteria are ubiquitous; we must constantly be alert to the possibilities for bacterial contamination of food anywhere in the food chain. Poor food-handling practices in the home and in restaurants account for most of the cases of food poisoning. This chapter contains pertinent information about the more common forms of bacterial hazards in foods. As homemakers we can all be on guard to prevent foci of infection in and around food preparation areas. Keep working areas, utensils, and storage bins clean and dry. Wash hands frequently, especially before working with some other food after handling fresh meat, fish, and poultry.

We want this section to be fun as well as informative. Be alert but not uptight about food myths, actions, and hazards.

EASY TO DIGEST

What are the most easily digested foods?

This raises the question of what criteria one uses to measure ease of digestion. Easily digested and quickly digested are not synonymous phrases in a technical sense. For example, sugars are quickly absorbed, while fats remain in the digestive tract for many hours; yet the normal human digestive tract is remarkably efficient in handling fats. Complex carbohydrates and proteins are digested at a different pace, somewhere between sugars and fats.

To imply that the digestion of the more complex nutrients is difficult is to underestimate the sophistication of the enzyme systems and the cooperation of organs such as the liver and pancreas, as well as the sophistication of the digestive tract itself.

Some components of foods are, of course, indigestible— cellulose, for example. However, the very fact that cellulose is indigestible makes it important to the diet as it is one form of roughage or bulk.

Many negative attitudes, which may be completely unwarranted on the part of the average person, have resulted in branding foods as "hard to digest," "acidic," or "heavy." (Frequently, the appropriate direction for the criticism would be toward the *amount* eaten. Foods often shoulder the blame for human indiscretions.)

DIGESTIVE JUICES

Does the odor of food cooking really stimulate the flow of digestive juices?

Yes. The sight and smell of food can initiate the flow of both saliva and gastric juices when the appetite is good and the person has had experience with the food. Stimulation without mouth contact is a learned reflex or a conditioned reflex. Therefore, "mouth-watering goodness" requires preconditioning or the feel or taste of food in the mouth.

Saliva flows as soon as food is placed in the mouth, sharpening the sensitivity to taste while performing its important functions of lubrication, dilution, and initial digestion of starches.

The secretion of juices in the stomach begins in earnest while food is being chewed, and continues until the stomach is empty several hours later. These juices are vital to proper digestion.

MEAT TENDERIZERS

How do meat tenderizers work? If they tenderize meat, won't they do the same to the stomach?

Most commercial meat tenderizers contain the enzyme papain which is prepared from the green fruit of the papaya plant. Papain breaks down protein in meat and tenderizes or softens the connective tissues as well as the muscle fibers. The action of the enzymes takes place during cooking and is greatest at temperatures between 140°F. and 176°F. As cooking continues, the papain loses its ability to split proteins. In the unlikely event that some of the tenderizer is not destroyed by heat, it will be destroyed by the gastric juices during digestion and, thus, poses no problem to the lining of the stomach.

PINEAPPLE AND GASTRIC UPSETS

Is there anything in pineapple that would cause gastrointestinal upsets?

Gastrointestinal upsets, if caused by a fruit, may be due to the fermentation of complex carbohydrates (fiber) in the intestinal tract which could cause the formation of gas and irritating organic acids. Undigested fiber may also promote water retention in the bowel.

Some raw fruits such as pineapple and papaya contain very active protein-digesting enzymes which may cause lip and mouth irritations in some people. It is doubtful that these same enzymes, even in large amounts, cause stomach or intestinal irritations in normal individuals.

Distress traceable to pineapples apparently is an individual reaction. A recent University of California study with healthy subjects failed to demonstrate any significant or general symptoms of gastrointestinal upsets resulting from the consumption of as much as one pound of pineapple per day. No bad effects were noted among seven young women who consumed either a pound of peaches or pineapple each day for four days along with otherwise conventional well-balanced meals. During the carefully controlled study accurate measures of intestinal functions were carried out.

The purpose of the study was to determine whether there were any physiological reasons to exclude pineapple from soft or low-residue diets. Peeled, canned peaches are allowed in limited quantities in such diets. Since there were no differences in the reactions to either peaches or pineapples, one can now question the rationale of eliminating pineapples from low-residue diets.

There appears to be no reason to exclude fresh or canned pineapples from the diet. Let your individual preference and experience be your guide.

FAT TOXICITY

Is it true that excessive amounts of fat in the diet will cause a serious toxic condition?

Under normal circumstances, the body is capable of metabolizing large quantities of fat without any acute danger. A condition called ketosis occurs, however, when fatty acids are not completely metabolized and when intermediary products called ketones accumulate in the blood stream. This condition causes metabolic changes that can be hazardous.

Ketosis may occur when the diet is practically devoid of carbohydrate and is composed mainly of fat. In this case, the oxidation of fat is increased because of the lack of carbohydrates to meet the body's energy requirements. Consequently, ketones are produced in larger quantities than the body can eliminate, and, as a result, ketosis often develops. Ketosis occurs often in cases of uncontrolled diabetes mellitus as carbohydrate metabolism is faulty. A healthy individual is not likely to develop ketosis unless his diet is excessively high in fat and drastically restricted in sugars and starches.

YELLOW SKIN

Can a yellowness of the skin be caused by eating too many carrots or other foods such as squash, sweet potatoes, pumpkin, mangoes, and persimmons?

A yellowish skin has been observed in some persons as a result of an excessive amount of carotene in the blood. The condition is known as "carotenemia," a pseudo-jaundice. The condition disappears with the elimination or reduction of the foods in the diet rich in carotene. Carotenemia occurs rarely, however, and anyone noting yellowing of the skin should consult his physician to rule out other possible causes.

All of the foods mentioned are excellent sources of carotene. If carotenemia is a problem, intake of these foods and certain others should be limited to a *maximum* of two or three servings per week until the yellowness disappears from the skin. Other foods high in carotenes are: green leafy vegetables (spinach, turnip greens, chard, and beet greens), green stem vegetables (asparagus and broccoli), yellow vegetables (carrots, sweet potatoes, winter squash, and pumpkin), and yellow fruits (apricots, peaches, and cantaloupe).

Although carotene is converted to vitamin A by the human body, carotenemia should not be confused with vitamin A toxicity (see p. 98). The body cannot convert massive doses of carotene to vitamin A fast enough to produce vitamin toxicity.

SLEEP ENHANCERS

Do certain hot beverages or a bedtime snack enhance sleep?

Some relaxation value may be found in hot drinks taken at bedtime; the relaxed state may then induce sleep. Individuals who go to bed truly hungry do not enjoy as restful sleep as those who are not hungry. This is probably related to the action of hunger contractions of the stomach to initiate waking.

Modest amounts of food just before retiring should not interfere with normal sleep, but there is no evidence that a bedtime snack, *per se,* will enhance sleep. No foods or beverages possess therapeutic powers for inducing sleep, nor do any of the nutrients. In recent years, some dubious "experts" have recommended calcium and magnesium supplements for nervousness and insomnia. Perhaps, because of the power of suggestion, this works for some people, but we think a dull book would be a better placebo.

CAFFEINE

Are coffee and tea harmful because of their caffeine content?

Tolerance to caffeine varies widely among individuals. A normal person can tolerate the amount of caffeine in most beverages without apparent discomfort, but people with such illnesses as active peptic ulcer, hypertension, and some cardiovascular and nervous system disorders usually must restrict their intake of caffeine-containing products because of the stimulating effect.

An average cup of coffee contains between 100 and 150 mg of caffeine. Instant coffee usually contains smaller amounts (80 to 90 mg per cup). The caffeine content of tea leaves is higher than that of coffee beans, but the beverages usually have about the same amount of caffeine. Although some persons are more sensitive to caffeine than others are, most of us will not be restless or sleepless unless we overindulge in the caffeine-containing beverages.

COLAS

What are the effects of cola beverages upon the body?

Claims have been made that carbonated beverages in some manner hasten gastric emptying. Theoretically, the more rapid emptying of the stomach would allow sugar or other nutrients to reach the absorbing intestinal mucosa more quickly. The beneficial effect obtained from "hastened" gastric emptying is still questionable.

Most cola drinks contain caffeine and, thus, could produce ill effects for some people. The amount of caffeine ranges from 35 to 55 mg in a 12-ounce bottle of cola.

Cola beverages are devoid of nutrients and (except for the low-cal) are generous in calories. If they are frequently used in place of more nutritious foods and beverages, however, the individual should be criticized, not the beverage. Also, remember that the ones containing sugar supply food to the decay-producing bacteria in the mouth.

SOFT DRINKS AND WATER RETENTION

Do carbonated soft drinks cause water retention?

Soft drinks should not cause water retention in normal, healthy individuals. The possibility exists that one may drink more of a soft drink than he would of water at one time. The large fluid intake, in addition to the carbonation release, may give a feeling of fullness with an impression of water retention.

Edema is generally associated with retention of water. In this instance, water is held in the extracellular spaces, meaning the spaces outside of the cells. Whenever illness, such as nephritis or cardiac failure, causes the retention of sodium, water accumulates along with the sodium in the extracellular spaces. The normal person can easily excrete sodium through the kidneys and thereby maintain water equilibrium.

Although a number of compounds containing sodium are used in soft drinks, the total amount of sodium is quite small, ranging from 15 to 40 mg in eight ounces of the beverages. Sodium benzoate, sodium saccharin, sodium citrate, and sodium chloride are some of the compounds used. Bottlers of soft drinks advise that the sodium content will depend to some extent on the sodium content of the water used as well. In any event, the amount is not excessive except for those on severely restricted sodium diets.

TOO MUCH SALT

How dangerous is it to use a lot of salt?

Salt contains about 39 percent sodium. Healthy persons will normally and promptly eliminate the usual amounts of sodium ingested from table salt and other sources. Persons with a lessened ability to excrete sodium often have problems with fluid balances in the body. In addition, excessive salt intake may aggravate a tendency toward hypertension.

HAZARDOUS SEEDS

Are the little seeds inside the stones of prunes, apricots, and peaches harmful? Some people like to eat the seeds or grind them for use as flavoring in cakes and icings.

The flesh of common fruit is wholesome and may be eaten with aplomb. The seeds of certain plants, however, contain amygdalin, a glycoside hazardous to man. Amygdalin occurs in large quantities in the bitter almond; some of the more common plant seeds containing amygdalin are peach, cherry, pear, plum, apricot, chokeberries, and cassava beans. Technically, amygdalin is known as a cyanogenic glycoside; hydrocyanic acid, a very toxic compound, is released from the glycoside during digestion. Although poisoning from the consumption of the seeds of these fruits is rare, it is unwise to eat the seeds or use them in any way in food.

In some parts of the world, it is rather common practice to eat the ground or marinated seeds of the peach, cherry, pear, and plum. Because they taste bitter, adults usually limit the number of seeds consumed at one time, but youngsters may not be so discerning. *The New England Journal of Medicine* on May 21, 1964, carried an article describing the poisoning of nine children during a six-year period due to their consumption of plum seeds. The toxic cyanide released from the amygdalin in the plum seeds was the poisoning agent.

WATER AT MEALS

Is it true that water and other beverages should not be taken with meals as they interfere with digestion?

There is no reason why a reasonable amount of liquid should not be consumed with meals; however, liquids should not be a substitute for foods and should not be used to wash down unchewed food particles. Thorough chewing of food is important, as it increases the opportunity for saliva to mix with foods; saliva contains an enzyme that digests starches. Water consumed with the meal leaves the stomach and does not interfere seriously with the normal digestion of foods. Even so, there is the possibility that drinking large amounts of fluids with a meal will leave one with a temporary full feeling before the meal is completed.

"BLOOD PURIFIERS"

Are onions and garlic of any medicinal or other value in the diet aside from adding flavor?

Onions have very little nutritive value; garlic has practically none. Both are used primarily as flavoring ingredients and neither is harmful. Various statements have been made in the past by indiscriminate persons regarding the use of garlic as a "blood purifier" or in the treatment of hypertension, cancer, and other diseases; such claims are simply not true.

CHOCOLATE VS CALCIUM ABSORPTION

Can eating chocolate interfere with the absorption of calcium from milk products?

Chocolate in amounts usually consumed does not significantly interfere with calcium absorption and utilization. A number of studies were made some time ago on the influence of chocolate on the absorption of calcium, but few of these studies were performed with human subjects. Studies with animals, rats in particular, have demonstrated that chocolate in unusually large quantities will interfere with growth and calcium utilization. Reports of these findings have no doubt led to the unwarranted conclusion that cocoa and chocolate may also interfere with mineral utilization in humans.

Studies with college girls at the University of Illinois, however, demonstrated that chocolate had no influence on calcium utilization. In these studies, one ounce of chocolate (as cocoa) each day had no effect on calcium availability in diets supplying 600 mg of calcium.

Cocoa and chocolate contain small amounts of oxalic acid. Oxalic acid combines with calcium to form an insoluble calcium oxalate compound. Rats are incapable of utilizing calcium in the oxalate compound; however, it is not known that humans have this problem. In any event, the amount of calcium in the milk greatly exceeds the amount of oxalic acid from the cocoa or chocolate used, and, thus, a sufficient amount of food calcium can still be absorbed.

MILK AND DIGESTION

Does milk inhibit the digestion of meals by coating the stomach and interfering with the production of digestive juices?

Milk does not inhibit digestion, as the secretion of digestive juices continues any time there is food in the stomach or any time there is appropriate psychological stimulation. The mucous membranes of the lining of the stomach protect against a "coating action." Food containing a considerable amount of fat tends to delay the emptying of the stomach, but this cannot be equated with indigestibility. It is a natural physiological phenomenon and probably improves digestion.

IS MILK CONSTIPATING?

Is it true that milk is constipating?

No more so than any other food. However, when milk is used to the exclusion of other foods that assist in maintaining regularity, it may be misinterpreted as a causative factor in irregularity. Don't accuse a food of any ill effects until you ask yourself how much of that food you ate and how good the total diet is.

TOO MUCH SKIMMED MILK

Would drinking a half gallon of skimmed milk daily be a harmful practice?

In determining whether this is harmful, additional factors would have to be considered. For example, milk is quite high in sodium content, and two quarts of milk would provide approximately 1 gm of sodium to the diet. Under certain conditions, sodium should be restricted in the diet and, therefore, it would be necessary to limit the milk intake.

Although the number of calories supplied by nonfat milk is considerably less than that of whole milk, two quarts would provide approximately 700 calories to the diet. If there is a weight problem, the daily addition of this number of calories to the diet from a single food could be undesirable.

Generally speaking, no one food supplies all the nutrients needed for optimum nutritional health. If the amount of milk you consume prevents you from eating a variety of foods, you might not be getting sufficient amounts of other nutrients such as iron and vitamin C, since milk does not contribute appreciable amounts of these nutrients.

SAFETY OF NONFAT DRY MILK

Are the nonfat dry milk powders completely safe for consumption?

The nonfat powdered milks on the market have been approved by the FDA as completely safe for human consumption. Dry cow's milk may contain fairly high concentrations of orotic acid. Rats fed powdered milk containing certain levels of orotic acid develop liver damage. These results have caused some speculation about the effect of orotic acid on humans when large amounts of powdered milk are consumed. There is little, if any, reason for concern except for those individuals with the hereditary disorder known as *orotic aciduria*.

Nonfat dry milk is a safe and wholesome food which provides important quantities of minerals and protein as well as vitamins A and D.

ENZYME MILK

An "enzyme milk" has been promoted as being especially good for infants. Is this true?

Enzyme milk is ordinary milk that has been treated with enzymes which act on the milk's protein to make a softer curd, presumably formed while the milk is being digested. Enzyme milk is safe for babies; however, the American Academy of Pediatrics questions the claims made for enzyme milk and asserts that it has no real advantage over conventional milk formulas.

During the first year of a baby's life, it is very important that the amount of milk and its proportion of fat, carbohydrate, and protein be carefully controlled. This must be done for each child individually. For this reason, the medical profession believes that infant formulas should not be promoted directly to the public. The family physician or pediatrician is the logical person to advise on the feeding of infants and children, not the milkman.

GLUTEN BREAD AND ASSIMILATION

Gluten bread is purported to be high in protein and also to impair the assimilation of other foods. Is this true?

No scientific evidence supports the idea that gluten prevents or impairs the assimilation of other foods. Wheat gluten is considered to be a fair-quality protein. Its biological value (a measure of the amount of protein retained by the body for growth maintenance) is lower than that of milk, eggs, and meat, ranking it with the protein of oats, potatoes, and yeast.

GELATIN

Ads say that chronically brittle nails can be improved and strengthened by daily use of gelatin. Is this true?

Several years ago, clinical data claiming that brittle nails could be improved or restored to normal by taking 7 to 21 grams of gelatin per day for an average of three months were broadcast by a major gelatin distributor. The amount of gelatin needed and the time required for improvement, however, depended upon the individual. Claims for some benefit do seem justified, but it is still questionable whether split and cracked nails can be restored to a true state of beauty. As yet, no significant explanation exists for this therapeutic action of gelatin.

SPICY FOOD

Is there any reason why a person over 60 years of age should avoid spicy foods such as chili or barbecued beef?

Chili and barbecued beef are nutritious foods which can be eaten by the healthy individual with no untoward effects. The use of spices is entirely a matter of personal preference. Spices serve a most important culinary function by enhancing the flavor and odor of food. Black pepper can irritate the stomach lining but causes no harm for healthy persons; and, although "hot" peppers cause burning sensations, they also do no harm to the person with a normal digestive tract.

In certain gastrointestinal disorders, however, the use of foods prepared with spices and condiments must be curtailed. Unless the physician has restricted the use of spices in the diet, there is no reason why a person of any age who enjoys eating these foods should not continue to do so.

UNCOOKED OATS

Can "quick-cooking" oats be eaten as they come from the box, without cooking them first?

Quick-cooked oats have been precooked, then dried and rolled during the processing. The purpose of the one-minute cooking before eating is to rehydrate the oats. If this product is eaten "raw" with milk, the rehydration will probably take place in the stomach.

Denmark is the highest oats-consuming population in the world. During World War II, many people ate oats raw because of a fuel shortage, and the Danes still use a lot of raw oats with no reports of ill effects. When making oatmeal cookies, the baking time and moisture content of cookies do not allow for the oats to become cooked. This, then, is another form in which undercooked oats are eaten.

BAKING SODA ADDED TO VEGETABLES

Baking soda is sometimes used in cooking to intensify the color of green beans. Does it destroy the vitamins?

Baking soda is sometimes used to intensify the color of cooked vegetables; it is also used to decrease the cooking time of legumes by helping to soften the outer skin. Neither of these uses for baking soda is to be recommended for the home. There is reported to be an increased destruction of ascorbic acid, thiamin, and riboflavin during the preparation of the vegetables when soda is used. This alone would be enough to condemn its use. Another consideration, however, is that unless just the right amount of soda is used under the proper conditions, vegetables can become quite mushy.

SALMON AND KIDNEY TROUBLES

Does eating salmon frequently affect the kidneys? Is fresh, whole salmon more healthful than canned salmon?

There is no reason to expect an association between the continued consumption of canned salmon and kidney difficulties. There is nothing in canned salmon that should cause trouble. It is true that salmon canned with the bones contains from 150 to 225 mg of calcium per serving. However, this is not an inordinate quantity of calcium and would not be expected to promote kidney stone formation. Whole fresh salmon differs from canned salmon nutritionally, as its bones are not usually consumed and, thus, less calcium would be available.

BACON DRIPPINGS

Are drippings from bacon a cause of cancer? Exposure to intense heat is supposed to cause a chemical change that makes the fat drippings harmful.

It has been shown experimentally that fats heated above 500°F. begin to undergo changes, and if the fat is actually charred, the tars formed could be injurious. The temperatures commonly employed in cooking, however, are not high enough to cause undesirable changes in the fat.

FRUIT AND VEGETABLE JUICES

Does the consumption of fruit and vegetable juices—celery, carrot, apple—cure such diseases as arthritis and cancer?

A number of articles have cited the uselessness of attempting to achieve freedom from arthritis and cancer by the use of fruit and vegetable juices. The only advantage in liquefying these foods is an increase in palatability for some consumers, which perhaps makes it possible to consume more of a particular food. There is no evidence than an individual who is otherwise in good health will enjoy any unique health benefits by consuming foods in addition to those consumed in the usual diet. There certainly is no evidence that any of these juices will cure arthritis or cancer—would that it were so.

GREEN APPLES

Green apples are often associated with stomach aches. Is there any basis for this?

The immature raw fruit has difficult-to-digest flesh. Its starch cells are most difficult to break down. The intact cells absorb water in the stomach and resist digestion for some time. This mass of swollen, undigested starch cells moves down the intestinal tract and has been known to cause great discomfort.

192

Cooking green apples ruptures the starch cells or softens them sufficiently to permit more rapid digestion. Green apple pies are safe to eat and can be a real treat.

ACID AND ALKALINE FOODS

What are the acid and alkaline foods? Should they be balanced in the diet?

Foods are grouped as alkali-producing, acid-producing, or neutral. This is determined by the properties of the minerals each food contains. For example, foods like fruits (with the exception of cranberries, prunes, and plums), vegetables (except corn and lentils), milk, and nuts contain alkali-forming minerals, namely, sodium, potassium, calcium, and magnesium. When these foods are metabolized or "burned" in the body, they yield an alkaline "ash" and are thus referred to as alkaline foods. Conversely, foods such as meat, cereals, or eggs contain acid-forming elements (phosphorus, sulfur, and chlorine) and will yield acid end products.

As an adjunct to the treatment of certain diseases, the physician might prescribe an acid- or alkali-forming diet. For the average, healthy individual, however, there is no conclusive evidence regarding the practical importance of balancing the acid and alkaline foods.

The human body has a wide range of adaptability. Therefore, the emphasis on acid and alkaline foods and alkalizing compounds by food fanatics is unfortunate and misguided. Many of those foods sometimes denounced as "too acid" because they taste sour are actually alkaline in their reactions in the body.

RAW ORANGE PEELS

Do raw orange peels contain anything harmful?

Orange peel contains a small amount of oil to which many people are allergic. The sensitivity to the oil is rather common among infants and children. For this reason, the processors of citrus juices for infant feeding are careful not to express peel oils when the fruit is squeezed. The oil is also an irritant and prolonged contact with the skin leads to irritation and damage. The individual can be the best judge of whether the consumption of orange peel causes any difficulties. If so, substitute another tart food for orange peels to satisfy the "craving."

REFINED SUGAR

Does consumption of refined sugar cause destruction of calcium in the body?

No known scientific indication exists to show that refined sugar has any effect whatsoever on calcium metabolism or on the physiological equilibrium of bone tissue. Table sugar, like table salt, is essentially chemically pure as nothing carried over from the sugar refining process would have an adverse effect on the body. The small quantity of vitamins and minerals available in partially refined sugar is of little, if any, nutritional significance. In fact, the sugar industry is sometimes criticized for marketing a product so chemically pure.

An important question exists, however, concerning the effects of sugar in the form of fermentable carbohydrate and its promotion of dental caries under certain circumstances. Development of dental caries is not, strictly speaking, the destruction of calcium in the teeth, since calcium cannot be destroyed but only dissolved and excreted. The process of caries formation is thought to result from the action of bacteria which are nourished by carbohydrate. When conditions are correct—namely, the existence of an unclean oral cavity and a source of food for the bacteria, such as fermentable carbohydrate—the organism will form a plaque on the teeth. The acid by-products of bacterial metabolism cause a dissolution of the teeth enamel with a subsequent erosion of supporting structures. The degree of hazard from a sugar (carbohydrate) is related to its fermentability and to its stickiness. Anyone who is subject to caries should avoid sticky candies, for example, and must either brush the teeth following eating or rinse the mouth thoroughly with water.

DETERGENT FOOD

What is a detergent food?

Dentists refer to crisp, crunchy foods as detergent foods because they help to remove other food particles from the teeth.

Chewing crunchy, low-carbohydrate foods such as celery, carrot strips, and radishes can do much to remove sticky foods from teeth.

RAW BEEF

Many people enjoy serving raw beef tartare as an hors d'oeuvre. Can uncooked beef such as this be dangerous?

The ingestion of raw beef can cause disease in man. Though very rare, a beef tapeworm, *Taenia saginata,* can be transmitted to man and lodge in the human intestine. If one buys only beef with an inspection stamp on it, he can be assured of purchasing the most wholesome of meat which is almost certain to be free of all such disease-producing organisms.

Beef also may become contaminated through handling. Meat handlers with cutaneous infections can transmit staphylococcus organisms to meat. Staphylococcus enterotoxin acts primarily on the human gastrointestinal tract, with onset of symptoms after ingestion occurring usually within about three hours. Symptoms are acute and include nausea, vomiting, diarrhea, intestinal cramps, headache, and, on occasion, fever. In addition, meat handlers who recently have been handling other products containing salmonella can subsequently contaminate beef with salmonella organisms, leading to similar symptoms of "food poisoning."

It is best for one who insists on consuming raw beef to be cognizant of the possible dangers involved. The best ways to avoid these dangers as much as possible are to:

1. Buy only inspected meat.
2. Keep meat under refrigeration until ready to use.
3. Buy meat that is freshly cut in the presence of the purchaser (such as top round or sirloin); then grind at home with a grinder, being sure to eat it within 24 hours after it has been purchased. Or, if no home grinder is available, buy only meat that is ground in the presence of the person buying it so that one can be sure that it is freshly ground under the most sanitary conditions possible.

UNCOOKED FRANKFURTERS

Is it safe to eat uncooked frankfurters?

Frankfurters are always precooked. Franks that have been properly packaged and stored and handled under sanitary conditions may be eaten without cooking.

UNCOOKED EGGS

Is it advisable to cook eggs to prevent being infected by a disease possibly passed to the egg from infected poultry?

To avoid the possibility of illness from contaminated raw eggs, use only fresh, clean, and unbroken eggs. The eggs that don't quite measure up to these specifications should be used only in cooked products. The usual methods of cooking eggs assure a safe product. Very carefully chosen eggs are not necessarily completely safe, as residual salmonella organisms may remain on the outside of the shell even after washing. Invisible cracks in the egg shell may also permit passage of the disease organism.

An outbreak of Salmonella infection in Massachusetts was traced to the use of contaminated eggs in unpasteurized eggnog. To avoid this situation, eggnog should be pasteurized during preparation. The Massachusetts Department of Health recommends that the milk and eggs be heated in a double boiler to 160°F. (a temperature just below scalding). The mixture should be stirred during heating. The eggnog can be flavored after it cools and then should be stored in the refrigerator until served. Eggnog purchased from the dairy is pasteurized, however, as are commercially frozen, shelled eggs.

FOOD FROM VENDING MACHINES

Is food obtained from vending machines always safe to eat?

In recent years, there has been a phenomenal growth in the food-vending industry. It is now possible to get a complete meal. At one time, the only food items associated with the vending machines were gum, candy, and similar nonperishable items. However, vending machines now distribute potentially hazardous foods—milk, eggs, meat, poultry, fish, and shellfish for example—capable of supporting rapid growth of infections or toxigenic microorganisms. Not only must these foods be prepared under sanitary conditions but refrigerated vehicles must be used in transporting them. The vending machines for these foods must be refrigerated. And, of course, the food must be replaced frequently.

Generally speaking, the food-vending industry has made great strides in insuring that its new products are fit to eat. Guidelines for the development of state and local regulations were prepared through the cooperative efforts of the National Automatic Merchandising Association, the U.S. Public Health Service, and state and local health agencies.

SAFETY OF SHELLFISH

Are shellfish always safe to eat? Haven't there been outbreaks of disease as a result of persons eating contaminated shellfish?

There are many safeguards to insure that shellfish are free from contamination. In 1924, there was an epidemic of typhoid fever in which 150 persons died. This was later traced to the consumption of contaminated oysters and became known as the "oyster scare." As a result, we have today what is known as the National Shellfish Sanitation Program, a three-way cooperative of the federal and state governments and of industry. Occasionally, breakdowns in surveillance occur but they are of minor consequence.

The federal government, through the Food and Drug Administration, has established a Shellfish Sanitation Branch. FDA helps in coordinating and supporting state programs and issues a biweekly list of state-certified interstate shellfish shippers for use by food control officials throughout the country.

States have prime responsibility for control of the shellfish industry in their areas. All of the coastal states which produce shellfish follow operating procedures set forth by the National Shellfish Sanitation Program. They have adopted uniform regulations which are usually administered by health and conservation officials. Surveillance extends from shellfish-growing areas to regulation of the processing and distribution aspects of this commodity. States issue operating certificates to plants which meet the standards of the sanitation program. Shellfish which are shipped in interstate commerce from certified plants have an identifying number and are guaranteed to have been grown and packaged under strict sanitary conditions.

The problem of regulation remains an important one with the increasing pollution of our waterways. The trend has been to close more shellfish-growing areas because they cannot meet the strict sanitary requirements for water. Members of the National Shellfish Sanitation Program are working with conservation groups, water-protection agencies, and fishery groups to protect present shellfish-growing areas. However, there is an increasing need for more extensive pollution control programs to insure that our supply of shellfish will continue to remain safe for consumption.

TRICHINOSIS FROM PORK

Can pork be cooked to kill trichinosis organisms and still retain its palatability?

The pork industry may feel undue concern is expressed over the threat of trichinosis since it is easily prevented in humans. However, physicians will continue to worry about it until such time as the threat is removed entirely.

Trichinosis in humans results from eating undercooked pork containing *Trichinella spiralis,* a roundworm animal parasite which encysts itself in human muscles. Though a large proportion of cases are mild and escape diagnosis throughout an individual's life, some are severe enough to cause death. Fortunately, because of the temperatures commonly applied in roasting and pan-frying pork in the home, there is no danger of trichinosis.

Pork is not considered to be palatable until its internal temperature has reached 155°F. to 185°F., well above the critical temperature required to kill the trichinosis organism without causing an excessive dryness in the cooked pork. An internal temperature of at least 170°F. is recommended by the USDA. When a meat thermometer is used, it should reach the center of the cut and not rest against a bone. If a thermometer is not available, cooking recommendations should be observed carefully. For large baking cuts, such as a ham or pork loin roast, the required oven temperature is usually 325°F. to 350°F. for a specified period of time, depending on meat thickness. It is generally recommended that the thinner cuts of pork, such as pork chops ($^3/_8$ to $^1/_2$ inch thick), be braised after browning on each side. Braising a chop of this size for 40 minutes over a very low heat will definitely kill any trichinosis organisms which may be present. This would correspond to a setting of about 175°F. or slightly above on the temperature control dial of an electric frying pan. When cooking pork out-of-doors or on a rotisserie of any kind, do not forget to use a meat thermometer, as judging meat doneness by the way a cut looks or smells is inaccurate.

Freezing of pork cuts in a home freezer or in the freezing section of a refrigerator is also a good way to kill trichinosis organisms. The freezing time required depends upon the temperature of your freezer. A home freezing unit should be 0°F. or colder. The following table will give you an indication of the time needed to kill all trichinosis organisms in a freezer:

Temperature of freezer	pieces or cubes of up to 6″·	Time required for freezing pork pieces with a diameter of between 6″·and 27″·
5°F.	20 days	30 days
−10°F.	10 days	20 days
−20°F.	6 days	12 days

By using either adequate cooking or cold storage in the freezer, one can enjoy preparing and eating the many cuts of pork available today without fear of dryness or of acquiring trichinosis.

OUTDOOR BARBECUING

Is the smoke emitted from charcoal in an outdoor barbecue grill harmful? If this is true, how can one prevent it?

It is unlikely that anyone would inhale enough smoke from a barbecue fire to cause any harm. Charcoal, except during the initial ignition period, emits very little smoke. Presumably the reference to "smoke" concerns that arising when drippings of meat fat hit the live coals; the smoke is caused by fuming or incompletely combusted fat. This process is called the thermal decomposition of fats, or in other words, a breaking down of fat at temperatures under those required for its ignition. The same thing happens when fat used for frying begins to smoke when overheated.

It has been shown that fat which is partially decomposed by heat produces substances suspected of being hazardous, but no incidences of harm traceable to food have been reported in man. Research with animals likewise has failed to demonstrate any hazard. Even so, it is well to avoid the possibility of fat combustion as much as possible by careful preparation of the barbecue fire bed. The National Live Stock and Meat Board recommends that meat be cooked by the heat from the coals, not by fire. Any fire should be quickly extinguished by water. Coals should also be spaced so that no two touch and adequate room should be provided so that fat drippings will not come into contact with coals. Ideally, a pan should be used to catch fat drippings before they hit the hot coals; an adequate "drip" pan can be made from aluminum foil.

FOOD POISONING

So many people seem to have intestinal upsets lately. Is food poisoning on the increase?

Intestinal upsets have many causes, ranging from viral flu-like infections and microbial food poisoning to simple food allergy. The most common symptoms of food poisonings are probably familiar to us all: nausea, vomiting, abdominal cramps and pain, diarrhea, and fever.

Dysentery encountered in many parts of the world is less frequently transmitted by food and water in the United States and is not a major problem. Botulism, caused by the most toxic of the microbial contaminants, is now rare. The most commonly reported causes of food poisoning are Salmonella, Staphylococci, and *Clostridium perfringens*. Salmonellosis, a disease characterized by nausea, vomiting, cramps, diarrhea, fever, headache, and prostration, is apparently increasing in prevalence. The U.S. Public Health Service has initiated a massive campaign to control salmonella and is optimistic that its incidence can be greatly reduced in the near future. Salmonella occur rather commonly but are killed at pasteurization temperatures. Poultry, eggs, and certain other animal products are common carriers of the organism. Heat treatment of animal feeds is one method of controlling microbial infection, but without proper sanitation in the feed plant, on the farm, and in food processing plants, reinfection of the foods may occur. The ultimate control of salmonella requires adherence to careful sanitation principles throughout the entire food chain from farm to table and back to the refrigerator.

It has been estimated that about one-half of the human population carries staphylococci organisms; therefore, the chance for food contamination is very high. The organism, but not the toxin it produces, is easily destroyed by heat. The control of staphylococcal food poisoning requires that humans carrying the infection be prevented from handling food during its preparation and that the food itself be properly handled, prepared, and stored to prevent growth of the organism. Staphylococci grow with wild abandon—in soft, creamy foods such as cream-filled pastries and many chicken and egg dishes—when the food is infected and permitted to stand at room temperature.

Another very common organism causing food poisoning is *Clostridium perfringens.* These organisms are more heat resistant than staphylococci; therefore, control is more difficult. Improperly handled cooked meats and meat dishes are the most frequent cause of Clostridum infections.

The true incidence of microbial food poisoning is not known, as there is a wide gap between suspected and reported incidence. Salmonellosis may produce only a mild nausea or may be severe, even life threatening for the elderly, infants, or persons in poor health. Staphylococcal food poisoning is characterized by such symptoms as nausea, cramps, vomiting, diarrhea, and prostration. *Clostridium perfingens* causes abdominal colic and diarrhea. Since the patient usually recovers quickly and since people learn to tolerate minor episodes of discomfort, thorough surveillance by public health authorities is difficult. Frequently, the contaminated food has already been discarded. Unless the physician is consulted and he, in turn, reports to public health authorities, these incidences will go unreported.

Few foods are sterile. Sterility is not necessary when proper methods are employed in food preparation, preservation, and storage both commerically and in the home. The homemaker can take certain steps to reduce the possibilities of food poisoning—the most important being the elimination of bacterial growth in the food bought and prepared. Reducing the time that any food remains at room temperature is the simplest way. When frozen or "cold" food is purchased, the homemaker should not cart it around for hours while finishing downtown shopping. Organisms originally present in insignificant numbers can reproduce rapidly in food left in a warm automobile and in a few hours can reach critical levels. Frozen foods should never be permitted to thaw until just before they are to be used, if thawing is required. Most frozen foods are designed to go directly from freezer to the oven. Return unused foods to the refrigerator or freezer immediately after use, packing them in sufficiently small containers to assure rapid cooling. Custards, cream-filled pastries, meat dishes, poultry, and milk are examples of foods which should not remain very long at room temperature. It is not necessary to wait until food has cooled before storing it in the refrigerator. Prolonged cooling of a quantity of infected food can create ideal conditions for growth of any organisms present. Prompt cooling to refrigerator temperatures will do much to eliminate any hazards. Remember also that simple reheating of foods will not always make them safe since a number of organisms produce toxins not destroyed by heat.

All kitchen utensils should be kept clean; however, it is especially important to wash with hot, soapy water those utensils, cutting boards, or counter tops that have been in contact with raw meats, poultry, and eggs.

The incidence of foodborne microbial disease is said to be like an iceberg as the vast majority of cases are submerged and never reported. When all participants in the food chain become aware of the steps necessary to reduce hazards of microbial food poisoning, it will no longer constitute a public health hazard.

THE THREAT OF BOTULISM

Is it true that eight ounces of botulism toxin could eliminate the entire world population?

That's approximately correct. There is little doubt that the toxin produced by *Clostridium botulinum* is the most lethal of foodborne poisons. Fortunately, outbreaks of botulism are rare in this country. When botulism occurs, it can nearly always be traced to underprocessed, home-canned foods. In the past 45 years there have been only three outbreaks of botulism from commercially canned foods. One death in 1941 was caused by canned mushrooms; improperly sealed cans of tuna caused two deaths in 1963; and in 1971 one death was caused by canned vichyssoise. Considering that about 25 billion cans of food are produced each year, the risk of botulism from commercially canned foods is extremely small. Each year, however, there are two to five deaths from botulism contracted from home-canned foods. Since 1960, nine deaths have resulted from botulism in commercially smoked fish. Seven of these deaths occurred in 1963. After this tragedy, the FDA appointed an expert committee to study the problem. Processors and handlers of smoked fish hastened to follow FDA recommendations in resolving the problem.

Clostridium botulinum is an anaerobic bacterium, one that grows only in the absence of air. This is why improperly home-canned food from which air is excluded can be ideal for the growth of this dangerous organism. The bacterium is killed and its toxin destroyed when held at 212°F.; if the spores survive, they grow to produce the bacterium and its deadly toxin.

The botulism bacteria will not grow in an acid medium; therefore, acid fruits and tomatoes when precooked can be safely processed in waterbath canners. However, not all fruits are sufficiently acid to assure complete growth inhibition of botulism. As the acidity of fruits can vary, the homemaker should not depend upon mild acidity alone to insure against bacterial growth; heat treatment is also required. Although pressure-cooker canning is preferred over both the cold- and hot-pack methods, satisfactory results can be obtained with the hot-pack method. Care must be taken, however, to follow directions implicitly. Only recommended fruits should be canned by the hot-pack method; the fruit is precooked and placed in the jar while still hot and the hot jar is immediately immersed in a boiling water bath.

Low-acid foods—meats, vegetables, and mildly acid fruits —must be exposed to temperatures higher than possible in boiling water, as the temperature of 249°F. for 10 to 15 minutes is required to destroy the botulinum spore. A pressure canner must be used and directions carefully followed as temperatures to destroy the spore cannot be achieved in the cold-pack and open-kettle methods. As the *Clostridium botulinum* bacterium will not grow at low temperatures, frozen storage is also a safe preservation procedure so long as packaged foods are not allowed to thaw and remain at room temperature for long periods. The U.S. Department of Agriculture provides booklets on safe handling and preservation of foods.

Preserved food that is at all suspect must not be sampled until properly cooked to destroy the bacterium and its toxin. Cook such food a few minutes at 212°F. Foods contaminated by *Clostridium botulinum* do have off-odors, but these are difficult to detect and vary somewhat with the characteristics of each food. Unfortunately, there is no easily recognized, characteristic putrefactive odor of spoiled food nor do cans or jars always bulge, a conventional signal of spoilage. Avoid tasting suspect food "to be sure" before serving since many botulism victims do not live to describe the "suspicious odors" associated with botulism contamination. In one instance, a woman tasted a few beans from a suspect jar of her home-canned product and, satisfied that they were all right, cooked and served them to her family. She died, having tasted the beans before the botulism toxin was destroyed by cooking; her family, however, experienced no difficulty.

Six types of *Clostridium botulinum* exist in nature and many of these types are widespread. Each bacterium produces a specific toxin, four of which are known to affect humans. The bacterium can be found in a great variety of organic substances. One prevalent strain, type E, is found primarily in water (and thus in fish) and soil. Food grown in or near such soil or water can easily be contaminated. The bacterium does not invade growing fruits and vegetables but contaminates the surface of the products. When these foods are improperly preserved and inadequately cooked before consumption, conditions may become advantageous for the growth of the organism and the production of its toxin.

Botulism poisoning does not occur from the ingestion of spores or the parent bacterium, as the toxin itself must be swallowed. Furthermore, neither the spores nor the vegetative form of the bacterium produces the toxin after ingestion. The toxin is absorbed from the intestinal tract into the blood stream and then begins to affect the nervous system. The time required for the onset of symptoms will depend upon the amount of toxin ingested; it varies from a few hours to several days. Usually the first symptoms are fatigue and muscular weakness followed by double vision, drooping eyelids, dilated pupils, dryness of mouth, swelling of the tongue, and difficulty in swallowing and speaking. In fatal cases, respiratory failure occurs. Antitoxins have been developed, but they are effective only when small amounts of the toxin have been ingested and when treatment is initiated promptly. Probably because of the wide availability of the antitoxin, the death rate from botulism has now been reduced to about 25 percent of reported cases.

The best procedure with suspect food is: when in doubt, throw it out!

-9-
food preparation and storage

———

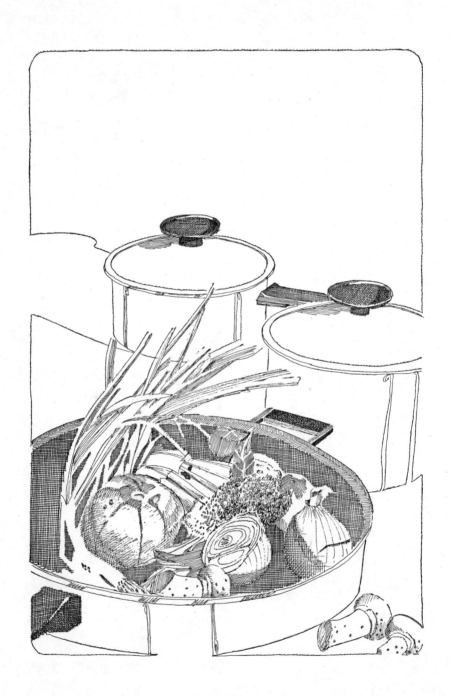

Consumers share responsibility for food quality once the food has been purchased. The processors and vendors have done what they can to assure wholesome and nutritious products with maximum shelf life. Once the food is in the consumer's possession, he must protect his purchases and prepare them for maximum personal and family satisfaction.

Departing from the cookbook approach, we have concentrated on preparation and storage to help preserve the nutrients and goodness of food and to assist in the never-ending battle against spoilage and food poisonings.

Conservation of food, the protection of our most precious commodity, is a responsibility that must not be taken lightly. Who knows how much longer we can continue our wasteful ways? Americans throw away more food than anyone else in the world. It has been stated that millions could be fed, perhaps better than at present, by the food we discard. The wasting of food is so consistent and predictable that scientists can establish studies of dietary habits by analyzing people's garbage! This is an interesting switch, for archeologists characterize ancient civilizations with much the same techniques.

The high cost of food, probable shortages, publicity about starvation, and growing export demands for the products of our farms should make the point very clear. We must stop carelessly wasting food.

The conservation of food requires proper use of storage facilities—pantry, refrigerator, freezer, or cool, dry holding areas. This increases in importance as more consumers search for food bargains and buy staples in quantity. Home gardening is on the increase and many families will face the new experience of storing, freezing, and canning perishables.

The conservation of food to help our food supply go further and to stretch the food dollar should not be taken for granted, nor should the conservation of the nutrients in food.

AVERAGE SERVING

What is an average serving?

An average serving can be defined in many ways. A serving of mashed potatoes is about the same size as a large scoop of ice cream, which is also a serving. A serving of meat is usually considered to be 3 ounces, a serving of juice about 3 ounces or half a cup, and a serving of blueberry pie is usually 1/6 of a 9 inch pie. A serving of vegetables is a scant cup—a scant cup is about as easy to define as a pinch of salt. According to the US Department of Agriculture, a serving of dill pickle is one pickle, 1 3/4 inches in diameter, 4 inches long, and weighing 135 grams. A serving of egg is the whole thing, and a serving of crêpes suzette is all in the art of it!

PACKAGE SIZES

The package size of conventional food items, such as breakfast cereals, changes frequently. Why is this?

The food processor must compete for shelf space in the market and for the shopper's attention; thus, package design is a constant challenge to the industry. A number of rational explanations are available for changes in package size; most are based on the economics of merchandising. Manufacturers may react to rising labor and material costs by holding prices constant and taking a reduction in profit; however, this is not a good way to please stockholders. They can also raise prices and hope the buying public will not become irritated, or they can reduce the amount of product and size of package while maintaining the price at which the product was originally sold.

If a manufacturer decides on the last method of economizing—that is, to reduce the weight or volume of his product—he also might take advantage of this opportunity to redesign the package or container for the product. Consumer demand for more functional sizes may also change the shape of containers. The change from gigantically tall to stubbier cereal boxes was a happy one. These boxes now fit in a kitchen cabinet perfectly! Another factor which influences package size is the probable length of time an item is stored at home after the package is opened. A perishable or semiperishable food will be packaged in sizes that can be used up rapidly. Inner bags and better package liners are helping to lengthen the shelf life of packaged foods.

Only a fraction of a second may be available to attract the customer's attention with an eye-catching package as he charges down the aisle. In fact, the processor might also find himself advertising with the front, back, or side of his package depending on the whim of the stockboy who stacks items on the shelf. Unfortunately, many product package designs and label contents are often misleading to the customer, if not confusing. The density or volume of a product per unit or weight often causes further confusion. For example: 1) a box of flakes or chips may have been filled to capacity in the plant only to shake down in handling. Most manufacturers now warn on the package that this may happen. 2) Prices of breakfast foods in packages of similar size may not be strictly comparable because of different densities. This means that products of the same weight may each occupy different amounts of space; therefore, the volume of an item is not necessarily the best way to judge a product's value. The performance or acceptance of the product by the consumer is often a more valid criterion.

AGE OF FOOD WHEN PURCHASED

How can a person tell how old non-refrigerated packaged or canned food is at the time of purchase? And how long can you safely keep these foods at home?

All packaged and canned goods are coded by number or letter, indicating either the manufacture date or expiration date. The latter is also called the "pull" date—the date the grocer must remove the item from the shelf. The codes vary, and the manager or information service at your local store will tell you how to interpret their particular code.

How long can you keep the products at home before they lose their nutritional value? This depends on the freshness of the product at the time of purchase, the type of packaging, and the temperature of the storage area.

Canned goods should be stored below 70°F. to maintain vitamin C and thiamin (B_1) content. Avoid dented or punctured cans. Swollen cans contain spoiled food, so toss them out.

If cereal products are stored in a dry, cool spot, they'll keep for six months. If stored in airtight containers, they're good for one year. Unopened packages of prepared mixes—such as cakes, puddings, biscuits, casseroles, and instant potatoes—can be kept for one year, but once opened, the contents should be used within two months.

Flour, sugar, and other staples will keep almost indefinitely if properly sealed to keep out insects, dust, and moisture. Ground herbs and spices lose their flavor after six months; whole herbs and spices after one year.

It's a good idea to mark the purchase date on all pantry items and plan to use and replace the stock within six months. If you find it necessary to keep foods for prolonged periods of time, store them in the coolest areas of the house and use the oldest items first.

CHOICE OF COOKWARE

What type of cookware is the best all-around choice?

The choice of cookware should be determined by its intended use and the amount of care the homemaker is willing to lavish on it. Attractive matched cookware to enhance the kitchen decor is an important but not overriding criterion. In some cases, it may be desirable to purchase unmatched cookware chosen solely for utility. Other factors include size, ease of handling, and the design of handles and knobs for safe and convenient use.

Generally, the heavier materials assure the best heat distribution if the stove heating surfaces are in good condition. Even heat distribution reduces the probability of bumping and spot burning during cooking.

Great strides are being made by the industry in developing non-stick surfaces. The Teflon coatings have been improved, but the problem of scratch-proneness has not been completely solved. Reasonable care in use will assure long life for the coatings. Ceramic-lined skillets and dutch ovens and metallic utensils with highly polished surfaces are easily cleaned.

Of course, when any of these modern surfaces are abused and become scratched or pitted, cleaning may be more difficult. Cast-iron cookware that is properly seasoned and maintained in good condition is easily cleaned under most conditions.

The issue of safety is occasionally raised in discussions of cookware. An unscrupulous salesman may attempt to malign aluminum, iron, or steel on the basis that hazardous amounts of minerals are dissolved during cooking or that the metals cause destruction of essential nutrients. Little data substantiate such claims. It is true that copper in pots, which may be in contact with the material being cooked, will cause oxidation, for example, of vitamin C. The only examples we know about may be found in the Near East and Asia where improperly tin-lined copper or bronze kettles are sometimes used. The solution of minerals from modern utensils must be small indeed and in certain respects may be more of a blessing than a hazard. Ultra-clean foods may be somewhat limited in essential trace minerals. When iron can be picked up from the cooking utensil, this is a boon.

Another consideration in choosing cookware is the style of meal service frequently used. Attractive oven-to-table cookware can be put to great use if one enjoys casual entertaining.

IRON POTS

A dutch oven made of iron is such a nuisance to clean. Is there a kind which is more easily cleaned?

An iron dutch oven may be a blessing in disguise—hold on to it. Iron cookware, once a tradition, is rapidly disappearing from the American scene. Disappearing along with it is a rich source of dietary iron. A large amount of very desirable iron is dissolved when acid foods are cooked in iron ware. One of the penalties of well-wrapped, wonderfully clean food cooked in plastic bags or in nonmetallic pots is that there is no chance for iron to dissolve in the foods. The available iron in food can increase by as much as 100 to 400 percent when iron cookware is used! This is of considerable significance to children and women because of their high require-ments for iron. So save that iron dutch oven; cleaning it will be good exercise.

TEFLON

Are teflon-coated skillets safe?

Teflon skillets are perfectly safe to use. Teflon is a coating material applied on the surface of the skillet to prevent food from sticking. When the product was introduced, concern was expressed that the coating material would decompose, releasing toxic materials.

The Food and Drug Administration reported that careful testing has been done with Teflon utensils; no danger can come from normal kitchen use or from overheating the utensils.

PRESSURE COOKING

Are more nutrients destroyed when using pressure cookers than when using the old, low-heat way of cooking? Do canning factories cook their products at excessively high temperatures?

Foods should be cooked in a tightly covered pan with a minimum amount of water and for just the length of time it takes to make them palatable. This will result in maximum retention of the nutrients naturally present in the food. While pressure cooking is done at a higher temperature than when using a saucepan, the cooking time is much shorter; the nutrient retention will usually be about the same in both ways of cooking. Many homemakers tend to overcook food and to use too much water, resulting in nutritionally inferior products. The methods used by the modern food-processing plants (canning, freezing, dehydrating), however, are those which retain the maximum nutritional value of the food; in many cases, the commercially produced foods will be superior to similar food prepared at home.

DEEP-FAT FRYING, PAN-FRYING, PAN-BROILING

What are the differences among deep-fat frying, pan-frying, and pan-broiling?

The term deep-fat frying designates the cooking of food in a deep, covering layer of fat. Pan-frying refers to the cooking of food in a small amount of fat, while pan-broiling indicates the cooking of food uncovered in a frying pan with the fat being poured off as it accumulates.

CHINESE COOKING

I am told that the Chinese food I have always enjoyed is Cantonese. Many people seem to like a different kind called Mandarin. Can you explain the difference?

There are actually four kinds of Chinese foods that originated from the four major regions of China. Mandarin food is derived from the northern region of China (Peking) and is well known for its combination of strong flavors (e.g., sweet and sour dishes and Peking duck) as well as light, subtle specialties such as chicken velvet. Garlic, bean sauces, scallions, and heavy soy sauce are commonly used in northern cooking. Northern cooks differ from those in other regions in that they use wheat flour for basic foods like steamed dumplings, breads, and noodles.

People of the coastal regions, like people in the remaining parts of China, rely on rice as the main staple. Their foods are generally cooked longer than are Mandarin foods, and often they are stewed with gravy and more soy sauce; salt and sugar are also used. Spring rolls and lion's head are examples of coastal foods. Spring rolls are similar to egg rolls but have a crisp, thin covering and more meat and spices. Lion's head is a large, subtly spiced pork meatball of a soft, light texture. The name is derived from the appearance of a lion's head which results when the meatball is served on a platter, surrounded by Chinese cabbage. As expected, much seafood is also used in coastal cooking.

Western inland regions (Yunnan and Szechwan) are unmistakably characterized by savory foods containing a great deal of spice—ginger, garlic, and hot peppers; examples are hot and sour soup and fish or pork in hot bean sauces. However, not all the food is spicy; an excellent dish of milder flavor is Yunnan ham, originating in the province of Yunnan and made of high-quality pork.

Westerners have been more exposed to Cantonese food from the southern region (Canton) because the Cantonese were the first to popularize Chinese cooking in the western hemisphere. They introduced foods such as egg rolls, roast pork, and egg foo young. This type of Chinese food is characteristically light, fresh, and less seasoned than that of the other regions. Stir-frying and stewing are the cooking methods used to retain the natural flavors. Specialties are shark's fin soup and roast suckling pig.

Historically, the harsh conditions, with scarcity of food and fuel, led the Chinese to place emphasis on the preparation and variety of their cuisine.

BEATING EGG WHITES

Occasionally beaten egg whites do not seem to foam or rise as much as at other times. What might be the reason?

Substances added to the egg whites before they are beaten can have a pronounced effect on the volume and stability of egg white foams. A small amount of egg yolk is often the villain, as the fat content of the yolk can prevent desirable egg white foam formation. When breaking the egg to separate the white from the yolk, be careful not to get even a little bit of yolk in the egg white portion which is to be beaten. Also, be sure that no egg yolk remains on the beater if it is first used to beat an egg yolk mixture. In much the same way, the fat content of cream and milk added in significant quantities can be detrimental to egg white foam formation.

Adding sugar to egg whites increases stability of the foam. Adding sugar after a considerable volume of egg white foam has been achieved is recommended, as desired volume may be impossible to achieve if sugar is added before beating.

Other factors, such as type of beater used, type of container in which eggs are beaten, and temperature of egg whites when beaten also affect the final foam formation. Thick blades or wires are said not to divide egg whites as easily as do fine wires in beaters. Best for beating egg whites are bowls with small rounded bottoms and sloped sides in which the beater can easily manipulate the egg mass. Eggs at refrigerator temperatures beat less easily and quickly and to a lesser volume than do eggs at room temperature.

WHIPPING EVAPORATED MILK

What is the best method for whipping evaporated milk? Several recipes call for an ingredient such as lemon juice or vinegar in the process of whipping. Is there a reason for this?

Evaporated milk can be whipped into a very nice foam if the correct procedure is followed carefully. Chill the milk in the freezer to approximately 32°F. The milk should be chilled in the bowl in which it is to be whipped. Leave the milk in the freezer until fine crystals form in the milk around the edge of the bowl. The beaters to be used for whipping also should be chilled. When the milk is whipped, add two tablespoons of lemon juice or vinegar for each cup of milk. The acid increases the stability of the whipped product.

GOOD COFFEE

Is there a sure way of making a good cup of coffee every time?

A good cup of coffee means many things to many people; it is strictly a matter of personal preference. The coffee industry recommends that two level tablespoons of coffee be used for each cup. In the past, the recommended amount was usually stated in terms of one rounded or heaping tablespoon per cup of coffee. This, however, left much to the imagination as to what constituted a heaping tablespoon and allowed a rather wide degree of variation.

Why not start out by using the recommended amounts in brewing coffee and continue the practice if there are no complaints. If family or friends think it is too strong or too weak, cut down or add until you make the perfect cup of coffee.

Another method that will make a really delicious cup of coffee is: use one tablespoon of coffee per cup and add $1/4$ teaspoon cocoa and two or three dashes of salt to the water per eight cups.

CAFFEINE IN COFFEE

Does the method of preparation affect the caffeine content of coffee?

Yes. Drip and vacuum coffee contain the least amount of caffeine, percolated coffee contains slightly more caffeine than does drip coffee, and "boiled" coffee contains more caffeine than either drip or percolated. The caffeine contained in a cup of instant coffee is high, but the amount of coffee used will determine the caffeine content of the beverage. Generally, the average cup of coffee contains about 100 to 150 mg of caffeine; but this, again, will depend upon the strength of the brew.

SCALDING MILK

Some recipes call for scalded milk. How can milk be scalded without scorching it?

Milk scorches easily when heated directly over a fire. This scorching can be attributed, in part, to a film of coagulated milk protein—albumin—which sticks to the bottom and sides of the pan. The sticking can be somewhat alleviated by rinsing the pan well with ice-cold water just before pouring the milk into it. Stirring milk as it heats also helps prevent scorching but does not prevent it completely if the pan is being directly heated on the flame or coils. Caramelization of lactose (milk sugar) sometimes occurs; a brown-

215

ish product may also be formed. To prevent these undesirable results, a double boiler is frequently recommended. Of course, nothing substitutes for careful watching when heating a sensitive food over a flame or electric coils.

MAKING SOUR MILK

If a recipe calls for buttermilk, can homogenized milk be used as a substitute if it is mixed with something like lemon juice?

Yes, if one cup of buttermilk or sour milk is required, one tablespoon of vinegar or lemon juice plus enough sweet milk to make one cup can be used as a substitute. Let this mixture stand for about five minutes before using. The combination of 1 $3/4$ teaspoons of cream of tartar and one cup of sweet milk will also be equivalent to the cup of buttermilk or sour milk needed in a recipe.

MILK THAT CURDLES

Why does milk curdle? Does the curdling of milk affect its nutritive value?

Curdling results when casein, the principal milk protein, precipitates or coagulates. This may be caused by an increased acidity level in the milk due to natural souring or to the direct addition of acid. The casein of milk is usually not coagulated by boiling unless the milk is slightly acidic or if high temperatures, such as those in a pressure cooker, are used. A high salt content or tannins in food may also cause milk protein to coagulate.

Curdling does not usually decrease the nutritive value of milk. In fact, milk naturally curdles when it enters the stomach. Boiling the milk, however, does change the flavor and destroy some of the vitamin C and thiamin. Even in this instance, the nutritive value of the casein is seldom decreased.

WARMING BABY BOTTLES

Is it no longer necessary to warm a bottle of milk or milk formula before giving it to the baby?

Dr. Emmett Holt of New York has published research showing that infants responded normally when fed a cold bottle of milk or a bottle of milk from which only the chill had been removed. No harmful effects were noted, and the infants fed the cold or cool milk had growth rates similar to those of infants given warmed formulas. It might be well to check with the pediatrician before changing an infant's feeding, however, and certainly check it with the infant to see how he responds. The usual practice is to provide the formula at a temperature between room temperature and body temperature.

TO KEEP EGGS FROM CRACKING WHEN BOILED

When eggs are placed in water directly from the refrigerator, many of them crack. How can this be avoided?

Eggs should be at room temperature before they are slipped carefully into boiling water. Reduce heat immediately so that the water simmers. Boiling temperatures toughen egg white. If the eggs are cold, place them in cool water and heat to the boiling point. Reduce the heat to simmer and a soft-cooked egg will be ready within two to five minutes. A bit of experimenting should help to determine the time required to produce the desired firmness of white and yolk.

A Milwaukee physician suggests a simple trick: Puncture the round end of the shell with a pin (a safety pin is easiest to handle). The expanding gases escape, actually bubbling up through the water the moment the egg is put into it; nothing else happens. He has been "pinning" two of them at six every morning (at seven on Sundays) for lo! these many years, with nary a cracked shell to spoil the perfect record.

PREVENT WAFFLES FROM STICKING

How can waffles be prevented from sticking to the grill?

Waffle iron manufacturers recommend that the grill be well greased before making the first waffle. Let the first waffle brown well before removing; this seasons the grill. Discard this waffle and continue baking waffles without greasing. When, for any reason, the grill is washed, repeat the seasoning process. If waffles still stick, ask mother about inheriting her waffle iron.

VEGETABLE OIL FOR COOKING

Does it make any difference what vegetable oil is used in cooking?

The cooking characteristics of commercially available oils are essentially the same. Price and flavor differences, however, may influence personal preferences. Most salad and cooking oils are derived from soybeans, cottonseed, corn, and peanuts. Some of the oils are treated to delay their decomposition which occurs after prolonged use in deep-fat frying. Modern oils do not decompose; therefore, they do not smoke at temperatures conventionally used in frying.

The qualities of cooking oils emphasized in advertisements often reflect differences in their saturated and polyunsaturated fatty acid content. Cottonseed oil and peanut oil have from 21 percent to 26 percent saturated fatty acids, while corn and soybean oils contain about 15 percent. Corn, cottonseed, and soybean oils have about the same amount of polyunsaturated fatty acids, that is, from 50 percent to 58 percent, and peanut oil has about 28 percent. A medically prescribed diet in which the kinds and amounts of fats are controlled would most likely indicate which salad and cooking oils are to be used.

SAFFLOWER OIL

What is safflower oil? Can it be used in cooking?

Safflower oil is pressed from the seeds of a plant that is grown on the West Coast and some Pacific Islands. It is a most unusual oil because of its extremely high content of linoleic acid (polyunsaturated). It contains nearly half again as much linoleic acid as corn, cottonseed, and soybean oils and almost twice that of peanut oil. Safflower oil contains 75 percent linoleic acid; 16 percent oleic acid (mono-unsaturated) and 8 percent saturated fatty acids. Refined safflower oil is bland in flavor and almost colorless. It may be used as a salad or cooking oil. Total production is limited and, therefore, the oil is more expensive than other vegetable oils.

FRIED FOODS

Restaurants and snack bars seem to specialize in fried foods—french-fried potatoes, potato and corn chips, fried hamburgers, chicken, fillets, eggs, bacon—everything is fried. Does this constant use of fats for cooking not boost our caloric intake needlessly? Are fried foods also hard to digest?

Slow down—one cannot legislate against human preference. Restaurant people will cook what their patrons prefer. Do not blame the cook; blame the customer. Although most people feel that fried foods are more difficult to digest, what they mean is that it takes longer to digest fried food. Digestion is still essentially complete.

Frying is only a way to cook at high temperature in a medium that will permit extremely rapid heat penetration of the food. Thus, thin potatoes can be deep-fried in just a few minutes if the temperature of the fat is about 390°F. Proper frying, either deep-fat or otherwise, requires careful temperature control and preliminary food preparation. In deep-frying if the temperature is too low, a crust will not form on the food and fat will be absorbed more rapidly, greatly increasing the caloric content. If the temperature is too high, the fat may smoke, giving the food an unpleasant flavor. Large food particles also require longer cooking, which means an increase in nutrient losses.

In general, frying increases the caloric content of food because of the oil or fat absorbed. Pan-frying and deep-fat frying drive moisture from the potato and permit more fat to be absorbed. French-fried potatoes can absorb enough fat to increase the caloric content by 400 percent. Three ounces of french-fried potatoes contain about 275 calories; the same amount of fried raw potatoes (shallow pan) contains 270 calories. Contrast this with the caloric content of a three-ounce serving of boiled potatoes—65 calories.

Since the emphasis today is on reduced caloric intake, many people prefer baked or broiled meats and baked or boiled potatoes. Broiling permits much of the fat to drip from the meat, leaving a leaner product. The method of frying, however, is an art, and many nutritious and delectable dishes can be prepared by pan-frying or deep-fat frying. Care should be taken, however, to avoid undue oil absorption and long cooking at low temperatures to prevent vitamin destruction.

FATS IN BAKING RECIPES

Are butter, margarine, soft margarine, and shortenings interchangeable in recipes for baked goods?

Butter and margarine are interchangeable, but are interchangeable with shortening only in recipes in which the amounts of water and fat are not critical. Amounts of water and fat are critical in certain cake and cookie recipes. Butter and margarine contain 80 percent fat and about 15 percent water; shortening is essentially pure fat. Allowances would have to be made for this difference in composition when substitutions are made in certain recipes. More butter or margarine but less liquid would be used in recipes calling for shortening. Too much water in the preparation of certain products causes the development of an undesirable texture.

Soft margarine can be used interchangeably with hard margarine in most recipes. One must, however, keep in mind the characteristics of the product used. Soft margarines contain liquid oil compounded with a semi-solid foundation. Therefore, recipes which require the shortening to remain intact may not adapt well to soft margarines. Generally speaking, soft margarines can be considered an intermediate between stick margarines and oils. Soft margarine could not be used successfully in pastries which require a hard dough such as "puffed" pastries which are alternate layers of dough and shortening, chilled between application of layers. And soft margarine would not adapt well to recipes in which the shortening has to be "cut in" as in pie shells.

MINERAL OIL IN SALAD DRESSINGS

Is it advisable to use mineral oil in salad dressings?

Do not use mineral oil except as directed by a physician. Mineral oil interferes with the absorption of the fat-soluble vitamins, especially vitamins A, D, and K, and should not be used on or in foods.

KEEPING LEFTOVERS

How long can leftover foods be kept in the refrigerator?

Simple refrigeration reduces the temperature of foods to about 42°F. At this temperature, organisms inducing spoilage are inhibited. Enzymatic action, causing excessive ripening and deterioration in fresh foods, is also stopped at this temperature.

Refrigeration preserves the quality of food and prevents spoilage, but it cannot do these things indefinitely, as food quality and nutritive value slowly deteriorate at these temperatures. Foods should be *held* in the refrigerator, not stored indefinitely. Cooked meat, if promptly refrigerated, can probably be held safely for a week; however, there will be small losses of thiamin upon reheating. There is little if any nutrient loss when meat is served cold without reheating. Cooked vegetables, on the other hand, rapidly lose ascorbic acid (vitamin C) when held. After refrigeration for 24 hours, cooked vegetables have three-fourths as much ascorbic acid as when freshly cooked; after being kept for 48 hours they have only two-thirds as much. It is best not to keep leftover vegetables for longer than a day or two.

COOLING FOOD BEFORE REFRIGERATION

Is it necessary to cool foods before placing them in the refrigerator?

Moisture or increased humidity is not a problem in modern refrigerators with today's moisture-proof containers. Modern refrigerators recover quickly when warm foods are placed inside. Thus, with few exceptions, no valid reason exists for cooling foods before refrigeration. Those foods that require slow cooling as a finishing process—for example, the finished texture of custard—are exceptions; these foods should not be cooled too rapidly.

When faced with the problem of refrigerating or freezing a large quantity of food, the best plan is to separate it into smaller units to insure rapid cooling throughout the food mass. This is particularly important with moist, creamy material such as chicken salad. If this is not done, the internal temperature of certain foods may not reach a safe temperature for many hours, and bacterial growth may be maintained for long periods of time. The nature of packaging materials also may further delay cooling. Prolonged cooling can become a very serious problem if the food has been contaminated or has previously stood for many hours at room temperature.

CARBOHYDRATE, PROTEIN, AND FAT IN FROZEN FOODS

Is there any information available on the protein, carbohydrate, and fat content in frozen foods as compared to fresh foods?

The protein content of frozen foods is not affected by the freezing process. These foods compare favorably with the fresh product. One possible exception, however, might be certain fish or shellfish. If held in the freezer for extended periods of time, the protein might be somewhat less digestible than that found in fish that is fresh or fresh-frozen.

The carbohydrates in frozen foods are nutritionally as good as those in fresh foods. The starch remains virtually unchanged, although sucrose does undergo a change during extensive freezer storage. It is broken down into two simpler sugars—dextrose and levulose. Since this is the same action that occurs during the digestive process, it is of no nutritional importance here.

Fats do not undergo any change during freezing or storage unless improper conditions exist. Any number of factors could affect the nutritional value of fat—the fat might be of poor quality to start out with; the product might be improperly packaged; the temperature used might be too high; or the food might be held in the freezer for a long period of time. If any of these factors or combination of factors are present, the fat may become rancid. When this occurs, the fat is oxidized and the vitamin A which is dissolved in the fat would also be oxidized, rendering it of no nutritional value.

FREEZING MILK

Would it be practical to buy the amount of milk needed for a month and then freeze it?

It is not known whether the freezing of milk affects its nutritive value although it might make some slight difference in its taste. If the milk is homogenized, the freezing process will probably cause the cream to separate. If milk is frozen, it should be thawed at room temperature in order to prevent unnecessary vitamin destruction.

Do not overlook the convenience and economical advantage of using powdered milks. Whole or nonfat dry milk powders are nutritious, tasty, and convenient. Using powdered milk at least in cooking could help conserve precious storage space for regular fluid milk.

REPEATED FREEZING AND THAWING

Would repeated freezing and thawing of frozen foods be expected to impair their nutritive value?

No evidence proves that the freezing process itself destroys the nutrient value of foods, nor does it bring about rejuvenation of the nutrient value of a food either. Freezing simply prevents further deterioration in food quality. Deterioration is not a serious problem when frozen food is stored for reasonable periods in the freezer at temperatures below -10°F.; most food can be successfully stored up to six months. Food slowly undergoes some quality deterioration at 0°F. and above, and it is well to check freezer temperatures occasionally. The keeping quality of frozen foods cannot, however, be judged simply by the apparent hardness of the frozen product as most foods are hard at temperatures of 20°F., temperatures too high for proper maintenance of frozen foods.

If the package of frozen food when thawed has not been damaged or its contents exposed to air, only a slight nutrient loss occurs and then primarily in the vitamin C content. If, however, frozen foods are allowed to warm to room temperatures slowly, are then refrozen, and then warmed again for table use, nutrient loss is greater.

When food packages are still hard or there is evidence of ice crystals, foods can usually be refrozen without serious damage, but refreezing should be done as quickly as possible. If foods are soft or completely thawed, they should be cooked at once to prevent bacterial growth and poisoning. If foods, either by odor or appearance, cause suspicion of their safety, dispose of them without tasting.

STORING GIBLETS

What is the best way to store giblets which come with some fresh poultry? Can they be frozen for later use in casseroles or gravies?

Giblets are the edible internal organs of poultry, such as the heart, liver, and gizzard. Usually the neck is also included in the package containing the giblets of a bird. Giblets are highly perishable and must be stored in the freezer if they are not to be used within a day or two after purchase. They should be frozen until ready for use and then cooked as soon as possible after thawing. It might be added that, for safety's sake, it always is advisable to keep any part of a frozen chicken unthawed until the day it is to be used.

Giblets and the neck may be roasted or simmered in water. If they are to be roasted, they can be salted and sealed in aluminum foil, then roasted on the rack with the fowl. For simmering, the gizzard, heart, and neck require about one and one-half hours, while the liver requires only about one-half to one hour. Giblets make excellent additions to gravies, stuffings, and casseroles.

FREEZING CURED MEATS

Is there any harm in freezing cured meats such as ham, bacon, and wieners?

The freezer storage life of cured meats varies somewhat but, as a general rule, is significantly shorter than the storage life of other meats and poultry. It would seldom be worthwhile to freeze cured meats instead of other meats that could occupy the freezer space for a longer period. However, if freezer space permits, these products can be frozen for the recommended time period with little change in quality.

Fresh pork can be kept frozen for three to six months, but cured ham and pork sausage should be used within two months after freezing. The usual storage recommendations for bacon are: refrigerator shelf—up to eight weeks; freezer—less than one month. Wieners may be freezer-stored up to three months.

The salt added to many cured meats can hasten the onset of rancidity, while added spices and thorough smoking may retard rancidity. A tendency which pork products have for becoming rancid can be aggravated by the length of storage before the products reach the home freezer. The good quality of bacon and table-ready (luncheon) meats is more easily assured now, partly because of new packaging methods and materials developed in recent years.

The main objective in packaging cured, smoked, or table-ready meats is to exclude both oxygen and light, either of which can cause color deterioration. Opaque labels are often used to prevent light infiltration. Lack of oxygen, of course, retards rancidity (fat oxidation). Skintight vacuum seals for bacon are now fairly commonplace. In packaging sliced meats, oxygen is excluded and then sometimes nitrogen is added to keep the slices loose. Occasionally, an antioxidant is incorporated into the packaging material.

"FREEZER BURN"

What causes meat to change color when frozen?

The change in color in meat which has been frozen is most likely due to a condition commonly referred to as "freezer burn." "Freezer burn" or loss of moisture (dehydration) occurs when meat or fowl is not properly packaged or when the package becomes torn so that moisture is lost even when the meat is frozen. When dehydrated in this manner, beef may acquire the appearance of light brown paper, while the skin of poultry and the surface of meat take on a bleached and dry appearance. Meat to be frozen should be removed from the original package and wrapped in a moisture-proof package before being placed in the freezer. When frozen meat becomes dehydrated, it is safe to eat although the palatability decreases.

FREEZE-DRYING

What is freeze-drying as used in the preservation of foods?

Conventional dehydration is done either at high temperatures or with prolonged drying at lower temperatures; these methods can affect the characteristics of the food as well as its nutritive value. Freeze-drying is a process in which moisture is removed from the food while it is in a frozen state. The advantage of freeze-drying is that the water is removed in a manner that does the least physical damage to the food itself. Freeze-dried foods reconstitute easily when water is added. The process still is rather expensive and is used for processing only certain kinds of foods. The cost of the process, however, is absorbed by the decrease in shipping cost or is passed on to the consumer.

Some of the shrimp used in restaurants has been freeze-dried. Shrimp is available and popular all over the country today because of the savings afforded by not having to ship water and because the reconstituted product is little different from fresh shrimp. Freeze-dried shrimp, however, are rather fragile and may break in shipment. Most of the cocktail shrimp is now shipped fresh or frozen. Some of the ingredients of dried soup mixes also are freeze-dried, while the remaining are dried by conventional methods.

FOOD MADE IN QUANTITY

Are there any helpful hints in serving food to large numbers of people?

The most important of the many factors to consider when serving large groups is the safety of the foods prepared. Food poisoning at school and church picnics has resulted from careless handling of food or from the use of foods which spoil easily at room temperature when refrigerator space is limited. Also the equipment available for preparing, refrigerating, and serving large quantities of food to groups should be carefully evaluated. Proper refrigeration of foods which have to be prepared ahead of time is of vital importance in preventing spoilage. Employment of wise storage procedures before serving food potentially susceptible to bacterial growth is imperative. Use of proper storage temperatures, storage of foods in places free from insects that might be bacterial carriers, and storage away from other contaminating ingredients or containers are necessary.

If the meal is to be a hot one, plan to serve foods that use both the oven and top burners so that one food item will not have to be taken from the oven to make room for another; this will protect against bacterial growth and also prevent cooling of the product before serving.

The most common type of food poisoning that occurs when preparing large quantities of food results from the presence of a preformed toxin of staphylococci bacteria in the food. As these bacteria are widely present in the environment, it is best to exclude from the menu foods in which the staphylococci can grow with ease—foods with eggs and cream fillings, puddings, custards, white sauces, and hollandaise sauce. Staphylococci will grow in stuffed fowl, fish, and meat and meat products if they are not kept at correct refrigerator temperatures. In addition, almost any warm food or food permitted to stand for very long periods, particularly in the warm summer weather, provides an ideal medium for rapidly growing staphylococci. These deceptive organisms do their damage without leaving signs of spoilage, so choose foods for quantity food service wisely.

Unless the food service will be of the potluck type, with each person bringing a contribution, reliable recipes for quantity cookery also should be collected. Most of the recipes in standard cookbooks serve from four to eight people and doubling these recipes usually can be done satisfactorily, but be very careful before attempting to triple or multiply them further. To preserve the original quality of the product, it is usually best to make several moderate-size batches of one recipe when using a standard cookbook, rather than simply multiplying the recipe. When serving large crowds, a special cookbook for quantity service is a wise investment. Finally, one of the most difficult parts of preparing meals for large groups is the finishing touch that makes the food look especially tempting and personalized. Plan well ahead to use garnishes such as parsley, maraschino cherries, watercress, and pimentos to brighten up foods for the serving table. If a holiday is near, plan to make a decorative centerpiece or have napkins and table cloths which carry out the holiday or party theme.

Preliminary instructions for kitchen helpers will be helpful and should include a short discussion of the importance of personal cleanliness and sanitation in food handling. Instruction in the use of cooking utensils and equipment for quantity cooking may be helpful, too.

A first-aid kit should be available for anyone who suffers a burn or cut. If electrical equipment such as large coffeemakers and electric skillets will be used, it might be wise to find out from the building custodian just what can be used and where so that overloading of electric circuits can be prevented.

PICNIC FOODS

It has always been a problem to prepare picnic food that will keep all day. Can you provide some guidelines?

Foods which spoil quickly must be avoided on picnics. Generally, these contain cream sauce or cream fillings.

The temptation to make egg salad or chicken salad must be tempered by good judgment if the food is to stand for any length of time without refrigeration. Mayonnaise, being an acid food, is safe by itself. When mixing it with foods the acidity is neutralized and it could become a good medium for bacterial growth. If potato salad is a must, mix all of the ingredients except the mayonnaise. Take a small, unopened jar of mayonnaise and add to the salad just before serving.

Portable ice chests can be very useful and worth the investment if picnicking is a frequent pastime. Start with a cold box and place only well-chilled food in it. Warm food should not be placed in the chest since its effectiveness will be reduced proportionately.

Vacuum jugs and well-made ice buckets will keep foods hot or cold for relatively long periods of time. Casseroles wrapped in thick layers of newspaper or kept in insulated bags will stay hot for several hours. Meats for barbecues can be packed while still frozen.

Foods which spoil easily should not be held over from lunch to dinner on an all-day outing unless given special handling. Food which was safe at lunch may become spoiled during the warm afternoon. It is best not to use leftovers that can spoil as portable cold chests are not able to rapidly cool food that has warmed up on the picnic table.

LOSS OF VITAMIN C

Is very much vitamin C lost when orange juice is held in the refrigerator? Is the same true of the vitamin C in powdered and ready-to-use fruit drinks?

The instability of vitamin C has been overemphasized. The vitamin is remarkably stable in orange juice when it is properly stored in closed glass, plastic, or wax containers in the refrigerator.

A recent study compared the stability of vitamin C in fresh, frozen, and canned orange juice preparations. The juices were prepared for consumption and stored at room temperatures and in the refrigerator in closed glass containers. Even after eight days, the vitamin C content was essentially unchanged regardless of the storage temperature. Samples of orange juice stored in closed or opened, wax or glass containers retained more than 95 percent of the vitamin C even after one week of storage in the refrigerator.

Vitamin C is also quite stable in powdered fruit drinks after mixing and refrigerating as loss of vitamin C can be minimized by storage at temperatures lower than 50°F. Ready-to-use fruit drinks, however, tend to slowly lose vitamin C which was added during manufacturing. Extended storage of fruit drinks in warehouses or on the grocery shelf also may result in less vitamin C than the label claims. The Canadian Food and Drug Laboratories reported that the content of vitamin C in different fruit drinks gradually declined during simulated household storage. The fruit drink cans were opened and the contents were stored in closed glass or plastic containers in a refrigerator for up to one week. After three days of such storage, many of the drinks were found to contain less vitamin C than the label statement claimed. The loss of vitamin C in fruit drinks is greater than the loss in fruit juices under normal conditions of use. This would suggest that the natural juices contain agents which protect vitamin C from oxidative destruction.

BOILING

Doesn't boiling destroy a lot of nutrients in meats?

Some water-soluble nutrients of meat will be extracted during boiling; the same can be said for boiled vegetables. To get the full nutritional value from boiled foods, the cooking liquid should also be used, for example, in soups or gravies.

ROASTING

Is much thiamin lost when meat is roasted?

Under standard methods of roasting from 75 to 100 percent of the thiamin present in fresh meat is retained. According to recent research the maximum retention occurs when meat is cooked for the shortest time at the lowest possible temperature.

WARM MILK

Is the nutritional value of milk decreased by heating it to lukewarm before drinking?

As long as the milk is not scalded during the warming process, *no* loss of nutritive value will occur. Properly scalded milk, that is, not overheated, retains most of its value, however. The best procedure is to put a glass of milk in a pan of very warm water and stir it occasionally.

BEST WAY TO PREPARE POTATOES

What is the best way to prepare potatoes in order to preserve their nutritive value?

Only slight nutritional differences are found among boiled, baked, and fried potatoes. The potato is a fine contribution to the vegetable portion of a meal and is an especially good food to purchase when economic factors must be considered in meal planning. In addition to providing small amounts of many nutrients (niacin, riboflavin, thiamin, iron, protein, and calcium), both white potatoes and sweet potatoes are relatively good sources of vitamin C; sweet potatoes also contain large amounts of carotene (vitamin A).

Unfortunately, potatoes seem to have the reputation of being a "fattening" food. Many people are surprised to find that one medium potato has only 65 calories by itself; of course, each teaspoon of butter or margarine added will increase the calories by 36. Standard servings of hashed brown or french-fried potatoes are considerably higher in calories than a boiled or baked potato, but they can contribute valuable nutrients to a meal while providing far fewer calories than do some of the rich desserts which are frequently eaten "instead of a potato."

SOAKING VEGETABLES

Soaking carrots, celery, and peppers in ice water makes them crispy. Is this advisable?

Some of the water-soluble nutrients, such as vitamin C, are no doubt lost by leaching when cut vegetables are soaked in cold water for long periods. A preferable method is to sprinkle vegetables with water, wrap them in a damp cloth, and then store them in the refrigerator. This accomplishes the same thing, and the decreased volume of water will greatly reduce the probability of nutrient loss.

SAFETY OF HOT WATER

Is it safe to use water from the hot water faucet in hot drinks?

There is no health reason why water from the hot water faucet cannot be used in making hot drinks. It's really a matter of taste; better beverages can be prepared by starting with cold water. Water which has passed through the water heater will have a flat taste and will not produce as lively a cup of tea or coffee.

KEEPING VEGETABLES FRESH

How can vegetables be kept fresh?

Do not store soft or bruised vegetables with firm ones. Most

vegetables should be kept in the refrigerator, except potatoes, dry onions, and cucumbers which require a cool, well-ventilated storage place. Salad greens and leafy, green vegetables should be washed before refrigerating. Sweet corn should be left in the husk until ready to be cooked. Carrots, beets, and radishes stay fresher longer if the tops and root tips are removed before storing.

EGG SIZES

How many different sizes of eggs are there? Is there any relationship between size and quality of eggs?

The size of eggs is determined by the minimum weight per dozen. The most common egg sizes available on the market are:

Extra Large	27 oz. per dozen
Large	24 oz. per dozen
Medium	21 oz. per dozen

You may somtimes find other sizes listed on the carton also, e.g.:

Jumbo	30 oz. per dozen
Small	18 oz. per dozen
Peewee	15 oz. per dozen

The size and quality of eggs are in no way related. The grade of egg refers to the interior quality of the product as well as the condition and appearance of the shell. Therefore, it is possible to have eggs that are extra large in size but of low quality.

MILK SPOILAGE

Milk seems to spoil within a very few days in my refrigerator. I have considered complaining to the grocer, but I really don't know how long milk should stay fresh after purchase.

The U.S. Department of Agriculture has reported that milk keeps an average of seven days in household refrigerators averaging temperature of 45° to 50°F. Recent tests have shown that by lowering the temperature to freezing or slightly above, milk can be kept as long as seven weeks! Before registering a complaint with the grocer, check (and experiment with) the temperature of your refrigerator.

RUBBER CHEESE

Cheese, when cooked, frequently becomes rubbery and tough. Is there any way to prevent this?

The most important thing to keep in mind when cooking cheese is that it is very sensitive to high temperatures and to prolonged periods of cooking. When properly heated, cheese melts to a creamy consistency. Further heating leads to separation of the fat in cheese, stringiness of the protein, and general hardening. Overheated cheese usually forms a rubbery curd and tends to toughen after cooling.

It is wise to follow recipes carefully when using cheese. Cook cheese dishes at low or moderate temperatures only until cheese has melted into a smooth, creamy form. It is best to grind or grate the cheese before combining it with other ingredients as this insures that the cheese will melt more quickly without overheating.

Cheeses are generally very high in nutritive value, being particularly known for their fat, protein, calcium, and vitamin A content. Those cheeses from which the fat has been removed, such as dry cottage cheese, have little fat-soluble vitamin A but do have the high-protein value of most cheeses. In general, the amount of heat applied during home cooking does not affect the nutritive quality of cheeses.

DARKENING OF CATSUP

What causes some tomato catsup to darken at the top of the bottle? Is the catsup edible or should it be discarded when this happens?

The change in color of tomato catsup is caused by a browning reaction somewhat similar to changes which occur on the cut surfaces of fruits and vegetables. Catsup that has turned dark may develop an off-flavor, but it is safe to use. The industry sometimes uses corn syrup instead of sugar to sweeten the catsup. Corn syrup reduces the amount of darkening, assuring a better appearance.

COLOR CHANGE OF MEAT

In the preparation of sauerbraten, there is a color change in the meat after it has been soaked in marinade for several days. Is the meat safe to eat?

The acidic nature of marinades causes reactions in the meat which change color and flavor. This in no way affects the edibility of the product. Marinated meat will lose this color during final preparations and will resemble meats prepared in the usual manner. Marinades used with meat, fish, and poultry make possible new flavors in familiar cuts of meats.

COLOR CHANGE OF POTATOES

Why do potatoes lose their bright white color when boiled? Does the added salt cause this?

If potatoes, cauliflower, onions, or rice turn a creamy color or light yellow, it may be due to softened water. Fortunately, there is an easy remedy for this. Just add a pinch of cream of tartar to the water and the white vegetables should stay white.

DISCOLORED EGGS

Are eggs which have a greenish-black color around the yolk safe to eat?

The color described is caused by a chemical reaction between the iron in the yolk and the sulfur in the egg white. The ferrous sulfide which is formed is in no way harmful or toxic but can detract from the appearance of the cooked egg. The degree of discoloration depends on the length of time and the temperatures used in cooking the eggs. Cooking eggs slowly at low temperatures will help prevent discoloration. In addition, it is advisable to place eggs in cold water immediately after cooking them. In this way, the hydrogen sulfide which is formed from the sulfur in the egg white is allowed to diffuse to the outer surface of the egg rather than combining with the iron in the yolk.

PRECOOKED MEATS

Is it safe to keep precooked meats and meat casseroles in the freezer for long periods of time?

This is a difficult question to answer without considering the other factors affecting the storage period for precooked meats and meat items: the quality of the ingredients used and the conditions under which the food was prepared and frozen. It is important to remember that freezing retards the growth of bacteria but does not eliminate the bacterial population already present. If food has been allowed to cool slowly at room temperature before freezing, bacterial contamination is a distinct possibility. For this reason, it is extremely important that precooked meats and meat casserole items be frozen immediately after they are prepared. A food product that is not prepared under sanitary conditions is a potential cause of food poisoning.

Precooked roast meats such as beef, lamb, chicken, and veal will most likely keep well for approximately four to six months at 0°F. Roast pork and turkey should not be stored longer than two to four months. Combination dishes such as beef, lamb, and veal stews; chicken and meat pies; hash and casserole dishes should not be stored for longer than two to four months. It is not wise to keep leftovers that were not frozen within an hour after preparation for longer than one month.

Don't overlook the quality aspect of freezing food. Since the flavor of some spices seems to intensify during storage, it might be advantageous to add the spices prior to serving. Also, care must be taken in the preparation of ingredients used in combination dishes. If spaghetti, macaroni, noodles, or vegetables are included, it would be better to undercook these items somewhat since they have a tendency to soften during storage in the freezer. To prevent meat from drying out or developing off-flavors, freeze it unsliced. If the meat is sliced, however, and is to be stored for future use, it is advisable to cover the meat with gravy or a sauce prior to freezing.

MEAT KEPT AT ROOM TEMPERATURE

After cooking meat, holding it at room temperature overnight seems to improve the flavor. Is it possible to get food poisoning from meat that is not refrigerated overnight?

Cooked meat should be covered and refrigerated as soon as possible. Uneaten portions of meat should be refrigerated at the end of the meal. When meat is prepared in a broth, both meat and broth should be refrigerated as quickly as possible. Meat broths make ideal growth media for microorganisms, including those that can cause food poisoning. Broths can be quickly cooled to room temperature by transferring the pot directly from the stove to a pan of cold water, making certain that no water spills into the broth.

When cooled, the broth may be placed under refrigeration still in its cooking pot until needed.

Cooked fowl and fish should be refrigerated after the meal is finished, since they also are excellent growth media for microorganisms.

The "aging" of cooked meat at room temperature is a different matter from aging raw meat. When raw meat or game is aged in a cooler to improve flavor, enzymes act naturally to alter slightly the composition of the meat. Some of these enzymes are inherent in the meat tissue, others are produced by molds and other microorganisms which grow on the meat as it hangs in a cooler. Before the meat is eaten, the crust of mold is cut off and the meat is cooked. Most of the microorganisms are thus removed or destroyed before the meat is consumed. Whether the "hanging" process actually does improve the flavor of the meat is a matter of personal taste. Personal taste also dictates the amount of time given to "hanging". In the Philippines, for example, poultry may be aged until the meat turns black.

As heat inactivates most enzymes inherent in meat tissue, they cannot be responsible for flavor changes after cooking. Any flavor changes in cooked, unrefrigerated meat may well be due to products of bacteria and other microorganisms that infected the meat after cooking. These microorganisms may be harmful to man, causing vomiting, diarrhea, and other symptoms.

The purpose of refrigeration is to slow the growth of microorganisms. Growth is not halted altogether; thus, if cooked, refrigerated meat is not consumed in a week or so, a slimy growth of microorganisms may become apparent on its exterior. The growth may appear earlier if the meat is moved in and out of the refrigerator over a period of several meals. Considerable flavor change, as well as a darkening of tissue, may be imparted to the meat by microbial by-products. While some persons may find the flavor desirable, the risk of illness is hardly worth the taste.

When in doubt about meat, throw it out.

SALT IN FROZEN FISH

Is salt used in the freezing process of all kinds of fish? How long can frozen fish be stored and remain safe?

Salt is not used in the same manner with the freezing of fish as with smoking or drying fish. In the latter case, salt is often used to hasten the drying process and to act as a preservative. Many grams of salt may be added in drying.

Iced salt water may be used to preserve freshly caught fish until it can be further processed for freezing. In some freezing processes, fish is given several layers of an ice glaze, which may contain salt to achieve a lower freezing point. Glazing with ice helps prevent moisture loss while protecting against spoilage. Patients on severely restricted sodium diets are advised to avoid frozen fish fillets for this reason. Washing with fresh water will remove some of the saltwater glaze.

The salt content of fresh fish depends on the species, not the environment from which the fish was taken. Ocean fish are not automatically high in sodium content just because they swim around in salt water.

A number of common preservatives are permitted in the holding and freezing of fish to inhibit bacterial spoilage. When stored at extremely low temperatures in the freezer, lean fish can be kept safely for about one year. Fatty fish tend to spoil faster because of slow oxidation of the fat. On the average, frozen fish have a safe storage span of approximately six months.

PREPARING RAW FISH

Sashime is a favorite type of raw fish dish. Since the fish is not cooked, how should it be cleaned to make it sanitary without causing a peculiar taste?

Though raw fish are eaten regularly in several parts of the world, principally in Japan, sections of Scandinavia and South America, there are some potential dangers. Fish often contain parasites—fish tapeworms—which can attach themselves to the small intestines of humans and grow to phenomenal lengths. The presence of these parasites can lead to some serious nutritional deficiencies in the host.

In many parts of the world where raw fish are eaten, they are first marinated, using some acid such as vinegar or lemon juice to coagulate the protein. Some evidence shows that this method decreases the activity of harmful organisms. Cleaning raw fish by washing in cold water or partial soaking in salt water may be helpful in decreasing possible risks, but it will not completely eliminate some of the potentially dangerous organisms that might be present. Generally, it is not a good practice to eat raw fish.

PINK PORK

What makes roasted fresh pork stay pink when done?

There are a number of explanations for the pinkness of fresh pork roast. It is possible that the pork roast was not free of blood, but it is more probable that the internal temperature of the meat was not sufficient to change the color of the myoglobin. The color change of pork myoglobin takes place at about 176°F. Myoglobin produces the red color in fresh meat juices. It is a compound similar to hemoglobin and is found in the muscle cells of meat. Myoglobin also gives rare beef its red color.

Fresh roast pork often tends to stay pink around the bone, but there is no harm if the pork is well roasted. Roast pork should reach an internal temperature of at least 170°F. Pork should be properly cooked to guard against the hazard of trichinosis. If a roast is cooked too quickly, even at a high temperature, the internal temperature of the meat may not reach 170°F.

Purchase a meat thermometer and use this when cooking thick pieces of pork such as roasts. The thermometer will help assure that the center of the roast reaches the proper cooking temperature and can be safely eaten.

SOAKING POULTRY IN SALT WATER

Is there any harm or benefit from the practice of soaking chicken or turkey in salt water for three to four hours before cooking?

The practice of soaking poultry in salt water before cooking probably dates back to the days when the use of wild game was common. Game such as venison, pheasant, and wild duck is sometimes soaked in a marinade or heavily salted water to "add flavor" or "freshen" the meat. Paradoxically, it is the unique flavor of wild game which sets it apart from the domesticated species. Meat soaked in salt water will absorb additional water, but it is questionable whether any tenderizing effect is achieved. Poultry need not and should not be soaked extensively in salt water.

STUFFING HOLIDAY FOWL

Is it safe to stuff a Thanksgiving turkey the night before it is to be roasted, provided it is put in the refrigerator overnight?

Stuffing any poultry too far ahead of time is not recommended. Both the poultry and its dressing can serve as mediums for the growth of contaminating bacteria. Salmonella bacteria are the usual culprits.

To assure that organisms present do not have the proper conditions for reproduction and toxin production, it is strongly recommended that poultry be kept under adequate refrigeration. Poultry should preferably be frozen if it must be held much more than 24 hours; for short-time household storage, poultry should be covered and placed in the coldest part of the refrigerator, 40°F. or lower, if possible.

A frozen turkey should not be thawed at room temperature, but in the refrigerator or under cool running water (at 60°F., or lower). To be on the safe side, prepare the stuffing the day before, if desired, but do not stuff the bird until just before it is to be roasted. As the dressing may also be an excellent insulator, one should allow sufficient time and temperature in cooking the stuffed turkey to destroy any possible salmonella in the center of the dressing. Unless this occurs, salmonella could multiply. Both the turkey and the dressing should then be cooled promptly to refrigerator temperature when the meal is over to prevent any further possibility of bacterial growth. This is best accomplished by stripping the carcass and transferring the leftover dressing to a shallow pan.

LEFTOVER RICE

Can leftover rice be reheated and served again?

Reheated rice is as good as new if you follow a few simple steps. Leftover rice should be stored in the refrigerator and should be kept for no more than a week. If you don't want to use the rice within a week, freeze it. Frozen rice can be stored up to eight months. The storage container should be covered so that the rice does not dry out; this will also prevent flavors from other foods permeating the rice. When you are ready to serve the rice, just add it to a small amount of hot liquid, cover the container, and simmer over a low heat for about five minutes.

KNEAD DOUGH?

Can the words "batter" and "dough" be used interchangeably?

238

No, they're not the same; and doughs are more fun. Although you can stir and pour a batter and dip things in it, a nice dough is something you can lift out of its bowl and play around with. Both are mixtures of flour, liquid, and other ingredients, but batters won't work when kneaded.

CORN INDIGESTIBLE?

Is corn, especially corn on the cob, indigestible? Is there any way to prepare it to increase digestibility?

As corn is primarily composed of starch, the majority of the kernel contents will be completely digestible when properly cooked and then chewed thoroughly to promote as much saliva production as possible. Saliva contains an important enzyme, ptyalin, which digests starches. If occasional kernels or hulls are noticeable in the stools, this probably indicates that the corn has not been properly chewed. Corn does contain a fair amount of indigestible hull, and if a large quantity is consumed at one time without proper chewing, these indigestible materials will be noticed in the stools.

Frozen kernels of corn are blanched before freezing and must be thoroughly cooked before eating. Follow the cooking instructions carefully, lengthening the cooking time if a softer product is desired. Since kernels of corn still on the cob are intact, they receive less water penetration and require longer cooking than frozen corn off the cob.

USES FOR LEEKS

Are leeks ever used in other combinations besides in soups?

In addition to flavoring soups, try adding shredded or chopped leeks to mixed vegetables. Leeks can also be served alone as a vegetable accompanying meat dishes. Boil them in salt water and serve hot or cold with melted butter or sauces, such as cream sauce or hollandaise sauce. Mayonnaise makes a good accompaniment for cold leeks. Another tasty vegetable dish is leeks au gratin— sprinkle boiled or sauteed leeks with a combination of grated cheeses and brown for a moment in the oven.

HOMEMADE ICE CREAM

Homemade ice cream becomes hard as a rock when stored in a deep freezer. Is there any way to prevent this?

Homemade ice cream does not store well at temperatures much below 25°F., about the temperature of the ice-brine mixture. Most home freezers are much colder than this. Therefore, most recipes suggest making only enough for immediate use. Very hard ice cream can be served more easily if the scoop is frequently warmed in hot water.

Commercial ice cream is especially prepared to remain relatively soft at home freezer temperatures. Special gelatin and stabilizers are used to prevent lactose (milk sugar) crystallization and to give ice cream the necessary body to stand up well over a wide range of temperatures. The graininess of some ice creams is not caused by ice crystals but by crystals of lactose which separate when the product is not made properly or is stored incorrectly. The proportion of total solids in ice cream must be carefully controlled in order to avoid graininess.

LENGTH OF STORAGE OF CANNED FOOD

How long may canned foods be safely stored on the shelf before using them?

Commercially canned foods may be stored almost indefinitely under proper conditions, because the sealed cans are heated during the canning process to destroy undesirable organisms that could develop during storage. The FDA, however, suggests a regular turnover about once a year. Although acid foods may react eventually with tin and iron in the can to cause off-flavors, the undesirable flavor is not an indication of spoilage. Canned foods should be stored in cool places to retard these reactions.

Storage at relatively high temperatures also causes a slow deterioration of certain vitamins. The Department of Agriculture reports that canned vegetables stored at 65°F. lose up to 15 percent of their thiamin in a year. When stored at 80°F., the loss is even greater, about 25 percent. Vitamin C loss in canned fruits and vegetables approximates that of thiamin at the two temperatures—10 percent loss after a year at 65°F. and up to 25 percent after a year at 80°F. The net loss of nutrients depends upon the type of food and the vitamin; some vitamins are more stable than others. Carotene (provitamin A) is quite stable in canned fruit and vegetables and very stable in tomato juice. Riboflavin is not affected by ordinary storage temperatures. The thiamin in canned meats, however, may be reduced by as much as 30 percent in only six months when stored at 70°F.

In some foods, changes in color occur during long storage periods, making them less appealing than the fresher product. Before opening any canned product, the can should be inspected for rust, punctures, and bulges. If this type of damage is found, it is safer to discard the food.

KEEPING CANS

Can the unused portion of canned food be stored safely in the refrigerator in its original container?

Yes, when certain precautions are taken. The food should be treated like other leftovers: (1) promptly refrigerated, (2) covered to prevent drying and development of off-flavors, and (3) used within a few days. Foods with a high acid content may dissolve a little iron from the can if they stand very long; this is not harmful, but the food may develop a metallic flavor.

If foods are often stored in the refrigerator this way, it might be more economical to buy the food in smaller size cans. Avoid eating directly from the can so that the food will not become contaminated.

STORING EGGS

How long can eggs be stored and still be usable?

To protect and increase the storage life of eggs, purchase them from a refrigerated display case and always refrigerate them immediately, large end up, when you have brought them home. Eggs will keep in the refrigerator for several weeks. However, for best results in cooking and for peak flavor, they should be used within a week.

There are several other rules to follow in storing eggs. Leftover yolks or whites should be stored in a tightly covered container in the refrigerator and used within a day or so. The yolks should be covered with cold water before storing. If you plan to store hard-cooked eggs, refrigerate them and use them within a few days. If the shells of the hard-cooked eggs have been removed, these eggs should also be placed in a container and covered tightly.

Whole eggs (without shell), yolks, or whites may be frozen. Nothing need be added to the whites before freezing, but the whole eggs or yolks will need 1 tablespoon of corn syrup or sugar per cup (mixed in with a fork) to prevent the yolks from becoming gummy. If you do not plan to use the whole eggs or yolks in sweet products, use 1 teaspoon of salt per cup instead of the syrup or sugar.

REFRIGERATING WALNUTS

How should walnuts be stored and how long should they be kept?

If walnuts are still in their shells, they can be kept at room temperature up to four or five months. If the outer shell is cracked, deterioration will be more rapid. Shelled walnuts will keep best in the refrigerator, preferably in the main section where the temperature is approximately 32-40°F., rather than the vegetable drawer.

Shelled walnuts are frequently packaged in vacuum-packed containers or in clear film bags. Once the container is opened, unused walnuts should be refrigerated in either the tightly resealed original container or in a tightly closed jar.

Walnuts can also be frozen. Taken from the freezer, however, they need time to dry, for they pick up moisture during the freezing process.

HOLDING AVOCADOS

How should avocados be stored?

Avocados ripen in two to seven days when held at room temperature. The best practice is to store them at room temperature until they begin to soften. At that point, they should be refrigerated until consumed.

Avocados which have been peeled should be sprinkled with lemon or lime juice and wrapped in an airtight plastic wrapper if they are not to be used immediately. This will retard the darkening.

Should the peeled avocado become dark, simply strip away that area and the remaining part will be fresh and retain its fine eating qualities.

Avocado growers have now succeeded in developing varieties which assure an almost year-round supply. The Fuerte variety is available generally from November to May. It is pear-shaped with a thin skin. The Hass variety appears on the market about May and is available until October, with the peak months being June and July. This variety has thick, pebbly skin, which turns black as it ripens. These two varieties are grown in the western part of the United States. Florida avocados are larger and shinier with light skin and are available from July to February. Avocados are not tree-ripened but are shipped to market at a stage of maturity which will permit the consumer to select the desired degree of ripeness.

STORING APPLES

What is the procedure for storing apples at home when they are picked in fairly large quantities from a nearby orchard?

Fortunately, apples have a better keeping quality than most other fruits, especially if they are picked before they are ripe and are properly stored. The ideal climate for storing apples is moist with a temperature of about 32°F. Under these conditions, apples can be stored for several months, allowing them to ripen slowly.

It would be wise to sort the apples. Those that appear ready to eat should be placed in the vegetable drawer of the refrigerator. In general, ripe apples can be stored for about ten days in this way. If apples are exposed to dry air, they lose moisture. Ripe apples can be stored only about a week in temperatures ranging from 60-70°F. Apples that are not ripe may be stored for approximately two weeks in this temperature range. Within that length of time, they should be ripe enough to make delicious eating. An additional reason for sorting the apples is that the smaller ones will keep longer than the larger apples and, therefore, should be set aside for future use.

REFRIGERATING CHEESES

I often buy quantities of different kinds of cheese, especially when traveling, and wonder about the best way to store it at home.

All cheese should be refrigerated. How long it will keep depends on the kind and how it is wrapped. For example, hard cheese, such as Cheddar or Swiss, can be stored for longer periods than the soft varieties, such as cottage or cream cheese.

The USDA recommends that cottage and fresh ricotta cheese be covered and used within three to five days. Soft cheese, such as cream and Neufchatel, should be lightly wrapped or covered and used within two weeks. Cheddar, Swiss, and other hard varieties will usually keep for several months if wrapped tightly. If surface mold develops on hard cheeses, you can trim it off and still use the cheese. However, if the mold has penetrated throughout, the cheese should not be eaten. (Sometimes mold is an integral part of the ripening process, as for bleu and Roquefort cheese. This mold can be eaten.)

Unopened jars of cheese spreads and cheese foods can be stored at room temperature. Opened containers should be covered tightly and refrigerated. They'll keep for several weeks. If you want to store a large piece of cheese, dip the cut surface in melted paraffin to keep it from drying out.

How about freezing cheese? This works best with brick, Cheddar, Edam, Gouda, muenster, Port du Salut, Swiss, Provolone, mozzarella, and Camembert. Small quantities of blue, Roquefort, and Gorgonzola can also be frozen if you want to crumble some later in salads or salad dressings.

The piece of cheese to be frozen should weigh under one pound and be no more than one inch thick. Wrap the cheese tightly and freeze at a temperature of 0°F. or less. Use it within six months, thawing it slowly.

MOLDS ON BREAD

How should bread be stored to prevent mold? Are the molds harmful?

The mold that grows on bread or cheese is generally harmless. Molds are microorganisms widely distributed in the air, water, and on exposed surfaces. Conditions favorable for bread molds are warm temperatures (usually about 80°F. or higher), a little moisture, and oxygen. In commercial bread preparation, mold inhibitors, such as sodium and calcium propionates and sorbic acid, are added to bread dough in amounts that effectively retard mold development without affecting flavor. These compounds can also be added to the bread wrapper for the same purpose.

Bread will remain fresh for two or three days if the original wrapper is intact. When opened, it will remain fresh for several more days if stored in a dry, ventilated bread box or drawer. Mold should not develop under these conditions. Bread may be stored up to a week at refrigerator temperatures. After that time, the texture begins to change and the bread seems stale. Bread can be held for extended periods in the freezer compartment if necessary.

If mold growth is extensive, it is best to practice certain precautions or discard the food. The cut should be made well away from the end of the growth since there is some diffusion into the area immediately outside the mold mat. Do not cut close to the moldy spot.

KEEPING YEAST

How is it best to store yeast which will be used for baking?

Yeast is a microscopic plant that multiplies rapidly under suitable conditions of temperature, food, and moisture. During this multiplication process, yeast ferments sugar-producing carbon dioxide and alcohol. Expansion of the carbon dioxide gas is the mechanism which makes yeast valuable in contributing to the light, porous quality of yeast breads and other yeast-leavened products.

Yeast is available on the market as either compressed or active dry yeast. Compressed yeast is a moist mixture of yeast cells and starch.

Yeast pressed into a cake form with starch used as a binder is in an active state. This type of yeast should be kept refrigerated at all times. It keeps well at refrigerator temperatures for only a few days. When it is fresh, it is creamy white in color, it is moist and easily crumbled, and it has a distinctive odor. When stale, the yeast cake dries out or becomes somewhat slimy and brownish in color, developing an unpleasant odor. Fresh compressed yeast will grow and multiply very rapidly when it is added to a dough and held at proper temperatures.

Active dry yeast is very similar to compressed yeast. The yeast and filler mixture has been dried, however, and then packaged in granular form in metal foil and sealed in an atmosphere of nitrogen to exclude air. Active dry yeast will become stale in the presence of air, moisture, and warm temperatures. Though dry yeast will keep quite well at room temperatures for several weeks, it will retain its activity even longer at refrigerator temperatures.

STORING POTATOES

In what way can potatoes be stored so that they will not sprout and become shriveled?

When storing potatoes, avoid using airtight containers. Although potatoes themselves should be kept dry, it is best to have some humid air circulating around them. Potatoes should never be refrigerated: direct contact with moisture consistently will cause decay in stored potatoes. Temperatures of 45°F. to 50°F. are best for long-term storage of potatoes, but room temperatures are acceptable for short periods of storage. Warm temperatures are likely to cause sprouting and shriveling. Temperatures that are too cold may give potatoes a sweet taste; excessively sweet potatoes can be improved by keeping them at room temperature for about a week before use.

HOLDING GARLIC AND ONIONS

Does either storage place or length of storage determine the flavor "strength" of garlic or onions?

Garlic can be stored successfully much longer than can onions. In classifying vegetables according to manner and length of storage possible, onions and garlic are often referred to as staples. Storage in a cool, dry place where there is air circulation is the usual recommendation. Air circulation seems a little more important than the temperature at which onions are kept.

The flavor of an onion is attributed to a sulfur-containing volatile oil whose concentration depends upon the moisture in the onion and the area where grown. White onions, for example, have the highest moisture content and thus are milder than the yellow or red varieties. Because of the greater moisture content, white onions are more perishable than yellow ones.

In contrast with the onion, garlic has such a powerful flavoring capacity that it can be used as an extract or can be sliced and preserved in dilute vinegar. When garlic cells are crushed in the presence of moisture, the volatile oil that is responsible for much of the flavor is released.

-10-
food safety and consumer protection

The food industry, responding to regulations and guidelines enunciated by the FDA, now provides more information about its products. The food label has become a statement of full disclosure. Nutrition labeling and other requirements place product information at the consumers' fingertips and within range of their bifocals. The disclosure of ingredients, nutrients, open dating, unit pricing, serving size, and servings per package better fulfill the consumers' rights to have complete information about the products they buy.

Consumers seem not to understand why so many food additives are used in the processing of food. At first glance one is suspicious—suspicious that processors use additives as substitutes for quality ingredients. Are all of the food chemicals in use today really necessary? Probably not. But the job of weeding out unnecessary ones is difficult indeed. Each chemical used must perform a useful function and its use should not otherwise reduce the nutritive quality of the finished product. Of course, the chemicals must be safe for human consumption. Thus, by virtue of the fact that a food additive has met these criteria, its elimination poses a difficult question for any review board.

The safety of any new additive must be proved by the industry before permission for its use is granted. An ongoing review of the safety of a group of materials generally recognized as safe is underway as an added precaution. Concerned scientists review the safety of food chemicals and follow new research when some doubt is raised about a given compound or class of compounds. The Food Protection Committee of the Food and Nutrition Board, National Research Council, continuously reviews the status of safety testing.

The FDA, on its own and in conjunction with other agencies, regulates the use of food additives. The USDA is responsible for chemicals used on the farm and in meat processing. The Environmental Protection Agency is responsible for the safe use of pesticides in and around food handling establishments. Even with myriad governmental regulations and guidelines, the first responsibility for the safe and proper use of food chemicals and for nutritious and wholesome foods rests with the food industry.

In the final section you will find responses to queries about many aspects of consumer protection. We invite you to become acquainted with the food label, with food additives, and with food safety. But mostly we want you to become acquainted with food for unending pleasure.

ROLE OF FOOD ADDITIVES

Why are so many additives used in foods?

Chemical food additives are necessary in preserving the high quality of many foods now available on the market. These chemicals are added by food processors to improve or maintain quality, or to give food some added advantage not found in its fresh state but desired by the consumer.

Most consumers are unaware of the vast preparation that goes into many of the foods that are found in today's market. The time and distances involved in moving products from farm to manufacturers and then to consumers are sometimes great, and it is difficult to keep food items at the peak of freshness throughout this entire journey unless food additives are used. It would be impossible to discuss all of the additives which help to keep foods high in quality until they are ready for use; however, they can be discussed as follows in general classes of additives.

Nutrient supplements composed of vitamins or minerals or both are added to some foods to improve their nutritive value. For instance, salt is iodized to furnish necessary iodine, certain milks are fortified with additional amounts of vitamins A and D, and some of the B vitamins and iron have been added to enriched flour and baked products.

Flavoring agents are added to some foods, making them much more palatable. These flavor-enhancing agents include not only monosodium glutamate and some natural oils, such as the oils of orange and lemon, but also non-nutritive sweeteners.

Preservatives include a vast variety of substances which are necessary additions to some foods that would otherwise easily fall prey to spoilage organisms or undergo undesirable chemical changes before being consumed. These preservatives include chemicals which act as antioxidants—the familiar BHA (butylated hydroxyanisole) and BHT (butylated hydroxytoluene) are examples. Calcium propionate and sorbic acid are chemicals used as mold inhibitors.

Emulsifiers are often used in bakery goods to improve the volume and fineness of grain and in dairy products to maintain a smooth, freely flowing product. Lecithin, monoglycerides, and diglycerides are used for this purpose.

Stabilizers and thickeners also are used for maintenance of smooth texture and to give "body" to certain foods. Pectin and vegetable gums are good examples.

Control of acidity or alkalinity is accomplished by the use of appropriate acids or alkalies. Neutralization of either acids or alkalies is often necessary. The production of quality baked goods, soft drinks, and confectioneries depends upon the availability of acids, alkalies, and buffers.

Other additives are used to mature and bleach flour, retain moisture, color, sterilize, harden, dry, leaven, and to carry out a number of other important functions. The propellant for food in pressurized cans is considered a food additive.

The Food Additives Amendment, passed by the Federal Government in 1958, requires that additives be proved safe for consumption; thus, a variety of carefully controlled tests are made before additives can be marketed. This law is enforced by Food and Drug Administration inspectors who continually check foods marketed through interstate commerce for compliance with the laws. Compliance includes not only the use of completely accepted additives, but also their use in only the small amounts necessary to produce the intended effect in the product.

TOXIC CHEMICALS

Why is the food industry permitted to add toxic chemicals to our foods?

The food industry is not permitted to use chemicals known to be toxic. Each substance must be proven safe for use in amounts normally consumed. Occasionally, the newer, more refined methods of assessment may demonstrate that a substance is not as benign as once believed. In this case, the substance is outlawed or the amounts permitted to be used are restricted to established levels of safety.

Differentiation is made between the hazard associated with the use of an additive and the toxicity of the substance. Toxicity is the ability of a substance to produce injury; hazard is the probability that injury will result from the use of a quantity of the substance in a given manner; safety is the practical certainty that injury will not result.

That food chemicals can be conveniently classified as being toxic or nontoxic is a common misunderstanding. No such simple grouping is possible. Some substances are highly toxic in small amounts and can be classified as such. Following this category, there is a scale of toxicity down to substances which are toxic only in extremely large quantities. It is at this end of the scale that common food chemicals are found. The hazard from use of these chemicals is very small.

Food, after all, is nothing more than a combination of chemical substances. "Natural" and "chemical" are mythical distinctions since there is no basic difference between the substances provided by nature and those produced by industry. The vitamin C found in oranges is the same as the vitamin C added to an imitation breakfast drink. Nature provides plenty of toxic substances along with abundant goodness. We have, for the most part, learned to avoid or to detoxify naturally occurring hazardous substances (e.g., the solanine alkaloid of potatoes or the enzyme inhibitors of some legumes). Trace amounts of toxic metals such as arsenic and mercury are found naturally in ordinary foods. Arsenic is a good example of a chemical which can be highly toxic and yet occurs naturally in foods in minute quantities. In such small amounts, it apparently can be consumed with impunity.

Without wishing to suggest that compromise with food or "food chemical" safety is desirable, it is important to realize that certain chemical additives are essential to the continuing provision of wholesome food by the industry. The current concern about chemicals in foods must not rush us headlong into a doctrine of chemical nihilism, lest we return to the uncertain food supply of the eighteenth century.

RELIABLE INFORMATION

How can the consumer be protected against unreliable information on nutrition and foods?

The consumer has no absolute protection and, thus, should make an individual effort to be discerning in obtaining information. It is astonishing that many people will question a physician's advice, look with suspicion upon government literature, view TV ads with cynicism, yet will assume that the health information in a book selected at the local bookstore is accurate and sensible.

Often when we are asked for an opinion on a certain book that requires a negative response, the questioner will exclaim: "But the author gives documentation, citations from medical journals, including quotations from physicians!" So? Anyone can give an impressive bibliography and supply quotations (often out of context) that *seemingly* support his views. It's an old racket. Who among the readers is going to seek out the cited references in order to verify the "documentation"?

The right to publish information, factual or not, is protected by our Constitution. There is, in fact, no effective mechanism for dealing with the proliferation of misinformation through the mass media. Federal agencies have limited jurisdiction over the written word or the verbal opinions saturating the air waves.

The Federal Trade Commission can act on misleading statements in certain areas of advertising and promotion. The FDA can act if such statements are used in connection with the sales activity of a specific product (i.e., misbranding). Postal authorities—the medical fraud unit—scan magazines, pamphlets, and other media that use the mails to detect fraudulent claims to promote the sale of foods, drugs, and medical devices through the mail.

The consumer can protect himself by seeking and comparing information available from several good sources: USDA, U.S. Public Health Service, AMA Council on Foods and Nutrition, Food and Nutrition Board of the National Academy of Sciences, American Institute of Nutrition, American Dietetic Association, American Public Health Association, American Home Economics Association, and, for specific problems, American Diabetes Association, Allergy Foundation of America, and American Heart Association.

Also, the consumer can ask for help in selecting reliable books. Write to one of the above or explore local sources of help: city, county, or state health departments; state agricultural extension services; food and nutrition departments of agricultural colleges; schools of public health; Dial-A-Dietitian programs; and clinics with nutritionists on their staff.

IMPROPER LABELING

What should I do if I think a package of food is improperly labeled?

The Federal Food, Drug and Cosmetic Act of 1938 stipulates that food labels must correctly identify the contents of the package. To report a violation of this federal law, or for more information about food labeling, contact either your local or state Food and Drug Administration office or write to: Bureau of Foods, FDA, 5600 Fishers Lane, Rockville, Maryland 20852.

In addition to listing the ingredients, food labels must contain the manufacturer's name, content weight, and chemical preservatives.

Artificial coloring must also be noted, except for cheese, butter, and ice cream products. A manufacturer violates the law if he uses a brand name other than his own on a product, fails to identify an imitation product as such, or misrepresents a product as a special dietary food. If a product label gives reference to a nutrient or if the product is considered a dietary supplement, all nutrition information must be given on the label. In short, a label that in any way deceives or misleads the consumer is considered in violation of the law.

A list of ingredients is not *required* on "standard of identity" foods such as preserves, jellies, chocolate and cocoa products, tomato catsup, salad dressings, and margarine. These products must meet certain requirements, regardless of brand name. For example, preserves and jellies must contain at least 45 parts fruit or fruit juice to every 55 parts water. If established requirements are not met, the product must be labeled "imitation." The FDA is now encouraging manufacturers of "standard of identity" foods to voluntarily list all ingredients on the label.

WHOM TO CONTACT ABOUT WHOLESOMENESS OF FOOD

If foreign substances like wood and stones are found in canned food, whom does one contact about the wholesomeness of food purchased?

Report the incident to the grocer and to the manufacturer or packer listed on the label of the product. Should one find foreign material in any food, save both the food and the original container with its label, and make note of the store where purchased and date of purchase. Refrigerate the contaminated food, labeled so that it will not be eaten, and hold it for the grocer's or for FDA inspection.

You may complain to the FDA by phone or by mail. In the telephone directory, look under U.S. Government, Department of Health, Education and Welfare, Food and Drug Administration. FDA has many regional and district offices, but you may also write to headquarters: FDA, 5600 Fishers Lane, Rockville, Maryland 20852.

The FDA does not have jurisdiction over all consumer products. Other agencies you should know about for registering complaints include:

USDA	Meat and poultry products
Federal Trade Commission	False advertising
Local health authorities	Sanitation of restaurants; products made and distributed locally

PRESERVING FRESHNESS AND WHOLESOMENESS

The label on a package of dry cereal states that BHT and BHA have been added to preserve freshness. Why are such things permitted in foods?

The food industry is not only concerned with protecting food from spoilage due to microorganisms but it is also concerned with the task of assuring that food products will remain fresh and retain their physical characteristics during shelf life. The most common cause of physical changes or spoilage of foods during storage is the oxidation of fat which produces an off-flavored or rancid product.

Much of the food industry's success in preventing rancidity and loss of wholesomeness has resulted from the wide use of antioxidants and the development of superior packaging. Antioxidants function generally by interfering with reactions which cause rancidity—stopping the oxidative process or chemically binding elements or compounds which might catalyze or speed up the reaction, such as oxygen, metals, or peroxides. Antioxidants also protect against nutrient loss since some of the vitamins would otherwise be destroyed by oxidative reactions.

Three antioxidants commonly used to prevent fats and oils from becoming rancid are BHT (butylated hydroxytoluene), BHA (butylated hydroxyanisole), and propyl gallate; sometimes these compounds are also used in combination. When a fat or oil containing these antioxidants is used in the manufacture of a food item, such as a baked product, this fact must be stated on the label of the finished product. BHA may be used in active dry yeast, in beverages and desserts prepared from dry mixes, and in dry, diced glacéed fruit; BHA and BHT singly or together may be used in dry breakfast cereals, potato flakes, potato granules, and sweet potato flakes. Other antioxidants are used in baked and fried foods and in films used for coating food wrappers or containers. Some substances in specified amounts, such as citric acid or citrate monoglyceride, are also added to food products to enhance the effectiveness of antioxidants. Such products act as "scavengers" (synergists or solubilizers) by forming complexes with metals, preventing them from catalyzing oxidative reactions.

The use of antioxidants in specified amounts has been carefully evaluated for safety. Their use should not be looked upon as an example of artificiality in processed foods, but rather as a technological process which has permitted the manufacturing of wider varieties of convenience foods that hold their freshness.

The food industry uses a variety of other techniques to protect food freshness. Special packing techniques include the bottling of cooking oils with air replaced by nitrogen so that oxygen is excluded, the use of airtight or vacuum packs, and the use of antioxidants in package liners. Cold storage of fat-containing foods, like butter, which contain naturally occurring antioxidant compounds also retards fat oxidation. Foods containing natural inhibitors of oxidation do not remain fresh indefinitely, however. Ascorbic acid used in canned peaches is a good example of a naturally occurring, water-soluble antioxidant, and the vitamin E found in vegetable oils is an example of a fat-soluble antioxidant—both are used by industry to a certain extent. Altering the chemical composition of a fat by various techniques, such as controlled hydrogenation, to reduce its reactivity with oxygen is another technique in protecting food freshness. Soybean oil is hydrogenated to prevent rancidity from developing as quickly as it might otherwise.

As industry must contend with several kinds of fat oxidation, it has or is developing appropriate techniques to deal with each of them. *Fat oxidation (self-starting) at room temperature* will be accelerated by light, the presence of unsaturated or highly reactive fatty acids, and catalysts such as copper. *Fat oxidation at high temperatures* during deep-fat frying presents additional problems for the food processor. Oxidative reactions at high temperatures differ from those at room temperatures, and the same antioxidant cannot be used for both processes. Some fats go through undesirable chemical changes at high temperatures and become unsuitable for further use, while certain fatty acids polymerize or form more complex molecules when heated, which also changes the characteristics of the oil and eventually makes it unsuitable for use. Although methyl silicones are sometimes used to protect fats against change at high temperatures, other special techniques must be employed to deal with many of these problems.

The food industry has managed to develop a number of antioxidants that significantly retard most oxidative reactions for at least as long as the conventional shelf life of the food product. These food additives, such as the antioxidants and synergistics discussed previously, fall under the purview of the Food and Drug Administration. Their use is regulated by the amount of the compound required for proper function, but amounts used must be within the limits for human safety. Federal regulations state that their use also must be consistent with good manufacturing practices; therefore, no food additive may be employed to mask the use of inferior raw materials or to cover up inadequate processing practices. The food industry takes pride in the wholesomeness of its products. It achieves this by carefully selecting raw materials by using the best manufacturing and storage methods available, and by encouraging a rapid retail turnover of food items likely to spoil in a short time.

NUTRITIONAL QUALITY GUIDELINES

Please explain the FDA's nutritional quality guidelines.

The Nutritional Quality Guidelines are not compulsory regulations, *per se*, but principles to be followed in describing nutritional characteristics of a given class of food. If the manufacturer of a product voluntarily complies with the guidelines, the label may carry the statement that the product "provides nutrients in amounts appropriate for this class of food as determined by the U.S. Government."

Guidelines for heat-and-serve (TV) dinners were the first to be developed under this new FDA regulation. To comply with a guideline and be able to carry such a label statement, a TV dinner must contain:

1. One or more sources of protein derived from meat, poultry, fish, cheese, or eggs. These sources, excluding their sauces, gravies, etc., must provide at least 70 percent of the total protein in the frozen dinner.

2. One or more vegetables or vegetable mixtures other than potatoes, rice, or cereal-based product.

3. Potatoes, rice, or cereal-based product (other than bread or rolls).

Frozen dinners that comply must provide at least the following quantities of nutrients for each 100 calories or for the total of the three major components, whichever is greater:

Nutrient	for each 100 calories of the total components	for the total components
Protein, grams	4.60	16.0
Vitamin A, I.U.	150.00	520.0
Thiamin, mg	0.05	0.2
Riboflavin, mg	0.06	0.2
Niacin, mg	0.99	3.4
Pantothenic acid, mg	0.32	1.1
Vitamin B-6, mg	0.15	0.5
Vitamin B-12, μg	0.33	1.1
Iron, mg	0.62	2.2

MEAT INSPECTION AND GRADING

Why do inspection stamps and grades appear on some, but not all, meats?

Inspection is an evaluation of wholesomeness. All meat and meat products that enter interstate commerce are inspected by USDA experts. Thus, over 80 percent of the meat available to the consumer is inspected by the federal government. The remainder must be marketed under state or local supervision, as meat both produced and sold within the state need not be inspected by federal authorities. To be assured of wholesome products, however, check with the butcher to make sure he is using only inspected meat.

The federal program of food inspection requires examination of the live animal, its carcass, and all parts of the carcass during processing, as well as the ingredients of packaged meat dishes. Sanitary inspection of the plant, equipment, and human food handlers also is required. The federal government also checks and confirms the accuracy of product labeling. According to the USDA, final approval on carcasses and large meat cuts is designated by a small round purple stamp with the letters "U.S. INSP'D. & P'S'D." followed by a number that identifies the establishment where the meat was prepared. (Since inspection stamps appear on the wholesale carcass, not every individual cut prepared for retail by the butcher will carry them.) The same assurance in print, "U.S. Inspected and Passed by Department of Agriculture," is on the label of federally inspected canned meat and other meat products, including frozen meat pies and meat-and-vegetables plates.

The *grading* of meat by federal graders is performed only on request and is an evaluation of quality. It is not a requirement that meat must be graded before entering into interstate commerce. Many meat packers and grocery chains often prefer to employ their own grading guides. The local market manager, however, can and will identify the grading system used on the meat in his store. The federal system, when used, indicates gradations of quality for beef, veal, and lamb. "Prime" is the highest grade for meat and denotes meat of tenderness and flavor. The supply of prime beef is quite limited and is seldom available in retail outlets, as it is sold to restaurants and hotels. "Choice" is the highest retail grade of meat generally available to the consumer. The next grade, "good," has a lower fat content and, thus, slightly lower taste appeal. Two of the lowest grades sometimes found in retail markets are "standard" and "commercial." They are more frequently used in the preparation of specialty meats. Additional care in cooking these lower grade meats is required because of their toughness.

EGG GRADING

258   How are eggs graded for quality?

The egg is examined under a bright light; this is called "candling," as a candle was the original source of light. An egg of high quality has only a small air space, a well-centered yolk, and a large portion of thick white. The USDA describes grade labeling of eggs as follows: "The letters U.S. mean the eggs were officially graded, and the letters AA, A, B, or C designate the quality. AA is the highest grade. The grade mark is an assurance of the quality specified if the eggs have been kept under good conditions after grading."

CALCIUM PROPIONATE

Many bread labels state that calcium propionate has been added to prevent spoilage. Is this chemical harmful?

The baking industry employs calcium propionate to prevent mold spoilage. Even though the baking process destroys the spores of molds that may be present, baked goods are exposed to spores present in the air and on bakery equipment. Calcium propionate inhibits the growth of mold and bacteria that would eventually render the bread inedible. Propionate is metabolized by the body and is completely harmless. The FDA specifies the amount of this chemical that may be used in foods; such an amount is well within the limits of human tolerance. Calcium propionate is preferred to sodium propionate in baked goods because the calcium contributes to enrichment.

MONOSODIUM GLUTAMATE

Is monosodium glutamate safe to use, especially during pregnancy?

Monosodium glutamate (MSG) is safe to use. It has been used for centuries in the Orient and for several decades in the U.S. without apparent ill effects. The Japanese, having used dried seaweed as a flavor-enhancer for centuries, isolated the ingredient, MSG, from seaweed about 65 years ago. MSG can now be produced from many vegetable protein sources such as wheat, soybeans, and corn, as well as from yeast and sugar beet molasses.

Contrary to the widespread misconception, MSG is not a meat tenderizer nor a preservative but is merely a flavor-enhancer that seems to work best with meats, soups, gravies, and some vegetable products.

Although no evidence has been found of any hazard associated with the normal use of MSG, some persons apparently have an intolerance to it. This reaction, now called the "Chinese restaurant syndrome," includes transient symptoms such as headache, "tightening" of the face, numbness or tingling sensations, flushing, sweating, chest pains, and dizziness. (Chinese restaurants are encouraged not to be too generous with the MSG.)

In a report on the safety of MSG, The National Academy of Sciences–National Research Council recommended that MSG be permitted in processed foods with labeling indicating its addition, for those persons who want to avoid it. In case of MSG sensitivity, read the labels.

SAFE USE OF SACCHARIN

What is the current opinion about the safety of saccharin?

The Food and Drug Administration has issued an interim regulation restricting the use of saccharin to its present levels in foods and beverages, pending completion and evaluation of additional safety reviews. Also, the FDA advises adults to limit their saccharin intake to one gram a day. (One gram equals 60 small saccharin tablets, or the amount of saccharin in seven 12-ounce bottles of diet beverages.)

Several safety studies are still underway or have yet to receive careful evaluation. Other studies have been completed and have indicated that very high levels of saccharin in the diet may produce bladder tumors in rats. It is important to recognize that such animal studies are not necessarily relevant to hazards for humans. Further, the adverse effects with rats occurred at levels of saccharin equivalent to about 875 bottles of artificially sweetened soft drinks per day!

Saccharin has been used by humans for over 80 years without apparent harm. The FDA has acted judiciously with its interim regulation and, of course, the safety reviews will continue.

SALT IN BABY FOODS

Is iodized salt used in making commercial baby foods? Is there any harm to babies from the salt in baby foods, whether or not it is iodized?

Iodized salt is not used in preparing commercial baby foods, except for dry cereal, which does contain iodized salt.

A few years ago the question was raised concerning the possibility of too much salt in baby foods. Although there was no evidence of hazard from the amounts previously used, in 1970 the manufacturers of baby foods reduced the amount of salt added to their products.

Baby food manufacturers must design their products to be attractive to adults—the purchasers—as well as safe and wholesome for children. The former was the basis for the criticism that baby foods were salted to appeal to the mother's taste buds rather than the infant's.

One manufacturer has reported that the reduction of salt in baby foods has resulted in a decrease in sodium intake of approximately 30 percent during the first six months of life. During the second six months of life, when salted table foods are introduced to the infant, the sodium intake may be as high as ever.

The relationship between high-salt intake in early life and the development of hypertension in later life is not clear-cut. Studies with rats that were bred to be salt-sensitive showed that hypertension developed when the rats were fed salted foods. This is not necessarily meaningful for human beings. It may be that certain infants have a genetic predisposition to hypertension that would be aggravated by moderate to high levels of salt in the diet. A family with a history of hypertension should report this to their infant's pediatrician.

ANTIBIOTICS

Why are antibiotics fed to animals? Is this safe for the people who consume the animal products?

Low levels of antibiotics are widely used in animal feeds to stimulate growth of the animals. Livestock and poultry producers save in feed and overhead costs because the animals are kept a shorter time. The antibiotics may also be helpful in preventing diseases in the animals.

There is a *theoretical* hazard involved in this practice. A major concern is that bacteria that are pathogenic to man may develop a resistance to the antibiotics that are so widely used in feeds. The FDA has called for research to determine whether any threat to human health does exist because of this practice, and results from the research should be available very shortly. In the meantime, certain antibiotics remain "approved" for use in feeds. This interim policy, as well as the research being undertaken, represents a joint effort on the part of the FDA and Canada's Health Protection Branch to answer the questions about theoretical hazards and develop uniform policies on use of antibiotics.

METAL SLIVERS

What would cause small pieces of metal to appear on top of canned food when the lid is removed?

The pieces of metal probably have been cut off of the can by the can opener. When can openers are out of line, which occurs often when the cutting edge is slightly bent, thin slivers of metal may be made when the lid is cut. Both manual and electric openers may do this if they are working incorrectly.

Do not take any chances. Discard the opener or have it repaired if it represents much of an investment. Small pieces of metal can be very dangerous if swallowed.

CITRIC ACID

Citric acid is used as a food additive. Is it dangerous in small amounts?

Citric acid is the naturally occurring acid which helps to give citrus fruits their zippy flavor. The human can metabolize citric acid completely; therefore, there is no reason to be concerned about consuming citric acid. It is, in fact, an intermediate in normal body metabolism of carbohydrate.

Citric acid is added to some foods to perform important functions in addition to imparting flavor. It can act as an antioxidant, as an acidulant, and as an agent which binds undesirable minerals. Citric acid will keep certain minerals in solution, thereby preventing precipitation and the development of cloudiness.

SASSAFRAS

I have heard that sassafras causes cancer and that it is no longer used as a flavoring agent in root beer and other carbonated beverages. Is this true?

Sassafras was used as a flavoring agent in beverages, candy, and chewing gum prior to 1959. At that time, the FDA issued a formal order that safrol (which constitutes about 80 percent of sassafras oil) and oil of sassafras could no longer be used. This action was taken because laboratory evidence on rats indicated that these compounds were "weak hepatic carcinogens." The effect of sassafras consumption on humans has not yet been determined.

LEAD FROM EARTHENWARE

Is there any danger from lead released from earthenware?

Pottery that has been improperly glazed may release lead when mildly acid solutions are placed in it. Lead is an important ingredient in glazing, giving a smooth lustrous finish.

A few years ago, the FDA warned consumers to stop using Mexican pottery and earthenware for storing and cooking of foods because of the possibility of lead leaching from the glaze. The Agency had tested a number of samples of Mexican cookware and found in 26 out of 28 pieces tested that lead in varying quantities had leached from the glaze. (Paint and clay are other possible sources of lead contamination in earthenware.) The FDA now has a sampling and testing program for both domestic and imported earthenware. Other organizations (U.S. Potters Association, International Lead Zinc Research Organization, Inc., and the National Ceramic Manufacturers Association) assist in protecting the consumer from improperly produced earthenware.

MERCURY IN TUNA

Does the amount of mercury in tuna constitute a health hazard?

The amount of mercury in tuna is not thought to be hazardous. The FDA takes regulatory action against any fish product or other foods, either imported or in interstate commerce, found to contain 0.5 parts per million (ppm) or more of mercury. The industry has agreed to establish and maintain an appropriate quality-control program to insure that future packs of tuna do not exceed 0.5 ppm mercury. On the basis of available information, it cannot be stated that all mercury residue in fish above 0.5 is unsafe. It has been estimated that the consumption of one pound of fish per week, containing 3 ppm or six times the limits set by the FDA, would not raise the blood level above the estimated maximum safe level.

BLACK SPOTS IN CANS

Is it hazardous to use canned foods when the inside of the can has black spots on it?

The FDA reports that discoloration of cans sometimes occurs during processing but is not harmful to the contents of the cans. Certain foods liberate sulfur, causing brown, blue, or black mottling of cans.

The Food Additives Amendment of the Federal Food, Drug, and Cosmetic Act prohibits the use of food containers that would transfer a harmful substance to the food in the cans.

COLOR ADDITIVES

What purpose do color additives serve in the food supply? Is such use justified?

Would you serve your guests a white margarine that looks like lard instead of butter? No? Undoubtedly most Americans would not. In modern food technology, particularly in the development of new products, color additives are considered indispensable. Without the addition of colorings, many products could not be marketed in a form that is appetizing for consumers. Dyes and pigments are also used in conventional foods that undergo objectionable color shifts during manufacturing or storage.

Although the color additives amendments were not part of the law until 1960, consumer protection against harmful color additives began in 1907, shortly after passage of the first Pure Food and Drug Act. The Amendments, however, gave the FDA authority to control the use of all colors, including amounts used. The Amendments also required reevaluation of safety of all colors—using new scientific methods for testing. Any color that produces cancer in test animals is automatically ruled out, even though there may be a maximum safe level for human beings.

PASTEURIZATION

Is pasteurization of milk absolutely necessary?

Pasteurization of milk has made rarities of the diseases that are spread from cattle to humans, and, thus, is a definite public health necessity. Pasteurization, however, does not eliminate the need for cleanliness in milk production. Pasteurization cannot make unclean milk clean although it can make unclean milk safer. Inspection of cows, barns, processing plants, and milk handlers also helps assure top quality milk.

TOXIN IN PEANUT BUTTER

Is it true that peanut butter contains a toxin that is harmful to humans?

Some peanut butter may contain minute amounts of aflatoxin that are not thought to be harmful. Aflatoxin, produced by a mold, *Aspergillus flavus*, may be found in almost any food held under improper temperature and humidity conditions. Nuts, oil seeds, and cereal grains, when stored under warm, moist conditions, support the growth of the aflatoxin producing mold.

The significance of aflatoxins on human health has not been fully established. The Food and Drug Administration, however, has taken action to remove products containing measurable amounts of aflatoxins from food cnannels. Toward this effort, the U.S. Department of Agriculture contributes with a program to remove contaminated peanuts from food channels at the earliest point of detection before continued dilution with other lots of peanuts. Testing starts shortly after peanuts are harvested and continues at each point in the marketing system until the peanuts have left USDA control. Many peanut processors continue the testing during processing and on the finished product. Industry, through the National Peanut Council and through the efforts of individual firms, has been most active in encouraging food producers, processors, and distributors to meet their obligations.

The FDA has set a tolerance of 15 parts per billion for aflatoxins in finished peanut products such as peanut butter. Smaller amounts are nearly impossible to measure. The tolerances are subject to change as additional information becomes available.

CARRAGEENAN

What is carrageenan, used in some processed foods?

Carrageenan is a vegetable gum that is easily extracted from the seaweed, Irish Moss (Chondrus crispus). This bushy, pink weed grows in abundance along the Atlantic coast of the United States and Canada.

Carrageenan is useful in processing because it forms gels (in puddings, pie fillings, and other desserts); acts as a suspending agent (in salad dressings and chocolate milk); and gives body (in dietetic foods, soups, sauces, and soft drinks). In toothpaste, carrageenan keeps the water from separating from the rest of the paste.

ASCORBIC ACID AS A PRESERVATIVE

Ascorbic acid is sometimes used in food preservation. What is its value?

Ascorbic acid (vitamin C) is commonly used in the freeze-packing of fruits and vegetables to prevent color and oxidative changes. It is especially effective when used to preserve the color of peaches. Most cookbooks will indicate how much to use for various fruits. Pure ascorbic acid is available at pharmacies.

index

BHA, 250, 255
BHT, 250, 255
bicarbonate, 103
bicycling, 22
Biochemical Nomenclature, Joint
  Committee on, 98
biochemistry, 109
bioflavonoid, 98
Biological Chemists, American Society
  of, 98
biotin, 5, 91
blenderizing, 153
blindness, night, 90, 95
blood, acidity or alkalinity, 103
blood cells, red, 97
blood clotting, 90, 98
blood fat concentrations, 20
blood hemoglobin, 99
blood pressure
    high, 72
    low, 52
"blood purifiers," 186
boiler, double, 216
boiling, 228, 229
bologna, 140, 141
botulism, 200, 202
    poisoning, symptoms, 204
    toxin, 202
bouillon, 173, 174
bread, 7, 10, 30, 245
    diet, 73
    enriched, iron in, 101
    fats in, 165
    French, 73
    gluten, 73, 189
    high-protein, 73
    Italian, 73
    storing, 244
    white, 73
    whole-grain, 164
    whole wheat, 73
    whole wheat, iron in, 101
breakfast, 31, 32
    eggnog, 32
    instant, 33
brewers' yeast, 110
broccoli, 92, 154, 183
broth, 173
brussels sprouts, 92
butter, 38, 147, 219, 220, 256
buttermilk, 146, 216

cabbage, 92, 98
    Chinese, 213
caffeine, 29, 76, 130, 131, 183, 184, 215
cake and cookie recipes, 220
calcium, 18, 19, 32, 34, 35, 37, 40, 64,
    72, 75, 101, 102, 103, 127, 142, 145,
    149, 151, 163, 167, 169, 171, 173,
    183, 193, 194, 229, 232

calcium absorption, 187
    balance, 10
    gluconate, 75
    lactate, 75
    oxalate compound, 187
    -phosphorus ratio, 101
    propionate, 244, 250, 259
California, University of, 181
calories, 3, 50, 82, 86
    balance, 10, 11
        positive and negative, 11
    counting, 4
    deprivation, 95
    in alcoholic beverages, 128
    per serving, 6
    requirements, adolescents', 28
    small, 8
    tables, 6, 7
calorimeter, 6
Canadian Food and Drug Laboratories,
    228
cancer, 186, 192
candling, 259
candy, 27, 29
canning
    cold-pack, 203
    hot-pack, 203
    industrial, 152
    pressure-cooker, 203
cans, discoloration of, 264
cantaloupe, 183
carbohydrates, 85
    alcoholic beverages, 128
    citric acid, 262
    dietetic foods, 69
    fermentable, 194
    frozen foods, 222
    gastrointestinal upsets, 181
    lack of, 182
    low-carbohydrate diet, 48
    pie crust, 166
    tooth decay, 34, 164
carbon dioxide, 55, 245
carbon for cell growth, 144
cardiac failure, 185
cardiovascular endurance, 22
carob powder, 74
carotene, 37, 94, 114, 145, 156, 159,
    182, 183, 229, 241
carotenemia, 182, 183
carotenoids, 93, 94
carrageenan, 266
carrots, 153, 184, 192, 195, 231
casein, 145, 216
cassava beans, 186
casseroles, 172, 223, 227, 234
castor bean, 55
catsup, 174
    tomato, 232
cauliflower, 71, 92, 98, 233

caviar, 70
celery, 71, 129, 192, 195, 230
celery salt, 69
celiac disease, 77
Ceramic Manufacturers Association, National, 263
cereal grains, 103
cereal products, 23
    whole-grain, 30, 31
cereals, 7, 10, 11, 83, 168, 193
    baby, 30
    breakfast, 208
    dry breakfast, 255
    quick-cooking, 165, 166
    regular, 165
    whole-grain, 37, 38, 39, 47, 156
chard, 183
cheese, 35, 37, 70, 74
    American Cheddar, 70
    bleu, 151, 244
    blue, 151, 244
    brick, 244
    Camembert, 244
    Cheddar, 150, 244
    cooking, 232
    cottage, 150, 151, 232, 244
    cream, 244
    dry cottage, 70
    Edam, 244
    fluoride in, 104
    freezing, 244
    Gorgonzola, 244
    Gouda, 244
    large-curd dry cottage, 70
    low-fat, 150
    mozzarella, 244
    muenster, 244
    Neufchatel, 244
    pasteurized processed, 70
    Port du Salut, 244
    processed Swiss, 70
    Provolone, 244
    refrigerating, 243, 244
    ricotta, 244
    Roquefort, 150, 151, 244
    rubbery, 231
    Swiss, 150, 244
Cheese Act, Filled, 151
cheese-making, sodium compounds in, 70
cheese spreads, 70, 244
cherries, 185
    maraschino, 227
cherry seeds, marinated, 186
chestnuts, 75
chewing gum, sugarless, 73
chicken, 174, 234
    dishes, 201
    meat, 141
    salad, 221, 227

chicory in coffee, 130
children, 26, 27
    and adolescents, development of, 64
    growth and development of, 52
    hyperactive, 115
    increased height of, 28
    need for food in summer, 25
    overweight, 51
chili, 190
chili sauce, 174
"Chinese restaurant syndrome," 260
chloride, 103, 104
chlorine, 193
chlorophyll, 159
chocolate, 187
    and acne, 64
    and cholesterol, 68
    bitter, 68
    hot, 131
    milk, 75, 131
    substitutes, 74
    sweet milk, 68
    white, 131
chokeberries, 186
cholesterol, 5, 65, 66, 67, 87, 103, 129, 143
    blood, 55
    levels
        plasma, 66
        serum, 40, 118
choline, 91, 118
chorionic gonadotropin, 49
chromium, 105
cider, hard, 162
cigarette smoking, 93
cirrhosis, 35
citrate monoglyceride, 255
citric acid, 24, 255, 262
citrin, 98
clay, desire to eat, 76
clostridium botulinum, 202
    clostridium botulinum bacterium, 203
    clostridium botulinum, type E, 203
clostridium perfringens, 200, 201
cobalt, 105
cocoa butter, 68, 75
coconut oil, 75
codfish, 142
coenzymes, 81
coffee, 33, 183, 214, 315, 230
    decaffeinated, 130
    whiteners, 129, 130
cola beverages, 184
cold, common, 117
colitis, ulcerative, 76
collagen, 90
colonic disorders, 76
color additives, 264

xerophthalmia, 95

yams, 155
yeast, 112, 245
    active dry, 245, 255

compressed, 245
yogurt, 74, 146

zinc, 5, 105, 114, 263